From Illiteracy to Literature

From Illiteracy to Literature presents innovative material based on research with nonreading children and reexamines the complex relationship between psychoanalysis and literature through the lens of the psychical significance of reading: the forgotten adventure of our coming to reading.

Anne-Marie Picard draws on two specific fields of interest: first the wish to understand the nature of literariness or the "literary effect", that is the pleasures (and frustrations) we derive from reading, and second, research on reading pathologies carried out at St Anne's Hospital, Paris. The author uses clinical observations of nonreading children to answer literary questions about the reading experience, using psychoanalytic theory as a conceptual framework. The notion that reading difficulties or phobias should be seen as symptoms in the psychoanalytic sense allows Picard to shed light on both clinical vignettes taken from children's case histories and reading scenes from literary texts.

Children experiencing difficulties in learning to read highlight the imaginary stakes of the confrontation with the arbitrary nature of the letter and the "price to pay" for one's entrance into the Symbolic. Picard applies the lesson "taught" by these children to a series of key literary texts featuring, at their very core, this confrontation with the signifier, with the written code itself. This book argues that there is something in literature that drives us back, again and again, to the loss we have suffered as human beings, to what we had to undergo to become human: our subjection to the common place of language. Picard shows complex Lacanian concepts "at work" in the field of reading pathologies, emphasizing close reading and a clinical attention to the "letter" of the texts, far from the "psychobiographical" attempts at psychologizing literary authors.

From Illiteracy to Literature presents a novel psychodynamic approach that will be of great interest to psychotherapists and language pathologists, appealing to literary scholars and those interested in the process of reading and "literariness".

Anne-Marie Picard is professor of French and Comparative Literature at the American University of Paris. Using a psychoanalytical approach, her research focuses mainly on French writers such as Colette, Sartre, Duras, Cixous, Angot and Houellebecq.

From Illiteracy to Literature

Psychoanalysis and reading

Anne-Marie Picard

Translated by Kristina Valendinova

Routledge
Taylor & Francis Group
LONDON AND NEW YORK

First published 2017
by Routledge
2 Park Square, Milton Park, Abingdon, Oxon OX14 4RN

and by Routledge
711 Third Avenue, New York, NY 10017

Routledge is an imprint of the Taylor & Francis Group, an informa business

© 2017 Anne-Marie Picard

This book is a translation of a work previously published in French as *Lire Délire, psychanalyse de la lecture* by Editions Erès (2010).

Translation into English by Kristina Valendinova

British Library Cataloguing in Publication Data
A catalogue record for this book is available from the British Library

Library of Congress Cataloging-in-Publication Data
CIP data has been applied for

ISBN: 978-1-138-79602-7 (hbk)
ISBN: 978-1-138-79603-4 (pbk)
ISBN: 978-1-315-65986-2 (ebk)

Typeset in Times New Roman
by Apex CoVantage, LLC

To Little Marie, a very determined clandestine reader of 12, my mother

To Marcel, my father, punished in school for using his mother tongue, Breton

Contents

Acknowledgements

I would, first of all, like to thank my translator, Kristina Valendinova, for her meticulous work of translation. She has helped me untangle some complex Moebius knots in my theoretical thinking. I would not have been able to have the benefits of her flair and skills without the financial support of The American University of Paris, which I am grateful for.

I am indebted to the Sainte-Anne Hospital in Paris, Unit of Psychopathology for Children and Adolescents, for having given me access to their consulting rooms and files, especially to Maïté Auzanneau. I also thank Marc-Léopold Lévy for his nuts and bolts approach to Lacan and psychoanalysis and his unfailing friendship.

I thank Madeleine LaRue for her close and rigorous reading.

Last, but not least, I thank my husband Didier for putting humour in my life and for supporting my intellectual endeavours with abiding love.

Epigraphs and longer translations of published works have been used by the kind permission of the following copyright owners, whom we thank gratefully:

Angot, C. *Normalement*, followed by *La Peur du lendemain*. © 2001 Editions Stock. Translated and reprinted by permission of Editions Stock.

Blanchot, M. *The Space of Literature* (1955). Transl. by Ann Smock. © The University of Nebraska Press. Originally published in French as *L'Espace littéraire*, © 1955 Editions Gallimard. English translation copyright 1982 University of Nebraska Press.

Blanchot, M. *Thomas the Obscure*. Copyright © 2015 for Station Hill Press. Reprinted by permission of Station Hill Press.

Burgelin, C. "Émile Faguet", © for L'Encyclopaedia Universalis. Translated and reprinted by permission of Encyclopaedia Universalis.

Calvino, I., *If on a Winter's Night a Traveller*, Transl. by William Weaver. Copyright © 2015 for Houghton Mifflin Harcourt. Reprinted by permission of Houghton Mifflin Harcourt. English translation copyright 1998 Vintage.

Cixous, H. *Dedans*. © 2015 for Hélène Cixous. Translated and reprinted by permission of Hélène Cixous, the author.

Cixous, H. *L'Indiade ou l'Inde de leurs rêves, et quelques écrits sur le théâtre.* Copyright © 1987 for Agence Althéa, éditions Théâtrales. Translated and reprinted by permission of Agence Althéa, éditions Théâtrales.

Cixous, H. *Or, Les Lettres de mon père.* Copyright © 1997 for Editions Des Femmes-Antoinette Fouque. Translated and reprinted by permission of the author and Editions des Femmes-Antoinette Fouque.

Cixous, H. *Osnabrück.* Copyright © 1999 for Editions Des Femmes-Antoinette Fouque. Translated and reprinted by permission of the author and Des Femmes-Antoinette Fouque.

Faguet, É. (1912). *L'art de lire.* Copyright © for Armand Colin 1992. Translated and reprinted by permission of Editions Armand Colin.

Haddad, G. *Manger le livre.* © 1984 for Grasset et Fasquelle. Translated and reprinted by permission of Grasset et Fasquelle.

Harpman, J. *La Fille démantelée.* © 2015 Espace Nord. Translated and reprinted by permission of Espace Nord Editions.

Hébert, A. *The Torrent: Novellas and short stories by Anne Hébert.* Transl. Gwendolyn Moore. Copyright © 2015. Agence Leimgruber. Reprinted by permission of Agence Leimgruber.

Lemoine-Luccioni, E. *Le rêve du cosmonaute,* Copyright © 1980. Editions Le Seuil. Translated and reprinted by permission of Editions Le Seuil.

Lévy, M.-L. *Critique de la jouissance comme Une.* Copyright © 2003 Editions Erès. Translated and reprinted by permission of Editions Erès.

Malka, V. *Mots d'esprit de l'humour juif.* Copyright © 2006. Editions Le Seuil. Reprinted and translated by permission of Editions Le Seuil.

Melman, C. *Nouvelles Etudes sur l'hystérie.* Copyright © Editions Erès. Translated and reprinted by permission of Editions Erès. Originally published by Editions Joseph Clims, 1984.

Millet, C. "Pourquoi et Comment". *La Vie sexuelle de Catherine M.* Copyright © 2002 Editions Le Seuil. Translated and reprinted by permission of Editions Le Seuil.

Pommier, G. *Naissance et renaissance de l'écriture.* Copyright © 1993 P.U.F. Translated and cited by kind permission of Presses universitaires de France.

Proust, M. & Ruskin, J. *On Reading* [1904]. Copyright © 2011 Hesperus Press. Reprinted by permission of Hesperus Press.

Rey, J.-M. (1982). "Petite préface à la lecture." *L'Ecrit du temps.* Copyright © 1982 P.U.F. Translated and reprinted by permission of Presses Universitaires de France.

Introduction

Dé-lire: the unconscious factors in reading

All words tell a story.

(Charles C., ten years old)[1]

As early as 1930,[2] the psychoanalyst James Strachey, reader and translator of Freud, raised the question of the importance of reading and writing in the psychic economy. It is true, Strachey explained, that even today these skills remain the prerogative of a limited number of individuals, not only worldwide but also in the West; at the same time, writing has been practiced by all highly organized societies and a given civilization may be judged by its percentage of illiterates. He then concludes that reading must indeed play a "considerable part in the deeper mental life of mankind" (p. 322). Is it not true that for both a child and an adult, reading always comes before writing? While speech is acquired in an "instinctual fashion", reading is the first intellectual activity that must be "systematically taught". On both the anthropological and phylogenetic levels, there is thus a time *before* and *after* reading. The flow of Strachey's text is somewhat disorganized, but the scope of his remarks open a way towards a psychoanalytic anthropology of reading. The subject (of both science and psychoanalysis) is the product of an alphabetic culture, a subject *to the letter*. Let us add another hypothesis: if we approach "illiteracy", the pathologies of reading, as a symptom – as a problem of sublimation – can the question of nonreading children (a term we will favour over "dyslexics", its much-used medicalized version) shed light on the metapsychology of the pleasures involved in reading and writing?

Reading as a mode of sublimation

To set up the paradigm that will guide our discussion, we first of all need to posit reading as a mode of sublimation. Let us return to Strachey. By referring to the problems of neurotics, the psychoanalyst shows that reading as an intellectual activity can sometimes be inhibited, particularly in obsessional neurosis. And yet he points out that this inhibition is not of the same nature as the numerous other prohibitions that also paralyze these patients: in the neurotic *alexia*[3] (problems or absence of reading), "special determinants" are at work. One of Strachey's patients reads with a pencil in hand, making a tick at the bottom of each page or paragraph that has been read and reread; another can read the seven columns on a page of *The Times* by simply moving his eyes slowly from the top to the bottom (p. 324). What happens in these difficulties – or in these strange abilities – should be understood in terms of *sublimation*, a process described by Freud, whereby "excessively strong excitations arising from particular sources of sexuality . . . find an outlet and use in other fields"[4] as they are *diverted* towards the production of a "suitable" object, that is one that is valued by culture. Strachey argues that in certain individuals, this process of derivation breaks down when a conflict exists between the sublimated unconscious tendencies, which supply the mental energy employed in reading, and nonsublimated unconscious thoughts that work to prevent and divert it. These "disturbing" thoughts are principally constituted by the oral components of nonsublimated drives. This is evidenced, for example, by various oral metaphors applied to reading – "to devour a book", "an indigestible book", "a voracious reader" or "a bookworm"; by our rituals of keeping cigarettes, snacks and drinks at hand; by our need for a couple of pages before sleep as a soothing "night cap" (Edward Glover quoted by Strachey, p. 325); or by the fact that we require silence and solitude and that the reader, fully absorbed, tends to react to any disturbance with irritation.

Our reading choices can therefore be categorized as deriving from two different attitudes which are themselves influenced by the two stages of the oral phase:

1   The first stage of sucking liquids is "pre-ambivalent" and easy (e.g. the "blissful absorption" of novel readers, "sucking it in"; Strachey, p. 325).
2   During the second stage of the chewing of solids, difficulties arise at every step (we "sink our teeth" into a difficult book, we "chew it up", and we finally "digest it"[5]).

Strachey reminds us that the articulation of the phonatory organs mimics this second stage of chewing because of the intimate relationship between talking and reading: we begin reading by *pronouncing* the written words aloud. However, while speech is a process of expelling something internal (namely thoughts) outside, reading, where we absorb the words of another, appears initially as its opposite. The analyst thus wonders whether the reader's ambivalence in the second stage of the oral phase can help us understand the difficulties of certain neurotics, where an incomplete sublimation combines with destructive sadistic impulses directed at the written words themselves. The laborious reading habits of a patient of Strachey's can give us a concrete idea of the workings of that ambivalence.

Scene 1

Each word is then felt as an enemy that is being bitten up, and further, for that very reason, as an enemy that may in turn become threatening and dangerous to the reader. It seems to be an uneasy doubt as to whether this enemy has *really* been disposed of, or whether he is not lurking somewhere, overlooked between the lines perhaps, or missed by some other mistake, that causes the obsessional reader to turn back, to read and re-read, to read each word aloud, to fix each word with a tick, and yet never to be reassured. But it must not be forgotten that the relation is all the time a two-sided one, and that he is simultaneously *loving the words, rolling them round in his mouth and eventually making them a part of himself.* Such are the *conflicts* which we may suppose to lie in wait for the reader who has any tendencies to regress to the second oral stage.[6]

The obsessional's way of reading, with its conflicts and strongly ambivalent attitude towards the text, stirred my curiosity since it casts a powerful light on the apparent simplicity of the act of reading, showing us the psychic economy of a reader at work, as if through a magnifying glass and in slow motion. While Strachey himself is primarily interested in the reader's regression to the oral stage (in the second part of this scene), his analysis of obsessional neurosis will allow me to prepare the ground, in this introduction, to then try to problematize the seemingly simple relationship between the reader and the written sign.[7] The study of the pathologies of reading in fact enables us to understand normal reading; in the neurotic's psyche, the constitutive elements of the relationship between a subject and text are fragmented, each of them likely to become the possible bedrock of a symptom.

Reading as a subjective positioning

The Latin meaning of *obsideo* (to occupy a place) is worthy of note as we proceed to define the two phases of the obsessional reading process: each of these two phases actually seems to represent a movement, a subjective positioning vis-à-vis the written word.

First a sadistic position, which tends to become defensive: reading is an actual combat between a reader who "bites" every word and a word that fights back, turning into a dangerous enemy lurking between the lines. As the anthropomorphized written sign is perceived as malicious, the reader must proceed with absolute vigilance: missing nothing, rereading, deciphering again, the reader ticks off each word when it has finally been "disposed of". Reading becomes a kind of exorcism; it partakes of black magic. What does the word want? What space is it trying to occupy inside the reader's mind? And consequently, what risk is there in letting one's eyes wander over the page? What danger is there in missing a word?

It is this very same line of questioning that makes up the compulsion to understand in Freud's Rat Man, a compulsion

which made him a curse to all his companions. He forced himself to understand the precise meaning of every syllable that was addressed to him, as though he might otherwise be missing some priceless treasure. Accordingly he kept asking: "What was it you said just then?" And after it had been repeated to him he could not help thinking that it sounded different the first time, so he remained dissatisfied.[8]

As Freud explains, this compulsion to understand is in fact a doubting mania: have I really heard what I have heard (p. 190)? It finds its counterpart (and its meaning) in the Rat Man's ambivalent love–hate relationship with his lady friend. In the same way, Strachey's reader hates the words and loves them at the same time.

The second motion, simultaneous with the first, is a regressive compensation: an amorous pleasure felt at the oralization and incorporation of words by the mouth. Strachey interprets this stage as the return of the unsublimated oral drive. It is certainly a bit more than that: by rereading each word aloud like a child, the adult *unlearns* to read, evades the laws of alphabetic writing, regresses deep into the (pre-Oedipal) past, to the time before the letter became the symbol of a sound, a phoneme to be joined with another to make a syllable; a mythical time when language, the body and the voice, still indistinguishable, formed an indivisible whole (as Sartre will help us understand later: see "The subject *avant la lettre*: a little believer"). The obsessional reader therefore seems to be rejecting the abstract, arbitrary nature of the sign. He calls upon the kinaesthetic memory of the body (see "Loudly and clearly: the Freudian *Lesen*" in Chapter II), in order to try and control the Symbolic instead of falling into its traps: he eats it to avoid being eaten by it. "In enforcing regression," Freud writes in 1926, "the ego scores its first success in its defensive struggle against the demands of the libido."[9] In what Strachey calls "a two-sided relation", the second regressive stage when the obsessional reader opts for pure oral satisfaction – a movement simultaneous with the defensive phase – should be attributed to the "ego's inclination to synthesis" (p. 117). This is essential: oralization allows for the reappropriation of the words written by the body. Black on white, the abstract sign is now articulated by the mouth and its visible nature is transformed into a gesture. It therefore seems that the obsessional neurotic is forcing the written sign to itself regress to a state before the letter, before the alphabet, to the time when it was a motion of the body, a praxeme. To what purpose? By changing the character of the sign, the subject renders it harmless.

The obsessional neurotic, Freud writes, is most disturbed by *"those elements that once belonged together but which have been torn apart in the course of his development"* (p. 121, my emphasis). The neurotic's process of reading teaches us something fundamental about the relationships between the written sign, the body and the (mother) tongue; we shall examine these relationships in detail in Chapters I and III. What is revealed by this strange regression to the oral stage of the libido, by the enjoyment derived from the chewing of the words one has been unable to master by the gaze, is in fact the failure of the obsessional strategies of defence. In our first case, doubt represented the deformed substitute of this defence, which reading threatened to remove. In this process, the repetition compulsion of the first defensive motion mimics what Freud in 1926 described as the characteristics of the obsessional symptom: the processes of *isolation* and *undoing*. Strachey's reader uses both of these defensive methods: he stops at every word, separates it from the others, reads it again aloud and makes a tick once it has been "disposed of". However, this is not enough because as soon as the eye falls somewhere else, what has been understood is immediately obliterated. The neurotic's way of "regarding an event as not having happened" partakes in magic thinking, Freud says (1926, p. 118). The subject pretends that the event never took place, thus negating any excess affect, any forbidden jouissance linked to it. The expressions used by Strachey – overlook, missed, turn back, reread – emphasize the reenactment of memory loss and the resulting necessity of rereading. Reading comprehension, the grasping of meaning, can be considered as a true event; it links words to their predecessors (co-textual signification) or designates the world outside the text (contextual or referential meaning). Both isolation and retroactive undoing are symptomatic processes that abolish any possibility of actual reading as they impede "affect and associative relations" (Strachey, p. 36): those free associations of thoughts and images that, alone, through the movement of retroaction and projection, can result in signification.[10]

The drive for knowledge, the drive for mastery and the scopic drive

The obsessional process of (non)reading is driven by unconscious factors and experienced as a sadistic assault on each word ("Each word . . . felt as an enemy that is being bitten up"). It is followed by an attack of doubt, as a self-reproach or a self-punishment for a feeling of guilt so violent that it must be undone through a regression to a space-time in which the body was not yet separate from language.[11]

We will remember that Freud describes the obsessional doubt as a "repudiation" of the "drive for mastery"[12] and of the sadistic jouissance that goes with it. Doubt is therefore an indication that the defence against the return of the repressed has failed; in the suffering of the obsessional reader we are indeed witnessing a "ceaseless struggle against the repressed".[13] The reader's reaction to the words is a defence against an unconscious thought which is warded off by accounting for all the objects, all words as objects, in a meticulous, tyrannizing fashion as a compensation for the failure of the primary defence against the drive's sadism. We encounter the same process in the Rat Man's obsession for understanding which effectively prevents him from hearing. The mechanism of obsessional neurosis believes to have sublimated and intellectualized the drive for mastery, replacing its sadism with the drive for knowledge.[14] Yet the latter is defeated: it no longer "holds its ground" (*obsideo*), no longer reaches its goal. The Rat Man cannot understand what is being said to him; the reader cannot understand what he is reading. The drive for mastery returns and launches into a ferocious attack against the words-enemies. Something in the process of reading (the object?) has removed the defence barring the forbidden jouissance. But *what* is it that the obsessional neurotic finds in reading yet wants to neither see nor understand?

Scene 2

Thomas stayed in his room to read. He was sitting with his hands joined over his brow, his thumbs pressing against his hairline, so deep in concentration that he did not make a move when anyone opened the door. Those who came in thought he was pretending to read, seeing that the book was always open to the same page. He was reading. He was reading with unsurpassable meticulousness and attention. *In relation to every sign, he was in the position of the male praying mantis about to be devoured by the female. They looked at each other. . . .* He perceived all the strangeness there was in being observed by a word as by a living being, and not simply by one word, but by all the words that were in that word, by all those that went with it and in turn contained other words, like a procession of angels opening out into the infinite, to the very *eye of the absolute*. Rather than withdraw from a text whose defences were so strong, he pitted all his strength in the will to seize it, obstinately refusing to withdraw his gaze and still thinking himself a profound reader, even when the words were already taking hold of him and beginning to read him. He was seized, kneaded by intelligible hands, bitten by a vital tooth; he entered with his living body into the anonymous shapes of words, giving his substance to them, establishing their relationships, offering his being to the word "be".[15]

In this scene penned by Maurice Blanchot, we find a strange personification of what Strachey's reader imposes on his own text. Here, reading is transformed into a real bodily combat, a struggle to death where one is destroyed by the other. The reader cannot escape the "intelligible hands" that eventually snap up his "living body". To read is to risk being read by the words, so that one's being is eventually only contained in the word "be". The horror experienced by Thomas the Obscure enlightens us and reminds us of *The Submissive Reader* in Magritte's painting,[16] an epiphany of being, the shocking revelation of having been written and represented. Letters and words have played their magic tricks; they have made me believe that they know, regardless of myself, what is it that I was looking for. Thomas, too, thought he could stay in control – and he was wrong. Yet how can the I avoid being seized by the "anonymous shapes of words" – words ready for the kill, gazing without seeing me; words which would treat anyone in the same manner, ignoring the majestic singularity of my "living body"?

"He pitted all his strength in the will to seize it, obstinately refusing to withdraw his gaze" – here, the scopic nature of the psychic position[17] necessary to reading, which Strachey leaves out, becomes obvious. The aim of the profound reader is to "seize" the meaning of this malicious "text, whose defences were so strong". What does it want to say (about me) that I do not want to know? Like

Strachey's obsessional patient, Thomas would paradoxically like to read without being placed, by the text, in the only position where reading is actually possible,[18] hence the impossibility of his struggle – of his *dé-lire*, a delirious *dis-reading*. Words appear like a rebus that cannot be worked out, unless we, too, agree to undergo a decoding. Words figure us out.

However, as long as the subject wants to fix the meaning of the word by his gaze, to keep the upper hand and to stay in control, no reading is possible. Meaning brims over: "He entered with his living body into the anonymous shapes of words, giving his substance to them, establishing their relationships." Blanchot's text helps us understand the Freudian idea that the action of the epistemic drive "corresponds on the one hand to a sublimated manner of obtaining mastery" and, on the other hand, "makes use of the energy of scopophilia".[19]

In this scene of reading, Blanchot shows us what Strachey has already hinted at: namely that the act of reading is in fact the moment (or the site) of a sublimatory weaving together of the drive for knowledge (D_k), the drive for mastery (D_m) and the scopic drive (D_{sc}); a binding made vivid and concrete thanks to Thomas's delirious *dis-reading* (*dé-lire*) which is here a meta-reading fictionalized by Blanchot, the theoretician of the literary effect:

> "Rather than withdraw (D_m) from a text whose defences were so strong ($D_m \rightarrow D_k$), he pitted all his strength (D_m) in the will to grasp it ($D_m \rightarrow D_k$), obstinately refusing to withdraw his gaze (D_{sc})."

By choosing doubt as his strategy, the obsessional reader rejects the ego's imperative to bind together the drives (in order to sublimate). The intense affect provoked by reading indicates that it concerns something else; an unconscious conflict has been displaced[20] onto the words, thus "allowing" the subject to *not* see what is before his eyes. What does it concern? What other question does the intensity of this reading stand for? What other terror is staged by these devouring words? What sense do they (unconsciously) make?

The diffident reading of Thomas the Obscure is a good illustration of what Lacan formulated between 1960 and 1964 in "The Position of the Unconscious":

> The effect of language is to introduce the cause into the subject. Through this effect, he is not the cause of himself; he bears within himself the work of the cause that splits him. For his cause is the signifier, without which there would be no subject in the real. But this subject is what the signifier represents, and the latter cannot represent anything except to another signifier: to which the subject who listens is thus reduced.
>
> One therefore does not speak to the subject. It speaks of him, and this is how he apprehends himself; he does so all the more necessarily in that,

before he disappears as a subject beneath the signifier he becomes, due to the simple fact that it addresses him, he is absolutely nothing. But this nothing is sustained by his advent, now produced by the appeal made in the Other to the second signifier.[21]

"He perceived all the strangeness there was in being observed by a word as by a living being, and not simply by one word, but by all the words that were in that word, by all those that went with it and in turn contained other words, like a procession of angels opening out into the infinite, to the very eye of the absolute" wrote Blanchot (p. 25); the subject, Lacan says, is only represented intermittently, between two signifiers; a signifier therefore represents the subject *for* another signifier. In reading, too, *ça parle*: the id, its enigma, speaks. The encryption is understood as actually addressing the drive for mastery. The double meaning of the French *sens* (both "meaning" and "direction") imparts the fact of language as a vector, as an address; a sign, Charles Peirce showed well before Lacan, is always "a sign for a subject". Blanchot's reader "apprehends himself" in the text and "he does so all the more necessarily in that, before he disappears as a subject beneath the signifier he becomes, due to the simple fact that it addresses him, he is absolutely nothing" (Lacan, p. 708). Blanchot's fiction justly portrays reading as a sacrifice: that of the (real) living body. The subject must pay a price, hand over a pound of flesh to the desire of the symbolic Other, thereby submitting himself to His Law (see Chapter I, "The subject to the letter").

Does this suggest that what finds itself displaced through the words (of the Other) in the obsessional neurotic's struggle is a refusal of this sacrifice? As he remains on the side of the unrepresentable, he prevents the word from becoming a signified, that is from giving him a sign, from addressing him and thus putting him in the locus of the universal. The neurotic defends himself against the sacrifice of his living, singular body and jouissance by slipping his own signified beneath the signifier visible on the page – be it a letter, a word or a phrase. What the obsessional *dis-reads* is hence the reiterated cipher of his unconscious, a message fearing interpretation and begging for it at the same time.[22]

Dé-lire

> *He recognized himself with disgust in the form of the text he was reading.*[23]

As Blanchot shows us so very well, what the reader is reading like an open book is his or her own madness, the madness of any human subject. The latter must, by definition, deal with language; when confronted with the written signs, he or she can either choose to ignore them (not to learn to read) or indeed be stuck with them and suffer the consequences. We could therefore say that "reading one's madness like an open book" is the very definition of the literary effect.[24] Reading (*lire*) is always a *dé-lire* – a deliration.[25] The literary reader's negation (I know they are only words, but still, I am in them) can then be summed up by the formula of our title: to read, to truly read, to let ourselves be affected by the desiring autonomy of the symbolic Other, means that, like Thomas, we have to risk the *dé-lire*. To *truly* read we must stop reading. If, like the obsessional neurotic, I put "all [my] strength in the will to grasp it, obstinately refusing to withdraw [my] gaze and still thinking [myself] a profound reader", no reading is possible. Words are going to swallow me up. *Dé-lire* is a portmanteau word, binding together Thomas's delusion (*délire*) of being hemmed in between the real of the body and the Other of language, and nonreading (*non-lire*), which suggests the forgetting of reading, its necessary negation. *Dé-lire* means letting oneself be "kneaded by intelligible hands, bitten by a vital tooth", full of the intelligible energy of being, which is symbolized (produced) as an effect of the letter, "for [the subject's] cause is the signifier, without which there would be no subject in the real".

In our civilization, the abstraction of alphabetical letters, once mere punch holes or traces, drawings of objects or gestures, in the end abolished the writer-engraver himself. Whereas once the traces of his body, pressing against wood or stone with his stylus, inscribed his presence, his existence, the letter has rendered the subject of writing ungraspable. Only his product remains: kneaded, assimilated, metamorphosed into an insect or a predatory rat by the (always) borderline reader, the imaginarized word testifies to its previous status as a human trace. The obsessional fantasy represents our own resistance to what is now, the arbitrary nature of the other's sign. In the context of its history, at the end of a chain leading from the pictogram to the ideogram, then from the hieroglyph to the phonogram, the letter is now supposed to symbolize only a sound.

But that would be too simple. In French, for example, mute letters can also represent nothing at all, just the relic of misguided etymological theory of a certain grammarian, dead for more than three centuries. Massin's wonderful encyclopaedia *Letter and Image* shows us to what extent the letter is both a pure symbol and to what extent it is part of a highly personal and fantasmatic alphabet. When it was brought to Europe by the Roman soldiers, its symbolic form, its outline, was "fixed" by the "adepts", who "inserted it in a fine tracery of lines", adding "the arcs and interlacing of the mystical golden number", "constructed round it the scaffolding which contented their spirit" and gave it "the majesty of a building or the cold beauty of a statue. Removed from the milling throng of words and separated from its semantic implications, the letter becomes an entity in itself."[26]

The animist logic of our private alphabet books (see Chapter I, "False theories and beliefs") continues to make us believe that the seen/written word is a symbol somehow motivated by its referent, that is its subject. In *Totem and Taboo*, Freud writes:

One of these taboo patients of my acquaintance had adopted a rule against writing her own name, for fear that it might fall into the hands of someone who would then be in possession of a portion of her personality She was obliged to fight with convulsive loyalty against the temptations to which her imagination subjected her, and so forbade herself 'to surrender any part of her person'. This included in the first place her name, and later extended to her handwriting, till finally she gave up writing altogether.

(pp. 55–56)

A certain ten-year-old boy comes to mind here: still unable to read, he was asked by a psychotherapist at the Sainte-Anne Hospital in Paris to type a word beginning with the letter N on a computer screen. Using all kinds of highly creative stratagems, including turning the computer off, he managed, for an entire forty-five-minute session, to avoid typing this particular letter,[27] the initial of his surname.

Whether they be phobic, obsessional, delusional or even psychoanalysts,[28] readers caught up in their acts restore to the letter and its abode – the word – their imaginary status, which the very process of learning to read seeks to repress (see Chapter II, "Words . . . revealed their meaning to me without my naming them"). To arrive at the signification of words (the signified), their sounds and the structural elements that compose them must first be erased – repressed. As long as we are paying attention to individual letters, we remain unable to read for content. It is precisely the return of this repressed materiality of the sign that impedes the obsessional's process of reading.

Scene 2 (continued)

For hours he remained motionless, with, from time to time, the word "eyes" in place of his eyes: he was inert, captivated and unveiled. And even later when, having abandoned himself and, contemplating his book, he recognized himself with disgust in the form of the text he was reading, he retained the thought that (while, perched upon his shoulders, the word *He* and the word *I* were beginning their carnage) there remained within his person, which was already deprived of any sense, obscure words, disembodied souls and angels of words, which were exploring him deeply.

(Blanchot, p. 26)

Nonreading children, unable to repress the thingness of words, also relate to us the same fear. One of these children, whose words I chose as the epigraph to this chapter – "All words tell a story" – describes his anxiety associated with reading.[29] Words tell a story in which the hero is always the ego (see Chapter III, "The book, Being's Native land") and this is exactly what Strachey's and Blanchot's readers understand.[30] Their bodies feel the address of meaning, the vectorization of language. This language seeks to locate them as subjects to the letter and in this way to place them in the locus of the universal, which they refuse to enter. The pound of flesh, of jouissance, to pay would be too heavy. Words are thus experienced as devouring enemies. The only thing that can save the subject from this announced castration is to attempt the impossible: to *de-reference* himself, to no longer be the addressee of meaning. In order to escape the word's gaze, the reader absorbs and devours it, hoping to leave empty the place where he came to, where he was to be subject(ed) to the Symbolic.

This place that writing assigns to the (subject as a) reader is indeed the place of any reader, a place from which every one of us can read everything, and this is precisely what nonreading children know and fear (see Chapter I: "Maintaining the status quo, dealing with the impossible"). Blanchot's Thomas provides a metaphor for this place, this locus of the reading subject: "the word *He* and the word *I*" were "perched upon his shoulders". That is to say, in the place of his own head (the seat of the ego), the two pronouns "were beginning their carnage . . . [and they] remained obscure words, disembodied souls and angels of words, which were exploring him deeply". Reading is depicted as a struggle to the death – a carnage: a battle between the body, caught in the savagery of the drives and incestual jouissance, and the "disembodied souls", the sexless and immortal (nonhuman) "angels of words". To read is to accept this carnage, to give in to the desire of words and thus to give up the belief in the majesty of our idiosyncrasy. Is it not true specifically of pronouns[31] that they urge the subject to accept becoming, albeit temporarily, just like everyone else?

Disbelieving that the word is the embodiment of one's own being is what allows reading to take place, what enables sublimation and lets us accept that culture and civilization do indeed concern us personally. Let me again cite Freud: we are "most disturbed" by "those elements that once belonged together but which have been torn apart in the course of [our] development." The symbolic law obliges the subject to accept that he is only but a "story told by words", to quote little Charles one more time.

In Chapter I, I am going to unfold the traumatic moment when the child comes to reading. Jean-Paul Sartre's delectable *Words* will help us grasp the psychical stakes at play in this subjective turning point, and explain why, as Strachey points out, most children need no "prompting" to talk but often have "to be encouraged or even obliged to read" (p. 323). If learning to read so often brings tears, it must be so because the boy, in particular, has much to lose in it. Little Sartre will show us that the pound of flesh to be paid to the Symbolic in order to become a human being is a measure of incestuous jouissance.

Notes

1 Charles, C., a young nonreading patient in the Biopsychopathological Unit of the Saint-Anne Hospital in Paris.
2 Strachey, J. (1930). "Some Unconscious Factors in Reading". *The International Journal of Psychoanalysis*, IX, pp. 322–331.
3 Etymologically "nonreading".
4 See Freud, S. (1905). "Three Essays on the Theory of Sexuality". In *SE*, VII, p. 104. Sublimation must therefore be differentiated from repression, since the latter by definition prevents the displacement and modification of the drive's aim. All human

aspirations, Freud says, a large part of the "works of civilization", have come about through this diversion, this redirection of the sexual tendencies. I will of course return to this later – for what, in fact, is the aim of reading?

5   Strachey, "Some Unconscious Factors in Reading", p. 326.

6   Strachey, "Some Unconscious Factors in Reading", p. 327; my emphasis.

7   The titles and references in parentheses indicate the chapters that develop the hypotheses and elements of interpretation that I am only able to briefly outline in this introduction.

8   Freud, S. (1909). "Notes upon a Case of Obsessional Neurosis." In *SE*, X, p. 189.

9   Freud, S. (1926). "Inhibitions, Symptoms and Anxiety (ISA)." In *SE*, XX, p. 113.

10 "One patient, for instance, found it almost impossible to read, although he pretended to be deeply interested in literature and to be extremely well read, and constantly inter-larded his conversation with quotations. In fact, I feel fairly confident that he had scarcely ever read a book through and had never read more than a dozen consecutive pages at a single sitting. He had, indeed, to contend against the most terrible difficul-ties" (Strachey, 1930, p. 323).

11 Freud analyzes this magic relationship in *Totem and Taboo*: the impossibility of sepa-rating the subject from his own name, or certain words from their referents, functions similarly for both the neurotic and the "savage". Just as it is the case for the latter, the neurotic's name "is bound up with his personality"; he reacts with the same "com-plexive sensibility" to uttering or hearing certain words or names. A great number of these patients' problems derive from "their attitude towards their own names" (Freud, S. (1913) "Totem and Taboo". In *SE*, XIII, p. 56). I will return to the question of the magi-cal thinking at work in the subject's relationship to language and the letter in more detail (see Chapter I, "The subject to the letter" and Chapter I, "To read or not to be . . .").

12 Freud, S. (1913). "The Disposition to Obsessional Neurosis, a Contribution to the Problem of the Choice of Neurosis". In *SE*, XII, p. 323.

13 Freud, "Inhibitions, Symptoms and Anxiety (ISA)", p. 112.

14 Freud, "The Disposition to Obsessional Neurosis", p. 323.

15 Blanchot, M. (1973). *Thomas the Obscure*. Translated by Robert Lamberton. Barry-town, NY: Station Hill Press, pp. 25–26. The emphasized passages should be read in parallel to those of Scene 1. (Translation note: The translation has been modified. I decided to use "sign" for *signe* where Lamberton uses "symbol" – this seems unnec-essary and even misleading here. Similarly, *le regard* is translated as "gaze" to more clearly reflect the register of the drive.)

16 René Magritte, *La lectrice soumise*, 1928 (private collection).

17 We will see that this position mimics and reenacts another fear (see Chapter II: "The reading thing and the reading body").

18 See the end of Chapter I: "To whom? The psychic place of the reader-to-be".

19 Freud, "Three Essays on the Theory of Sexuality", p. 193.

20 On the benefits procured by the obsessional neurotic from the process of displacement, see Freud, S. (1909). "Notes upon a Case of Obsessional Neurosis", especially pages 197–198.

21 Lacan, J. (2006). *Écrits*. Translated by Bruce Fink. New York: Norton, p. 708.

22 See Lacan, J. (1974). *Télévision*. Paris: Seuil, p. 22. This must of course be referred to the Freudian interpretation of misreading as a play of the letter and of desire: "For in a very large number of cases it is the reader's preparedness that alters the text and reads into it something which he is expecting or with which he is occupied. The only contribution towards a misreading which the text itself need make is that of affording some sort of resemblance in the verbal image, which the reader can alter in the sense he requires." Freud, S. (1901). "The Psychopathology of Everyday Life: Forgetting, Slips of the Tongue, Bungled Actions, Superstitions and Errors." In *SE*, VI, pp. 111–112.

23 Blanchot, *Thomas the Obscure*, p. 26.

24 See Chapter II, "The reading eros".
25 *Deliration:* we use this word, which the OED defines as a "frenzied, delirious behaviour", instead of *delirium*, which connotes pathology, to suggest at the same time a *delusion* and an *unravelling* of the reading subject.
26 Massin, R. (1970). *Letter and Image.* New York: Van Nostrand Reinhold, pp. 19–20. See also the André Levy's archeographic approach in *La leçon d'alphabet.* Paris: Editions Vert et Bleu, Coll. Archeographia (2004), and Marc-Alain Ouaknin (1997). *Les Mystères de l'alphabet.* Paris: Ed. Assouline.
27 Pronounced /ɛn/ in French, like the word *haine* (hatred).
28 See Strachey's flight of interpretation at the end of "Some Unconscious Factors in Reading", which transforms the written words into the father's penis: "For if the book symbolizes the mother, its author must be the father; and the printed words, the author's thoughts, fertilizing and precious, yet defiling the virgin page, must be the father's penis or feces within the mother. And now comes the reader, the son, *hungry, voracious, destructive* and defiling in his turn, eager to *force his way into* his mother, to find out what is inside her, *to tear* his father's traces *out of her,* to *devour* them, to make them his own, and to be fertilized by them himself" (p. 331, my emphasis). Should we therefore think that the ambivalence of the obsessional's reading may possibly be caused by a conflict between love and hate for the father, the mother's body becoming, in a sense, simply its playing field? Strachey never returns to the case of his neurotic patient. He eventually suggests a generalized version of the passage to reading as an act of sublimation, insisting on the fantasmatic violence it reignites (see my emphasis).
29 Could it be that his words also indicate a kind of knowledge about the very origin of writing? Ethnologists have in fact called the first graphs "mythograms", drawings that allude to spoken words and that storytellers use to orient themselves in narrative sequences. These kinds of memory externalizations are the first abstract, nonrepresentative traces which were united in a semiotic system fully equivalent to language. See Lafont, R. (Ed.) (1984). *Anthropologie de l'écriture.* Paris: Centre de création industrielle, Centre George Pompidou, p. 49.
30 See Scene 1: "It seems to be an uneasy doubt as to whether this enemy has really been disposed of, or whether he is not lurking somewhere, overlooked between the lines perhaps, or missed by some other mistake" (Strachey, 1930, p. 327), and Scene 2: "And so Thomas slipped toward these corridors, approaching them defencelessly until the moment he was perceived by the very quick of the word. . . . The words, coming forth from the book which was taking on the power of life and death, exercised a gentle and peaceful attraction over the glance which played over them. Each of them, like a half-closed eye, admitted the excessively keen glance which in other circumstances it would not have tolerated" (Blanchot, 1973, p. 28).
31 See Benveniste, E. (1971). "The Nature of Pronouns" (1956). In *Problems of General Linguistics.* Coral Gables, FL: University of Miami Press, pp. 217–222.

Chapter 1

Coming to reading

THE SUBJECT *AVANT LA LETTRE*: A LITTLE BELIEVER

> *All totemic societies have their initiation rites and the access to writing is part of them. What evidence can help us define the role that totemism plays in the genesis of writing? Is writing an act of the clan's initiates, of those who are not satisfied handling the mother tongue but set about killing the father, in whose name speech is fulfilled, and lay him down on paper?*[1]

The following clinical vignette may help illuminate the questions we are going to be dealing with and sum up the paradoxical issues a subject encounters in the human adventure of reading. In the course of a session, an eight-and-a-half-year-old boy, Valentin, recounts a nightmare to his analyst:

> I'm in a library. I'm very small, like a dwarf, and I'm looking for something I've lost. I'm surrounded by the books; they are really big. I know that I'm a dwarf and that their pages would like to crush me. I'm scared. I have to find something: my mother. I start running. . . . The shelves are filled with books, like in a dresser, red books with mathematics and French, and they are talking. They are saying wicked things: "You won't find your mother, you're lost!"

With the help of Sartre's *Words*, we will now try to understand the psychiatrist's report of his session with the boy: "[Except for the nightmare,] V. is doing very well . . . his school grades are very good, both in math and in French."[2]

The book, between totem and taboo

In his autobiography, which won him the 1964 Nobel Prize for Literature – which he promptly refused – Sartre begins the story of his quasi-religious relationships with books by picturing his grandfather officiating a ceremony of reading, during which he is handling books with remarkable skill and confidence.

> I began my life as I shall no doubt end it: among books. In my grandfather's study, they were everywhere; it was forbidden to dust them except once a

year, before the October term. Even before I could read, I already revered these raised stones; upright or leaning, wedged together like bricks on the library shelves or nobly spaced like avenues of dolmens, I felt that our family prosperity depended on them. They were all alike, and I was romping about in a tiny sanctuary, surrounded by squat, ancient monuments which had witnessed my birth, which would witness my death and whose permanence guaranteed me a future as calm as my past.[3]

To a child who cannot yet read, books appear to have a different status than the other ornaments or knick-knacks in the house. In the Sartre family, books are off limits and become true objects of worship; situated in a transcendental and ahistorical space, they reign over the family's condition and bond generations together. Because they precede the subject and his presence in the world, they give this world consistency; they "had witnessed my birth . . . would witness my death . . . [their] permanence guaranteed me a future as calm as my past". On these "raised stones" depends the family's "prosperity", since the grandfather not only handles them but also manufactures them. It is therefore very easy for the child to transfer to them the boundless admiration and fear inspired by the grandfather.[4] Fascinating, sanctified and untouchable, books seem to underlie the grandfather's omnipotence, which the child will seek to appropriate. In the family tribe, books have a totem-like status. Through its positive totemic effect – as opposed to, for example, the negative totemism of Freud's Little Hans,[5] whose father appears as a phobic metaphorical object, a horse – they function as metonymic substitutes for the grandfather himself.

I used to touch them in secret to honour my hands with their dust but I did not have much idea what to do with them and each day I was present at ceremonies whose meaning escaped me: my grandfather – so clumsy, normally, that my grandmother buttoned his gloves for him – handled these cultural objects[6] with the dexterity of an officiating priest.

(Sartre, p. 28)

"Before I could read . . . I did not have much idea what to do with them . . . the meaning escaped me": the nonreading child initially appears as an idol worshipper, blinded by the animistic fetish. He is the choirboy of a religion which consists in admiring his grandfather "hundreds of times" as he crosses his study "in two strides" to "unhesitatingly" pick out a "volume, without allowing himself time for choice", running through it "before he sat down", and finally opening it "with a flick 'at the right page'", "with a combined movement of his thumb and right forefinger" (p. 28). Subject to this implacable will, the book "creaks like a shoe".

In the beginning, the reader is therefore fascinated by the grandfather's actions. The mystery deepens as the child catches a glimpse of what lies inside the books. Their totemic opacity had transformed them into ordered and rigid "stones"; yet their mineralogical character (raised stones, bricks, dolmens, monuments) will quickly vanish when, like "boxes which opened like oysters", they reveal "the nakedness of their internal organs", a swarming, quasi-uterine life that is poly-morphous and thrilling. Their "pale, dank, slightly blistered pages, covered with small black veins" smell of mildew (p. 28).

The totem becomes a complex and dubious object. It is replaced by an ambiva-lent taboo,[7] reminding us of the famous pebble in *Nausea*:[8] rocky, dry, compact, unambiguous and reassuring on one side; muddy, moist, repulsive and unnamable on the other. How can one control this *thing*? Like the soggy pebble's "passive resistance" to naming (p. 187); *Nausea*'s narrator Roquentin's hand, which first morphs into a crab, then into a thick white worm; the root of the chestnut tree which captivates him in the Bouville public gardens, and transforms into a swol-len bruise: the insides of the book-totem seem indeterminate and terrifying, *unhe-imlich*, in-between sexes. The object seems to cover over an unnamable real; it looks contaminated by a grotesque sexual imaginary[9]: it seems that the topologi-cal duplicity – of a double phallus: penis/vagina, object/abject – embodied by the book of the child's animist religion spawned a whole series of dubious Sartrian objects:[10] it is their *proton*.

The child's ambivalence vis-à-vis the grandfather's phallic totem, an object of both veneration and repulsion, indicates the highly complex interweaving of epistemophilia and the family romance (see "The Marvellous child") and of the desire for knowledge and the knowledge about desire. The fantasy of the young Sartre hence allows us to approach the unapproachable: *das Ding*, the Freudian Thing, as it plays out in reading.

An idea comes to mind: does the book's slippery interior owe anything to its connection with the women of the house?

When the child attends the "religious service" in his grandfather's study, he witnesses a particular type of reading taking place, one that consists of a series of precise gestures: picking out a book, opening it with a flick, finding in it what one was looking for, shouting for joy and putting it back in its place. This magic act shows the drive for knowledge as a drive for mastery reaching its object. Yet another kind of ceremony, something very different indeed, happens when Lou-ise, the grandmother, sits down with a book:

> [She would] sigh with pleasure and weariness, and lower her eyelids with a delicately voluptuous smile which I have since discovered on the lips of the Mona Lisa; my mother would fall silent, inviting me to keep quiet, and I would think about Mass, death or sleep; I invested myself with a holy silence. From time to time, Louise would give a chuckle; she would call to her daughter, point at a line and the two women would exchange a conspira-torial look. Yet I did not care for these over-elegant works.
>
> (p. 29)

Once in female hands, the object changes appearance. Far from the majestic minerals of the grandfather's shrine, it is now a "shiny flexible" leaflet. Also, the grandmother seems to contemplate it with sighs of ecstasy; it seems to be a source of some incomprehensible pleasure (p. 29). The books, which have been brought home from a lending library, have an uncanny resemblance to those that had been returned there earlier. Carefully covered with paper, handled with great attention and tenderness, they are transformed into trinkets; they "remind one of New Year sweetmeats . . . bright, white, almost new" (p. 28). They cannot be appropriated, grasped by a man; on the contrary, they seem to provoke shock and a kind of feminization. The body unknowingly gives in to them; the reader loses all self-control.[11] Here, reading appears as a female *symptom*, a slightly terrifying auto- or homo-erotic addiction – certainly frustrating to any male observers, the grandfather and his grandson, who find they have been excluded from this female circle of complicity.

Before he is born into the Symbolic and its laws, Poulou's imagination as a nonreading child is thus dominated by two rival cults of reading:

1   The main cult, with his grandfather Karl as its high priest: his measured steps towards the precise book and the correct page in a way make the man. This reading in action is a forcing – a forceful *seizing of knowledge.*
2   A minor cult practiced by women: their moments of falling asleep and their conspiratorial smiles personify the strange shock of a different form of pleasure – clandestine as it is outside the master's law, and thereby relativizing the omnipotence of the only male in the household.

In their reading, women are fiddling with the *unheimlich* – their positions resemble a strange kind of hypnotic sleep, even death. As vestals of a rival cult, they initiate the child to the jouissance of reading,[12] in other words to a "genuine reading" (p. 47). The truth is that they hold a secret: they know something about jouissance, about the Other jouissance that makes Karl Schweitzer a stranger in his own home. The women's reading poses and conniving smiles suggest the existence of a third place, where pleasure and death coexist in an unworldly enjoyment, outside the realm governed by the grandfather's law of desire. It is by imagining this out there place visited by women that Poulou's ego world will open up to otherness and to desire. He is thus saved from possibly sliding into a phobia which would likely have prevented him from achieving the phallic mastery over the written symbol and from choosing reading and later writing as his preferred modes of sublimation.

Anne-Marie had taken my fake fits of rage seriously. She confided her anxieties to Mamie. My grandmother was a sure ally. . . . It would have been dangerous and futile to make a frontal assault on my grandfather: so they came in on his flank. During one of our walks, Anne-Marie stopped, as if by chance, in front of the kiosk . . . : I saw some marvellous pictures and their garish colours fascinated me; I wanted them and I got them; the trick had worked. . . . When I opened them, I forgot all else: was this reading? No, it was dying of ecstasy: my self-oblivion also gave birth to natives armed with assegais, the bush, an explorer in a pith helmet. I was *vision.* . . .

This reading matter was long kept a secret . . . aware of their unworthiness, I did not breathe a word of them to my grandfather. I was mixing with low company, taking liberties, spending my holidays in a brothel, but I never forgot that my true self remained in a place of worship. Why bother to shock the priest by confessing my misdeeds?

(Sartre, pp. 47–49)

Forgetting, death, ecstasy, oblivion, vision and, later on, bewilderment (p. 49): this "genuine" reading touches upon the question of the Other jouissance.[13] Forcing and ravishment: the reader imagines himself to be bicephalous and bisexed, caught between two positions of jouissance.[14] The transgressive female intervention leads to the constitution of a space outside Karl's panopticon: "away from the sanctuary, in our bedroom or under the dining-room table" (p. 47), hidden from the omniscient gaze, the child becomes the cult's (discrete) worshiper. His underground territory of reading defines a world outside the "sanctuary": it is a transitional space, "a brothel", where the child is allowed to delineate his private space, a salutary being-for-itself. The feminine Other jouissance can then be joined together with the male jouissance of the Master of Words, to the child's best advantage.

The marvellous child

The privileged topic of any writer's autobiography seems to be his coming to writing: how, as a child, did he begin? When did he choose to become a writer? The very fact of this announced act of writing is what retroactively makes the writer-child a heroic literary character (see Chapter III, "The ego: an effect of reading?").

Sartre explains his entrance into the world of writing by making a connection between reading and psychic structure. With acute psychological insight, the Sartre of 1964 tries to explain why, given his personal history, the child he was could only "make it" with the help of writing – in other words, by becoming Sartre. He draws his genealogical tree with a jubilatory sense of self-derision and a superbly sharp pen, in order to paint a picture of his miserable existence, that of an astonishingly neurotic child, the "undefined made flesh and blood" (*Words*, p. 27), nobody's son:

[My father] met Anne-Marie Schweitzer, seized on this tall, neglected girl, married her, gave her a child with all speed, myself, and tried to seek refuge in death. . . . I was lucky to belong to a dead man: a dead man had poured out the few drops of sperm which are the normal price for a child.

(pp. 12–17)

Let us notice that what the autobiographer is suggesting here, in such a casual manner, is the unconscious subject's self-authorization not to be governed by the fundamental laws of human existence. To deny the mother her desire for a man and deprive the father of his desire to live for her (and himself) in the name of an autoerotic, unsatisfying and deadly jouissance, is to deny that one is born of a man and a woman, that one must take up a position on one side of the sexual divide, that one is mortal. Here, the subject posits himself, ironically and covertly, as a marvellous child: "It was conveyed to me that I was the child of a miracle rather than a dead man's son" (p. 16). And as to the Oedipal rivalry, what rivalry can there be with a dead man? "In fact, my father's hasty retreat had conferred on me a very incomplete Oedipus complex: no Super-Ego, I agree, but no aggression, either" (p. 24). And the mother? It's Anne-Marie, the young girl the boy has all to himself, and who sleeps nearby every night.

> A young girl's bed had been put into *my* room. The young girl slept alone and woke chaste: . . . how could she have given birth to me? . . . I should marry her later on so as to look after her.
>
> (p. 16)

Sartre's *Words* reveal to us a fantasmatic family romance, hidden and exposed at the same time. As the psychoanalyst Jean-François Chiantaretto[15] writes, Sartre's claim – that his father's death left him with a "very incomplete Oedipus complex" – allows the subject to unconsciously "keep the mother all to himself". Writing *Words* would then enable Sartre to escape a terrifying thought, namely of being the fruit of an incestual union between a father and a daughter. What risks would such a thought carry for the subject? A terrifying and dazzling apparition would emerge: God the Father himself. Karl Schweitzer, the only man of the house, is in fact the two-headed Janus. At times he is frightening like the double of the fierce God of the Old Testament: his appearance at church one day actually makes the worshipers flee (p. 17). Yet most often he is delighted by the very existence of his grandson, treating him like the "wonder" he was no longer expecting (p. 17).

> My very presence satisfied him. He was the God of Love with the Father's beard and the Son's Sacred Heart; he would lay his hands on me, I would feel the warmth of his palms on my head, he would call me his little one in a voice bleating with affection, and tears would fill his cold eyes. . . . It was obvious that he adored me.
>
> (p. 17)

Is there no law restricting Poulou's incestuous jouissance? No submission to the desire of a third party, an other to the mother? "I did not bump myself on its corners, so I distinguished reality at first only by its cheerful inconsistency. Against whom or what could I have rebelled? No one else's whim ever claimed to be my law" (p. 19). Poulou's ego world is based on a fantasy of omnipotence, reignited by the toxic jouissance of his own image reflected in the gaze of others. Self-deprecatingly, the author describes himself as a four-year-old Candide: "It was

Paradise. Each morning, I woke in a daze of joy, marvelling at the [mad] stroke of [luck] by which I had been born into the most united family in the most beautiful country in the world" (p. 24). This *chance folle* (mad stroke of luck), a holophrastic oxymoron, nicely sums up the question of the marvellous child, to whom all is permitted and due, yet at the risk of falling into madness. And without the words of the book, without the call of the Symbolic in place of the Name-of-the-Father,[16] this would certainly have happened. It is in fact from the Symbolic itself that the first castration arrives, the beginning of the fragmentation of the maternal body, which, as we remember, has not been eroticized by any male gaze in the house.

*

> I wanted to begin my appropriation ceremonies on the spot. I took the two small volumes, sniffed at them, felt them, opened them casually "at the right page" and made them creak. It was no good: I did not feel that I owned them. I tried without greater success to treat them as dolls, cradle them, kiss them and beat them. On the verge of tears, I finally laid them on my mother's lap.
>
> (*Words*, p. 30)

The alexic child does not know what to do with books, besides imitate the poses of adult readers. Mimicking his grandfather, he tries to impose his will on the object in order to enjoy it in his own way; imitating a woman, he turns the book into a child he caresses. Yet what path is there to take, what trials to overcome, before one can psychically sublimate the drive for mastery and arrive at meaning and signification? We saw the first and terrible ordeal in Valentin's nightmare at the beginning of this chapter. It represents the wounding of the mother that must be suffered, the pound of flesh that must be paid in order to gain admission to the adult library, to those wicked books that seem to enjoy the very sight of Valentin's suffering. In *Words*, Poulou experiences the same trauma:

Scene 3

> On the verge of tears, I finally laid them on my mother's lap. She looked up from her work: "What do you want me to read, darling? About [*The Fairies'*] story?" I asked incredulously: "[*The Fairies*], it is *in there*?" I knew the tale well: my mother often told it to me while she was washing my face, breaking off to massage me with eau-de-Cologne or to pick up, from under the bath, the soap which had slipped from her hands, and I would listen with half an ear to an all-too-familiar story; all I wanted to see was Anne-Marie, the young girl of my mornings; all I wanted to hear was her voice, disturbed by servitude; I loved her half-completed sentences, her always slow-to-come words and her brusque confidence, quickly defeated and put to rout, which disappeared with a pleasant fraying sound, and then re-established itself after a silence. The story was secondary: it was the link between her soliloquies. All the

while she was talking, we were alone and private, far from man, gods and priests, two does in the wood, with those other does, the Fairies; I never could believe that a whole book could have been written to feature this episode in our profane life, which smelt of soap and eau-de-Cologne.

Anne-Marie made me sit down in front of her, on my little chair; she leant over, lowered her eyelids and went to sleep. From this mask-like face issued a plaster voice. [I lost my head]: who was talking? About what? And to whom? My mother had disappeared: not a smile or trace of complicity. I was an exile. And then I did not recognize the language. Where did she get her confidence? After a moment, I realized: it was the book that was talking. Sentences emerged that frightened me: they were like real centipedes; they swarmed with syllables and letters, span out their diphthongs and made their double consonants hum; fluting, nasal, broken up with sighs and pauses, rich in unknown words, they were in love with themselves and their meanderings and had no time for me. . . . These words were obviously not meant for me. The tale itself was in its Sunday best. . . . Someone began to ask questions. . . . It was as if a child was being quizzed. . . . But this child was not entirely me and I was afraid to reply. I did reply, though; my feeble voice grew faint and I felt I was turning into someone else. Anne-Marie, too, with her blind soothsayer's look, was someone else: it was as if I were every mother's child and she were every child's mother. When she stopped reading, I quickly took back the books and carried them off under my arm without a word of thanks.

(pp. 30–32)

The scene portrays an epiphany. First, a series of apparently trivial gestures performed by a child and his mother over a book unfolds before us. Because he is still a little mystic, the child asks to *see* (rather than to know): he wants truth without knowledge, without having to learn. Spitefully and helplessly, he lays the coveted book (coveted because of the jouissance it affords) in the mother's lap: the enigmatic object does not "work" properly, it resists his omnipotence. He does not even know about the alphabet. He does not know that what he wants is to *read*.

Hence, two troubling miracles, which could be easily mistaken for catastrophes, occur at the same time:

1   Language becomes autonomous: first, the child discovers that the story usually told to him by his mother *in vivo* and *ad lib* is "in the book", that it can be situated outside (the etymon of the Latin *ex-sistere*) the mother's voice, outside the intimate moment where it was told to the child while he was being bathed by his mother. However, although the autobiographer relates this separation as the first to happen, it only occurs once another, more radical and unforgiving instance of it has taken place.

2   The mother herself is made incomplete, de-completed: a part of her is lost; her gaze and her plaster voice no longer speak to the child; her mouth is full of

incomprehensible words: they are no longer her words, she is no longer mummy. Mummy has left her body and the child is about to lose its head because of it. This double separation triggers a moment of foundational disbelief.

What torment is she causing to him? The child's imaginary world filled with identification and imitation, that is to say a world of differentiation without separation, has suffered an irreversible narcissistic wound. It marks the brutal expulsion from the paradise of his childhood ruled by magic and omnipotence, and simultaneously the appearance of an "other" subject, a subject *to* something transcendent: the law of the Symbolic. "Elements that once belonged together," Freud said about the child's developmental stages, "have been torn apart" (Freud, 1926, p. 121). Sartre's account helps us understand the different steps on this journey.

Bathing in the maternal

The scene of the bath is recaptured in the narrative and logical (rather than simply mnemonic) order of Sartre's account. It allows us to compare the two performances of the same story, "The Fairies". In the first version, the story is told in the mother tongue as part of the profane ritual of the daily bath; in the second version it is frightening, made of insect-like words[17] crawling out of the book. An analepsis reverses the logical order: (1) one day, this happened, (2) while before, it was like that. The chronology allows the reader to grasp the child's terror when he is suddenly faced with the speaking statue; in the same way, it becomes possible for the subject to reconstruct what is found missing: the bath in the maternal music and touch and the young mother, enslaved by the child's needs, are now figures of the lost familiar (*heimlich*). "I knew the tale *well* [Cette histoire m'était *familière*]: my mother *often* told it to me while she was washing my face . . . and I would listen with half an ear to an *all-too-familiar* story [le récit *trop connu*]": the imperfect of the verb *be* (*je étais*), which in French links duration and frequency, marks a comforting recognition as well as a nostalgia for a time forever lost, a modality of being irreversibly vanished.[18]

Freud tells us that the etymological origins of the German word "familiar" – *heimlich* – include a reference to the scene of incest. *Heimlich* can refer to a secret kept hidden, concealed,[19] that which is deep-rooted and intimate, shadowy and occult. In the profane yet ritualized scene of the bath, these secret twins play their forbidden games outside the human law and its prohibition of incest. Contrary to the scenes dominated by the dazzling presence of the grandfather, what happens in here has nothing to do with monotheism. Here there is no transcendence to be worshipped. Profane and pagan, the scene returns us to the animal body and its organic jouissance: "All the while she was talking, we were alone and private, far from man, gods and priests, two does in the wood, with those other does, the fairies. . . ." Away from the grandfather's panopticon, which rules the outside world, the maternal bath is Paradise before the Fall, a Paradise Lost. In this hideout one can make mischief, tell silly stories about fairies and continue to believe in a magical world, that is in the consubstantiality of words and things, in the possibility of desire's satisfaction. Sartre says this clearly: "The story was secondary" (*L'histoire, ça venait par-dessus le marché* – to top it all off/on top of the deal). What *deal* have mother and son been part of? What illicit trafficking, what bargain has the child been enjoying, if not the mother's complete availability, her selfless giving as the primordial Goddess of Paradise? "All I wanted to see was Anne-Marie, the young girl of my mornings; all I wanted to hear was her voice, disturbed by servitude." The transformation of "every morning" into "all *my* mornings" is indicative of the infantile self-centeredness. Likewise, the reflexive verb used in French "*je me plaisais à ces phrases inachevées*" (I took pleasure in her half-completed sentences) is a direct shortcut to the truth of the autoerotism of primary narcissism, a time when the familiar other has not yet become a foreigner, a stranger struck by the Other's desire.

The scene of the maternal bath is a scene of fantasy, a myth of original unity, a consistency of the being of things, an essence represented by the tangle of the mother and child's bodies, a time-space in which the other and the ego, the word and the world, are in fact consubstantial, where they are *One*. The phrase "All the while she was talking, we were. . . ." (*Tout le temps qu'elle parlait nous étions*) could well be made into the melancholic motto of this land long lost, where language was a kind of music enveloping the two mingled bodies. The scene is born out of the imaginary of the marvellous child; it is a product of the magic world he inhabits, a world whose language is the "mother tongue", an idiolect spoken by only two speakers, where the Other's desire has not yet intervened. Sartre will not write the promised second volume of his autobiography; *Words* stops right before the moment when his mother remarries. By reconstructing the mother tongue, *après-coup*, after it has been lost, the subject remains faithful to his former omnipotence. By fantasizing a place lagging behind the Symbolic, he liberates the ego from the alienating effects of the signifier: he can call up the thing by its secret name, like a fairy does with her magic wand.

THE SUBJECT TO THE LETTER

The mother as a stranger: *who speaks?*

"She leant over, lowered her eyelids and went to sleep. From this mask-like face issued a plaster voice. I [lost my head]: who was talking?" When the mother, previously "all to myself", sits down with the book-object, lowers her eyes, "goes to sleep" and begins to speak with a "plaster voice", we witness an absolute catastrophe: the Whole-One collapses, the Real surges forth as pure nonsense. Before the child's frightened eyes, the icon of the Madonna and Child fades away forever, swallowed by the magic box in her lap. She is replaced by a being that only slightly resembles her: her gaze is that of the dead, her voice that of an oracle transported beyond. What the scene in fact so masterfully depicts is precisely the production of a *beyond*, of the mother's Other.

In its brutally sudden loss of belief, which the subject's uncanny feeling[20] marks as a trauma, the scene locates the original moment of the fantastic – a genre Sartre later revives in his first novel, *Nausea*. The moment puts an end to the child's assumption that the other is the same – a double not separated from the self.[21] The shared ego is split and the double is projected outwards, "as something foreign to itself" (Freud, "The 'Uncanny'", p. 235). "The 'double' has become a thing of terror, just as, after the collapse of their religion, the gods turned into demons."[22] This is precisely what is at stake here.

Who is telling the story? The question of *Che Vuoi?* (What does the Other want from me?) resonates in the child's terror. The mother is no longer "my fellow being, my sister" and wakefulness now resembles sleep, life resembles death. The terrifying image brings to mind Olympia, the mechanical doll in E.T.A. Hoffmann's "The Sandman". Like the wax figurine in the paradigmatic story, with her glass eyes and machine-like gaze, "the young girl of my mornings" has become an apparatus, a lifeless object (Freud, "The 'Uncanny'", p. 225). The adored twin is lost and the subject finds himself exiled, a wandering soul banished from the native land. In order to maintain some consistency, the ego tries to preserve the image of this first Mother intact (this is not her, it is something *in* her) by rejecting the "thing" out there.[23] Who is this monstrous alien? The question creates a place beyond the mother. She is now inhabited by an unnamable Other, one who deals the subject a terrible (and beneficial) blow, revealing not only the mother's incompleteness but also the subject's fundamental inadequacy to satisfy her desire. Violently ejected from the *heimlich* sweet *heimlich*, the ego is thrown into lack and alienation.

The boy's complaint "I lost my head" must then be understood literally: by a boomerang effect, the mother's absence from herself imposes an identical decomposition on the child's ego, a division between the *I* (the enduring image of the ego as undivided, as One) and the *head* (an extension, a small residue of the mother). Once aware of this irreversible fragmentation, the subject has to embark on a process of mourning, of coming to terms with the disappearance of the marvellous child, all-for-the-mother. Previously the recipient of "conspiratorial smiles", he can now envisage the possibility of their eclipse. As Lacanian objects "a", partial objects fallen from the mother's body, these *desired* signs of recognition become signifieds, parts of a signifying chain ready for the process of reading and writing.

The mother's voice becomes foreign and strange because it no longer addresses the child; he can no longer hear in it the desire to please him – it is not making sense any longer. The mothering language has stopped playing the little music of the ego. Before, its modulations functioned as an envelope, giving consistence to the shared imago. Now the "plaster" voice resonates from an *other place* (suggested by the French *en*, "from it") that cannot yet be imagined, splitting off from the mother's body.

> Sentences emerged from it [*en sortaient*] that frightened me: . . . they were in love with themselves and their meanderings and had no time for me: sometimes they disappeared before I could understand them; . . . they went rolling

on nobly towards their end without sparing me a comma. These words were obviously not meant for me.

(p. 31)

Previously the mother's voice and gaze were consubstantially linked to her words and the story told. In the same manner, the strangeness of the language spoken by the Other's voice is echoed by the strangeness of its address: Who is speaking? What language? And to whom, since I am not there? "And then I did not recognize the language. *Where did she get* her confidence?" (my emphasis). The child postulates the existence of an other place where the mother gets it. But this is not the place she is inhabited by the monster that makes her so terrifying, but a place where *it knows* something that she herself cannot know – a hypothesis of the existence of a speaking Other, as opposed to the unnamable *it*.

From the mother's tongue to the language of the book: *it speaks!*

"After a moment, I realized: it was the book that was talking." The Other becomes embodied in the previously mute object; the book is now the site of the Other's discourse and knowledge. Sartre's formulation – "I was wild with delight . . . I was allowed to wander in the library and I mounted an offensive on human knowledge. That was what made me" (p. 33) – finds its metapsychological explanation here. Standing in for the knowledge and language that divide the mother from herself and thus separate her from Poulou, destabilizing the figure of the marvellous child, the book in fact occupies the symbolic position of the paternal language. While the mother is usually the one bringing the objects of the world into existence by naming them, it is in fact the father who instils doubt and introduces play into the univocal designation of the maternal language. By doing so, he relativizes the signifier's motivation (the essential resemblance between the word and the thing, preserved in onomatopoeia) and undermines its magical mode of reference.

Once it has been separated from the maternal enunciation, from the mother's body and voice, the familiar tale lives on for Little Sartre as an utterance (*énoncé*), independent of the words used to express it, which in itself permits the hypothesis of synonymy. The *unheimlich* stirred by the speaking book then allows another radical operation to take place, one that constitutes an epistemological break. By understanding the story, despite its different wording, the child experiences disbelief and is forced to give up his false theory of language. Yet in the case of non-reading children, this false theory holds its ground, preventing the subject from recognizing the arbitrary nature of the sign (see the last part of Chapter I).

My mother would say to me a hundred times a day, not without intent: "Karlémami are waiting; Karlémami will be pleased, Karlémami . . . ," suggesting *by the intimacy* [*l'intime union*] *of these four syllables complete harmony between persons. . . .* The word shed its influence [*son ombre*] on the thing;

through Karlémami, I could maintain the flawless unity of the family. . . . My grandmother, suspect and sinful, forever on the verge of slipping, was *restrained by the arm of an angel, through the power of a word.*

(Sartre, p. 25, modified translation, my emphasis)

The couple's "complete harmony" is part of magical thinking. "The word shed its influence on the thing," Sartre says mysteriously. What does he mean? For the child, the word does not simply replace the object, thus exposing the latter's absence. Instead it is somehow inhabited by the object and becomes, in a sense, a thing in itself.[24] In this passage, language resembles a song of the child magician's body, ruling a world where he can summon the grown-ups simply by calling their names. "The intimacy of these four syllables" suggests "complete harmony between persons"; in *Karlémami* "the flawless unity of the family" remains intact. We see Sartre's insistence on this idea of unity, intimacy, harmony, flawlessness, completeness, maintenance. Here, the myth of the maternal language clearly expresses its powerful ideological grounding in primary narcissism – together with another belief, namely that there is such a thing as a sexual relationship.[25] The holophrase *Karlémami* transcribes a belief in the existence of a relationship between Karl the man and Mamie the woman; the "power of the word" prevents the grandmother from "falling into sin" as if she was "restrained by the arm of an angel". This "misspelling" – which comes before the advent of reading – helps the marvellous child preserve the unity of his world, by saving the grandfather's woman from descending into sexual difference and thus into lack.[26] The child's false (sexual and linguistic) theory binds itself to this belief in the unity of the world and in the division of its inhabitants, both internally and from each other. Conveniently, his own androgyny and immortality can thus also remain unquestioned.

"What is that?" a child asks. "A bird," the adult answers. The maternal language names and creates things at the same time. Like mothers, fairies too invent the world by pointing to things with magic wands. This univocal designation (which grants the object of desire) is the basis of the myth of the mother tongue – and that is no doubt the reason why the motif is so commonly found in fairy tales. How should we understand this?

1   By touching the object, the wand stops the sliding of meaning and precludes all ambiguity.
2   As a material representation of ostension,[27] it points out and isolates a segment of the real (hence creating a signifier, as Saussure would say) and transforms it into the object of jouissance.
3   Only the Good Fairy can use both the formula and the wand without risking death.

As to the magic formula that goes along with the gesture:

1   It is always idiosyncratic and discrete (different from all others) and only comprehensible to the one who utters it.

2   Each situation requires a different formula, since the latter can only produce a single miracle – hence the existence of a "Great Book of Spells" containing all possible spells for all the desired objects of the world, where each of them is accounted for and associated with a unique magical formula.[28]

Fairy tales depict a magical world populated by good fairies and witches, where everyone is rewarded according their deeds. For example, in Poulou's favourite story "The Fairies", the good girl's words are transformed into precious stones, while the wicked one spits out snakes and toads. The myth of the maternal language also presupposes that there is a (single) word for every thing, that things are in their proper place and that the members of a couple necessarily complete each other (Karl and Mamie, the rat and the mouse, the toad and the frog). The imaginary salience of the so-called mother tongue, as Marc Léopold Lévy tells us,[29] distinguishes it from all other languages of childhood, from the puns and expletives of the paternal language, which succeed in separating the word from the thing; and from the playground language of first socialization, where different laws come into conflict with each other (the law of the family, the law of the tough guys and bullies, the law of the teachers, etc.).

After the loss of the magical thinking which is concurrent with the mother tongue, the nostalgic subject will tend to locate this primary language closer to the body and its drives, and therefore closer to truth – as if it conveyed absolute certainties. For example, one Canadian boy told his father: "Mummy says *oiseau* for *bird*, but it IS a bird!" The mother tongue is of course not necessarily the language *spoken* by the mother (especially in the English-speaking world) but instead the one that names and therefore conjures up the objects of the world.[30]

This theory of language *avant la lettre*, before language is broken down into pieces (letters), occludes a fundamental fact, namely that in *any* language the word is separated from the thing and their forms are mutually independent. As we have known since Saussure, the word signifies (via the signified) but does not represent either the object or the subject. The "mother tongue" therefore has a strong affective, ideological charge; it is fuelled by our desire to believe that, precisely, in one's own language, no such gap between words and things exists. However, as Marc-Léopold Lévy points out, this gap is what

constitutes not only language and its laws but also the subject as a human being. The belief in the consubstantiality of the word and the thing is a fantasy that allows the subject to escape an unpleasant encounter: one that would confront him with the impossible. This impossibility not only resides intrinsically *in* language but is in fact part *of* it. It is what founds the human subject as such, i.e. as a lack of being . . . represented by language. This fantasy, equivalent to that of the "native land" which further magnifies it, construes reality as a mask against the impossible – we tell ourselves that "it would be different" were we not living in a foreign land. By adding to the fantasy of each human subject (that language re-presents the objects of the world), we have therefore decided that, as in the case of the native land, there is something different and special about the mother tongue, something that remains outside the symbolic law. The impossibility is thus doubly concealed.

(M.-L. Lévy, 2003, p. 104)

Therefore, the discovery that language has an independent mind is necessarily a terrible disappointment: the angel falls from the heavens and in the gap between the word and the thing, between my mother and myself, between a man and a woman, their ultimate emptiness is revealed.

The nonreader must seize upon this autonomous materiality of the Symbolic, these "pieces" of the mother's body, in order to learn to read. But how can we recognize and accept this initiatory loss, the blow to the mother's completeness, the pound of flesh that must be paid for one's access to reading? In Poulou's case, the passage is made easier by the fact that the tale read by the mother is the same one that she normally tells him during his bath. This sameness allows the child to tolerate the mother's transformation. The same mother, the same story/a different mother, not quite the same story. The difference between the two versions ("The tale itself was in its Sunday best. . . .") and the juxtaposition of its two signifying forms ("And then I did not recognize the language. . . .") together open up a new, confusing space, where the ego can no longer find its bearings. What Sartre will later call a "release [déclic] which tore me out of myself" (p. 32) is first a blurring (bougé), a trauma which must be understood as a beneficial symbolic castration, allowing the subject to emerge from it as a subject to the Symbolic. The future subject of reading can only arise from this time-space: from a break that engenders a lack-in-being[31] and restricts the drive for mastery.

The gap between the "two different mothers" and the "two different stories" therefore creates a space where language will be constituted as an autonomous dimension. The Symbolic emerges from a place where something is found missing. Something has become separate from the mother: her gaze and her voice, but also the ego itself, as this object-being previously reflected in the mother's loving face. Sartre indeed tells us that what the subject is missing, what is "torn out of himself" (p. 32), is in fact his ego (the ontological modality of *I was/je étais*). This gap presents a question to the subject – Who is speaking and in what language? – which leads the child to formulate the hypothesis of something being present in spite of its absence, present in absence itself. The speculation is then confirmed by the negative character of the signifier and its letters.

The book's voice shows us its words as "centipedes" – little insects swarming on the ground, where the subject too is now crawling after the collapse of his ego. These animal images seem to figure the Symbolic in its pure state, which is emerging here as Real because it is impossible to identify. Words can be separated from the mother's seductive voice. The uncanny feeling gives way to surprise: there is an Other and s/he is speaking without any desire for me. There is language that exists outside the body's consistency. It is saying something. It wants something. But from whom? And where do I have to place myself (*sistere*) so that it may speak *to me*, so that I can understand it?

To whom? The psychical position of the reader-to-be

What exactly must be lost, what illusion? And where should one stand so as to be concerned by the Other's question, to be able to make sense of what the Other is trying to say and what it means? The question "*Che Vuoi?*" is therefore naturally followed by "for whom?"

To whom is all speech and writing addressed? The answer is: to a human being. Once the subject can access this position, he or she is able to hear, read and comprehend anything – or at least understand that there is meaning that can be separated from its form. Once it has detached itself from the body and gaze, from things themselves, meaning (addressed to a specific subject) can be understood as (universal) signification and it can be written and read in the alphabetical code, and hence can become a *lectio* – a lesson we draw from reading.

Let us return to the end of Sartre's scene.

> Someone began to ask questions. . . . It was as if *a child* were being quizzed: what would he have done in the woodcutter's place? Which of the two sisters did he prefer? Why? . . . But this child was not entirely me and I was afraid to reply. *Nevertheless*, I did reply; my feeble voice grew faint and *I felt I was turning into someone else.* Anne-Marie, too, with her blind soothsayer's look, was someone else: it was as if I were every mother's child and she were every child's mother. When she stopped reading, I quickly took back the books and carried them off under my arm without a word of thanks.
>
> (p. 32, modified translation, my emphasis)

"*Someone* began to ask questions. . . . It seemed [to *me*] as if a *child* were *being questioned.*" We have three agencies here (me, they [*on*] and a child) which denote, respectively, the ego, the Other of language, and the universal place where the future subject must position himself. *A child? Who?* The ego turns back to look for the generic child who is "not entirely me" but to whom these peculiarly formulated questions are addressed. The strangeness (extraneity) of language "in its Sunday best", uttered by the mother, designates a place where the subject becomes a stranger to himself, divided by language that no longer *represents* him. Not knowing to whom and where these words are spoken, he loses both his head and his voice. The dead body of the plaster mother and the danger of his own abolition both fascinate and terrify him – and there is only language to hold on to. He therefore responds, as if usurping this new place of address, and by positioning himself as a point of reference: he is now both an addressee and an object in the world, a referent. Language becomes thinkable because it can now be separated from the mother's body, which remains as its relic: a "plaster statue", a simple mouthpiece "standing in" for the place from where "it" speaks. By answering, *nevertheless*, the marvellous child commits a suicide and a matricide at the same time, only to gain humanity instead.

Realizing that the "mother for myself" has disappeared, the hero of the family romance must suffer the same fate. The subject now exists outside the mother; he is able to imagine himself in a third place outside the consistency of their incestual bodily closeness. The "young girl of my mornings" fades away, giving way to the impersonal "they" (*on*) of anonymous enunciation. The place from which the plaster statue speaks is the same universal place that the child, in a kind of delirium (having "lost his head"), "usurps", and by doing so he becomes the "child of all mothers". By recognizing himself in the generic child, the subject accepts being represented as an element of the signifying chain (*child–mother*); this designation of a kinship structure collapses the incestual relationship of fusion and sublimates the Imaginary of the family romance and its particularities (its particular madness) into the Symbolic and universal. The word *mummy* now replaces and calls for the memory of the mother's caressing body. Expelled from the magical world of the mother tongue, the humanized subject can subsequently be represented by one signifier – *child* – for another signifier – *mother*. He is propelled along the infinite and one-directional passage of the symbolic chain, and there is no way back. From now on, the subject can merely hope to emerge intermittently, in a gap between two signifiers, where meaning – in the sense of a consubstantiality of words and things, of speech and the body – can only be the object of nostalgic desire. This lost paradigm is endlessly replayed in the *jouis-sens* of reading.[32]

"When she stopped reading, I quickly took back the books and carried them off under my arm without a word of thanks." Disguised as a reader, his mother has been unfaithful to him – not with the postman but with the Symbolic. The scene ends with a violent gesture: Poulou shows his mother that he has been rejected by her (as his mother) and, paradoxically, that he is also jealous of her (as a sister). He does not flee empty-handed. He snatches the incriminating object (of desire) from her hands because she failed to give him what he wanted – unconditional love, which magically would have made him the master of the book, without having to lose anything, without having to pay a price. His frustration shows that he already knows: in order to gain access to reading, to seize the keys that will allow him to sublimate the drive for mastery into the drive for knowledge, and thus hopefully gain control over his grandfather's books, this loss cannot be avoided.

> Then I became jealous of my mother and I decided to usurp her role. I seized upon a work called *Tribulations d'un Chinois en Chine* and took it away to a box-room; there, perched on a folding bedstead, I pretended to read: my eyes followed the black lines without skipping a single one and I told myself a story out loud, taking care to pronounce every syllable. I was discovered – or I let myself be discovered; there were cries of admiration and it was decided that it was time I was taught the alphabet. I was zealous as a catechumen; I even gave myself private lessons: I climbed on to my folding bedstead with Hector Malot's *Sans famille*, which I knew by heart, and half-reciting, half-deciphering it, I went through every page, one after another: when the last was turned, I knew how to read.

(p. 32)

The child leaves the world of needs and the incestual jouissance of the maternal language and submits himself to the law of the Other's desire – the Other who has now become the ultimate addressee of his speech and his future reading. What Sartre later marks as his birth begins here: this shocking aphanisis, this "exile", becomes a constructive tearing away. "In the long run, I came to enjoy this release which tore me out of myself" (p. 32). From the gap between the mother and the self, between the maternal and the universal language, springs the singular desire to be able to read and write.

As he recounts it in his autobiography, Sartre's story of his access to genuine reading, to *lectio*, to knowledge and signification, highlights the modalities of this brutal and final exit from the infernal paradise of childhood, ruled by magic and omnipotence, by monsters and merciless gods, where all is chaos of frustration and incomprehension. The jubilatory effect of the subject that is produced by this transition marks the entrance of the alexic child into the humanizing dimension of the written word. It represents a double break – epistemological as well as ontological. This brings to mind Christian Bobin's formulation: "One day you recognize a word on a page, you say it aloud and a little piece of God is gone – paradise suffers its first fracture."[33]

This fracture, which is prior to every human life and to humanity itself, is depicted in the parable of Genesis, as a metaphor of irremediable loss. Could we therefore understand God, Marc-Léopold Lévy wonders,[34] as the representation of what the human being lacks as a speaking being, what he loses due to the very fact of becoming human – his animal nature, the world of instincts governed by the natural order, the possibility of a total fulfilment. This Paradise is a nostalgic invention of a certain space-time where the drive finds its complete satisfaction and the human being remains a dumb animal, a happily purring cat; a world where there is no need to go through the Symbolic in order to formulate a demand, no subordination to the Other's language and desire.

Some subjects manage to linger in this "Paradise" at the cost of their psychic and social emancipation: this, it turns out, is precisely the case of certain nonreading children.

TO READ OR NOT TO BE: THE NIGHTMARE OF THE NONREADERS

We live our lives half asleep, so that the Other may keep his eyes wide open.
(Melman, p. 126)[35]

Before he can use the all-powerful Symbolic to bind the Imaginary and produce semblances through writing, Sartre must first suffer the loss of the Mother. She thus becomes a fragmentable mother – a plaster statue whose vacant stare plunges her son into a dreadful state of nonbeing (*manque-à-être*). Simultaneously, language can separate itself from the single meaning of the mother's address, and it emerges as a foreign language independent of her seduction: it means something; it wants something impossible because it does not yet exist. The subject can only grasp the fact of meaning (as both intention and signification)[36] once he has assumed the position of the "child of all mothers" to whom the editor of "The Fairies" is speaking. All language and writing speak to this universal position, from which anything can be read and understood – or almost anything.

Valentin's[37] nightmare (see the beginning of this chapter) can help illustrate this human adventure. In the dream he is very small and he is looking for "something he has lost" – his mother.[38] He is a little orphan menaced by the books that are going to crush him. The psychiatrist's report states that except for his nightmares, the boy is doing quite well and has "good grades both in math and in French". We are no longer surprised by this: we know that in order to make books speak, one must first de-complete the mother. That is the price to pay if one is to do well at school and have good grades. Understandably, some children see no point in losing the maternal Whole-One (this is especially true for boys). Indeed, some have no desire to occupy the position in which one accepts to be crushed by the Symbolic and must then wander alone through the various institutions of knowledge. Their theories of language thus retain their status of a dogma; as we can often observe in these children's drawings, they cling to the maternal language and its myth of fullness and consubstantiality. The disembodied and asexualized mother (see Figure 1.1), with her cartoon-like bubble of speech, fully controls the world and the child[39] – a subject with no desire of his own.[40]

In their book *Des enfants hors du lire* (*Children outside Reading*), the authors, psychologists and researchers at the Child and Adolescent Unit of the Sainte-Anne Hospital in Paris, explain the criteria that have led them to identify a particular group of children as the so-called *enfants non lecteurs*.[41] The name may seem a euphemism; however, it seems to me more fitting than the oft-used category of "dyslexia", which connotes a medical approach to the symptom; giving the child a psychiatric label may in fact prevent those around him from taking a respectful step back and listening to what the child has to say. What indeed is expressed in this mute speech, in this silent anguish? What unconscious gains can be drawn from holding on to this peculiar impossibility?

In order to be considered a nonreader, a child must meet the following criteria:

- be at least nine years of age at the moment of first consultation
- have been schooled in French from kindergarten onwards
- not suffer from any disabling psychopathological disorder such as psychosis and not manifest any linguistic dysfunction (such as dysphasia) or have any sign of a disease affecting the central nervous system
- possess normal aptitudes on at least two of the WISC scales (the revised Wechsler Intelligence Scale for Children – WISC R at the time), that is to have an IQ of more than 85 on the verbal or performance scale
- not come from a particularly impoverished or pathogenic family
- have serious reading difficulties.[42]

Figure 1.1 Drawings of their mothers by nonreading children

A.-M. Picard

When reading out loud and decoding a short text, nonreaders are children who, at nine years of age, do not exceed the level of reading comprehension of first-grade pupils. All they are able to do is slowly articulate the studied text; they can only grasp isolated letters; they juxtapose certain syllables; they recognize few words and sometimes none at all. When they cannot answer questions about the meaning of the story, they invent things based on whatever clues they can identify. This is one of their preferred strategies – pretending that all is well (see "False theories and beliefs: how *not* to arrive at meaning").

If a child fails to meet but a single one of these criteria, he or she is placed in a category of "weak readers" who are able to deliver a superior or swift oral decipher-ing (this population therefore approximates those children we usually see in similar kinds of studies, at least in France).[43] It is interesting to note that in this study:

- Nonreading children mostly came from middle-class backgrounds (several in the study were from families of unskilled workers, but some came from more highly educated families – their parents were executives or teachers).
- The father's level of schooling was often inferior to that of the mother.
- Their early childhoods were described as uneventful.[44]

However, in a number of cases, the arrival of children in the learning institution "had coincided with traumatic events (such as the death of the father)" or, which the researchers found even more puzzling, "with the revelation of family secrets (such as the death of a twin, a brother or sister that had been given up to social services, a diagnosis of a genetic disease concerning the child, etc.)". The child's entrance into the school system compels the family to reenter the social sphere and abide by its conventions, "provoking the disclosure" of these often very well-guarded secrets which had previously remained unknown to the child (Kugler et al., 2000, p. 488).

These secrets, whose unveiling sometimes coincided with the child's entry into the first grade, are of particular interest to us, as they were to the researchers at Sainte-Anne. The reason is that although the personality structures of these chil-dren "[attest] to no psychopathological disorder", they seem deeply inhibited and suffer from "limited imagination" (as demonstrated by Rorschach tests).[45] What is it they are afraid of and what effect may this fear be having on their desire to decrypt writing's code? When we speak to these children nothing seems peculiar at first; however, further tests show "a lack of fluency in all language games, par-ticularly concerning narrative behaviour: problems with shifters, repetitions, the excessive use of exophoric forms" (i.e. universal categories: *the* boy, *the* parents, *the* dog) and a "weak aptitude with respect to anything metalinguistic" (Kugler et al., 2000, p. 489). In other words, the child's weakness lies in the manner in which he or she "theorizes" reading. Let us not forget the key importance of what Freud calls "false theories" in the functioning of writing. The authors add:

> The cognitive aspects demonstrate a very specific way of dealing with infor-mation: fragmentation, isolation and poor prioritisation of the knowledge elements, especially when they are presented through language. The subject throws himself into action, giving himself no space for making hypotheses and assessing them. These procedures of isolation are particularly debilitat-ing with respect to the act of reading: each letter is enunciated separately;

there is no possibility of phonemic fusion. The lack of overarching hypothesis thus paralyzes any search for the overall meaning of the text.

(p. 489)

In terms of the development and prognosis of such children, the authors of the Sainte-Anne study (published in 2001, after fifteen years of experience with a steadily growing group of nonreaders) conclude: "The particular treatment and remedial work propositions" that are "associated with psychotherapy adapted to these disorders" demonstrate "incontestable" benefits, even though "progress is very slow, and non-reading is gradually replaced by poor reading and transcription skills" (Kugler et al., 2001, p. 489).

Can the myth of the maternal language that we have explored in this chapter, in order to show the complex psychic processes at play in reading acquisition, help us understand the private stage on which these children are "playing" and where the lack of a universal language prevents them from expressing their suffering, their *mal-à-dit*, as Lacan might say? Let's try to clarify the peculiar and even mysterious difficulties faced by these children, who have rather ordinary psychocognitive profiles, with the help of Sartre's *Words*. In our reading, we should keep in mind the previously mentioned tendency to isolate letters and words in ways that are highly reminiscent of Strachey's obsessional reader (see the Introduction).

False theories and beliefs: how *not* to arrive at meaning

Sonia is ten and half years old when she arrives at Sainte-Anne for her first consultation. She and her Portuguese family have been living in France for four years. They all speak Portuguese at home. Sonia cannot read. Still, her mother says, "she has the power to learn – but she is like my husband, he also needed help at school." And she adds, "Sonia is everything to her father." This is confirmed when we see them both together, sitting side by side in the waiting room, the girl's head resting on her father's shoulder. Mrs M tells us privately that she has had two miscarriages: one before and one after Sonia was born. Both have been kept a secret from her daughter. During the psychological assessment, we notice that Sonia is exceedingly attentive to the presentation of objects given to her: everything must be beautiful, perfect, neatly arranged. She says that she wants to be a hairdresser "like mummy was before".

When we ask Sonia what she expects from us, how we can help her, she answers: "I would like to learn the words I don't know." And in fact, when she is reading, she simply skips over the words she does not recognize.

"How do you think people learn to read, Sonia?"
"A *monsieur* taught my father all the words. He learned them from a big history book."
"And where do you find that book?"
"Don't know."

It is as if all words could be learned at the same time, as if they were all contained in a single volume. In the child's imagination, the theory of reading contains an impossibility which rids the child of all desire to gain access to it. How could we even imagine entering into this Whole-One that is in no way concerned with us, that consists of a boundless foreign place with no clear path to get there? The Magic Book cannot be simply acquired; it does not symbolize knowledge, but instead the truth of the maternal language. In Sonia's case, this language has been lost (deterritorialized from its native land), while simultaneously retaining all its signifying pregnancy in the *heimlich* of the family home – against all odds. Sonia does not know whether she wants to live in France or in Portugal. Something in the *heimlich* of the maternal language has become a family secret: a dialect spoken between only two or three people, in the physical closeness with her father, a musician.

The child's imaginary world figures a relationship to the knowledge about truth (the truth of parental desire): she creates a fantasy of what could have determined her own conception. Her attitude to knowledge, which is sustained by this convenient imaginary theorization, inevitably has an impact on her cognitive performance. The child has managed not to know. We find a similar psychic situations in other cases of the so-called severe learning difficulties, where a false theory of reading combines with an attitude of not wanting to know, and the former becomes an excuse for the latter.

Freud tells us about the effects of the drive for knowledge (*Wissensdrang*) and how it happens that a child stops being curious.

> It seems to me to follow from a great deal of information I have received that children refuse to believe the stork theory and that from the time of this first deception and rebuff they nourish a distrust of adults and have a suspicion of there being something forbidden which is being withheld from them by the "grown-ups", and that they consequently hide their further researches under a cloak of secrecy. With this, however, the child also experiences the first occasion for a "psychical conflict", in that views for which he feels an instinctual kind of preference, but which are not "right" in the eyes of the grown-ups, come into opposition with other views, which are supported by the authority of the grown-ups without being acceptable to him himself. Such a psychical conflict may soon turn into a "psychical dissociation". The set of views which are bound up with being "good", but also with a cessation of reflection, become the dominant and conscious views; while the other set, for which the child's work of research has meanwhile obtained fresh evidence, but which are not supposed to count, become the suppressed and "unconscious" ones. The nuclear complex of a neurosis is in this way brought into being.
>
> . . . in this field children produce many incorrect ideas in order to contradict older and better knowledge which has become unconscious and is repressed. . . . In some, sexual repression has gone so far that they will not listen to anything; and these succeed in remaining ignorant even in later

life – apparently ignorant, at least – until, in the psycho-analysis of neurotics, the knowledge that originated in early childhood comes to light. I also know of two boys between ten and thirteen years old who, though it is true that they listened to the sexual information, rejected it with the words: "Your father and other people may do something like that, but I know for certain my father never would."[46]

In order to remain a good boy or girl in the eyes of the parents, the child sacrifices curiosity and gives up on truth. The child submits to the grown-up's opinion and thus evades possible punishment or disapproval. Even though – or because – the discovery of "sexual things" is always loaded with forbidden excitement, children will repress the truth that was previously unveiled by their investigations in order to protect their bond with their Imaginary parents. They stop searching because finding could mean dissatisfying their parents. The drive for knowledge is blocked by a false sexual theory, which is then elevated into a system: it becomes the basis for a belief that protects the child from becoming dislodged from his position as the Mother's imaginary phallus. What the child could in fact find is the parents' desire, their lack, and therefore their castration, insofar as they are themselves subjected to the Other. The child would then be ejected from the primal scene – that of his own conception – where he revels in a misconception, a foundational impossibility of his own presence in the scene. Finding the truth, the child would no longer be the all-satisfying phallus; the latter is now with the Other, the divine One that inhabits the parental bodies during their sexual rapport. The two boys in Freud's discussion need to posit their father as an exception (everyone except him): if he remains outside the command of the Other's desire, he remains omniscient, enjoying all, like the Father of the primitive horde before his murder or Poulou's totemic grandfather prior to the female rebellion.[47] Equally there will be no play of language, no empty space and no symbolic elaboration, like in the game of the sliding puzzle, where it is the empty slot that allows us to move around the other pieces in order to create an image or make up a word or a phrase. Sartre has escaped by only a hair's breath.

To believe in the stork means to remain a good little boy – to avoid separation and having to work through the feelings of one's abandonment in and through the parent's desire. The false sexual theory protects the child – and this is the chief benefit of halting the drive for knowledge – from the anxiety of becoming estranged from one's own parents.[48] When little David tells us "Storks brought books to mummy," his mother being a librarian, his false theory of language is again attached to the myth of the Magic Book, to an image of conception which desexualizes the mother. Epistemophilia is bound up with a knowledge about desire, as we have seen in the case of Sartre and his bi-sexed books (the raised stones and the moist oyster). If nonreading children show very little curiosity about the facts of life, is it not because they already have their own theory, their own idea that has acquired the power of a dogma? We may wonder about the place that David assigns to himself in these rows of books that his mother is so interested in. After all, the stork brought him to his mother, too. Why does she pay more attention to them than to him? Books have become his love rivals. His theory of language is hidden under the loincloth of the image of a book, his mother's preoccupation, closed and filed on the library shelf. This allows him to avoid the troubling question: "Why did she make me? What desire do I come from?" What would be the danger of knowing the answer? In any case, it seems less dangerous not to know. Yet, as a consequence of avoiding this confrontation, of avoiding the knowledge that is forbidden because it signifies a lack (of satisfaction), the drive for knowledge is inhibited and the child cannot begin to desire, cannot hypothesize the existence of the object and therefore cannot sublimate.

In Freud's understanding, the false theories of children[49] allow them not to think any further: they focus on *how* (how children are made) instead of asking *why* (why did my parents make me), a question that articulates the parents' desires and ultimately the meaning of the child's existence.[50] As we have seen in the case of Sartre, his grandmother and grandfather form a unified (and asexual) couple, articulated by the holophrase *Karlémami*. Like children's sexual theories, false theories of language are part of the narcissism of the family romance and the convenient answers it offers to the question *why*. By not being able to read, certain children may therefore go on *not* wondering what their parents want, what they did or did not want earlier, or what they are hiding from themselves.

In *Des enfants hors du lire*, Carol Rose offers us a typology of the false theories of nonreading children. These can take a number of forms, for example:

- Reading is not a meaning-producing activity but primarily something imposed on the child by an other, usually by an adult.
- Reading means learning things by heart.
- Reading means naming letters and so forth.

These beliefs are compact and can only be questioned with difficulty. They are often induced in the child by some pedagogical figure, such as a parent or a well-meaning teacher (Rose, p. 179), and they are useful to the child psychically and narcissistically, primarily in that they allow him not to be responsible for his failures (which are often actively pursued). In addition to this, as dogmas they leave little space for doubt. Doubting would require speculation and thus a freedom to think and to exist; however, for these little troubled learners, both remain impossible (Rose, p. 178). Sonia's "theory" is based on a belief in the existence of a "Big Book" that supposedly contains all words. This book is held by a distant other and thus has no effect on the child's present situation. Her ideas remind us of Sartre's own childhood theory prior to reading, in which the grandfather's books functioned as totems.

David's storks and Sonia's Man with the Book are both figures of omniscience. Like divine messengers, the birds travel between the heavens and the earth, bringing books (and babies) to Mummy. And in the faraway land of Portugal, the lost land of childhood, an old sorcerer holds the keys to the father's knowledge – a father who himself had difficulties as a child. Like Poulou, on their way to the minor science of reading (as *lectio*), which represents the first step towards all future acquisition of knowledge, Sonia and David must first pass through the omniscience of the nonsublimated drive for mastery. As long as the belief in "God" – the omniscient Other – remains unbarred, taking the plunge is hard. Without the female plot against the grandfather's autocracy, Karl would have continued to play his divine role ("God the Father himself" [Sartre, *Words*, p. 16]), his knowledge unchallenged, and Poulou would have been unable to construct a world outside the law of his grandfather's gaze, a world he fittingly calls a "brothel".

Maintaining the status quo, dealing with the impossible

Nicolas, a twin, keeps putting letters together two by two, in order to decipher them. Yet sometimes he becomes stuck before a particular word:

"Why are you afraid, Nicolas?"
"I don't know this word because I haven't invented it."

Only the person who has invented a word can read it. When children like Nicolas are looking at a page of text, they tend to guess instead of deciphering. They turn into anguished soothsayers, trying to divine a complicated cypher while lacking the code. They prefer to leave all knowledge to the Other, who is not interested in them (so that there no threat of castration). They have no desire to question the statue of the commander,[51] to bring the Other down from the sky, nor to suffer the consequences: to hear him signify the subject's lack, his inability to satisfy the parent's desire.

Others rely on the divination of their mother, who embodies the Other in the father's relative absence (in the majority of consultations, the father is not present). These mothers know everything and prohibit nothing. Staying away from all knowledge means that it is best to leave everything to mummy.

"What is your date of birth?" we ask Valerie.
"I don't know. My mother's never told me," the child answers.
"How do people read?" we ask the mother.
"You must read everything," she answers. "You put two letters together. . . ."

Nicolas and Valerie prefer to leave knowledge to the Other, who indeed knows "everything". The consistency given to this Other by the parent, often the mother, means that there is no place where the child could exist. What else could then one want, other than the status quo? These children can continue living in the magical world of the maternal language, the Paradise of imaginary incest, where they are all for daddy or all for mummy. This is the reason why, as Maïté Auzanneau points out, children with severe reading disorders function in the mode of "all is well, all must be well at any cost". After years of failing to learn to read, when "shame, guilt and a certain secretiveness are added to the specific problem of reading", these children end up developing

> inadequate strategies, they do their best to come up with the maximum range of solutions to make themselves a protective shell in which they feel, after all, relatively "ok": their dependency on their mother, or on the other generally, and later their recognized status give them access to welfare aid and specific training programs. All is done to trigger rejection and failure.[52]

These strategies and solutions, based on "convenient" theories of reading, can be seen as examples of what Joyce McDougall calls "dream solutions" to the "desire of the impossible".[53] The impossibility of the desire lies in the fact that, paradoxically, it is trying to maintain the status quo to preserve the imaginary (incestual) scene of the private theatre for all eternity. This desire of the impossible marks all human dramatizations and beliefs.

> How do we manage to bind the wounds to our narcissistic integrity caused by external realities – the impossibility of being one with the mother; the failure of the illusion that one can control another's thoughts and actions; the fact of aging; and finally, the inevitability of death? Most of us manage to make unstable adjustments to these realities, but there is little doubt that in our unconscious fantasies we are all omnipotent, bisexual, eternally young, and immortal.
>
> (McDougall, p. 9)

The mythic counterpart of the configurations that these dream solutions are trying to preserve – ultimately in order to avoid division and separation, as well as to prevent the "fragmentation" of what in the child's psyche remains a totality – is the Paradise before the Fall. Like any other belief system, the apparently solid, "rigid and walled-up" beliefs of certain children (Rose, p. 178) allow the subject to "earn her way to heaven". However, such preservation comes at the cost of sacrificing one's desire (for knowledge) and hence one's creativity and the possibility of participating in the cultural sphere.

WATIZDIZ? Preserving the unreadable

In a study of the narrative behaviour of nonreading children carried out by Catherine Ferron and her colleagues several years ago, the authors noticed[54] a strong tendency to use exophoric forms of reference (*the* boy, *the* mummy, *the* car). They equally comment on the high degree of referential indeterminacy in the children's narratives: the heroes unknown to the listener are never introduced, the antecedents of pronouns are simply assumed and so on. These presumptions imply a strong belief that knowledge is shared by everyone and that it is therefore possible "for the addressee to reconstitute or identify the reality [the child] is referring to"

(Préneron et al., p. 208). We could add that this shared knowledge is the objective possibility and indivisibility of the referent as *One* (the totem). This is the object the child is trying to look for in the eyes of the listener, who is herself seen as the (more or less) Good Fairy, able to bring word objects (sometimes recognizable, sometimes monstrous) into being through speech. But what is she speaking about? What does she want (from me) with her question and her pointing finger? WATIZDIZ? "Non-reading children are missing indexed coordination," Ferron observes (1987, p. 111), "the subject of enunciation only speaks through its absence" (1990, p. 262).

> In the session, children speak minimally, making schematic, holophrastic statements: "There is, there is." They have nothing to say, no story to tell. Where can the therapist find something that she can use as a basis, a support of desire?
> The creation of the signifier and the holophrase are two sides of the same lack. . . . Their voices seem to have no bodily support; their gaze often becomes lost in a maternal elsewhere, against which their symptom is their only defence. They are subjects of their mother's dream.
>
> (Ferron, 1990, p. 264)

In these children, the prohibition on thought leads to the formation of a symptom: inhibition, lack of autonomy, problems of concentration, rigidity, escapism and stereotypical repetitions (Auzanneau, p. 377). But equally there can be agitation or apathy, absence of curiosity, anxiety with a dominance of guilt – no doubt "successfully" instilled in them by the social and institutional gaze which plays the role of the (otherwise missing) third term.

Not knowing how to read means that the subject, who finds a way out through the Symbolic (more exactly through the parental relationship to the law and thus to desire) and only has the Symbolic to rely on (by appropriating the position of the universal subject), is refusing to take the only outlet to freedom available to him. The nonreading child has created a belief that hermeneutically seals off any space for hypothesis, for doubt and speculation, so that thought is reduced to nothing. The child experiences this sealing off as both oppressing and satisfying.

> The non-reading child cannot consent to the sacrifice of recognizing the mother's body as separate from his own. He remains in a kind of interior exteriority, in an outside-inside of the fantasmatic sexual relationship, a negation. The analytic work therefore lies in helping to bring about repression, to vectorize the intention, because to consent to sacrificing the maternal One means to have to account for oneself, to become separate from the mother.
>
> (Ferron, p. 264)

Nonreading children want to know nothing about the trials of castration and separation. We could formulate this differently: it is because of what they do not want to know that certain children manage not to learn how to read. The sacrifice, which would have woken up the dozing Other (see Charles Melman's epigraph to this chapter), will not have taken place; the child continues to rely on magical thinking because it lets her go on believing that the object of jouissance has been created *sui generis*. Believing in the Magic Book means waiting for the lost Paradise to return; a stroke of the magic wand will reveal the meanings of words and things, which in turn will continue to reflect each other, thanks to the omnipotence of the maternal language. In the meantime, children avoid the confrontation with signification – that is with the difference and arbitrariness of the symbolic code – by not reading, scared to know what it is that one wants from them and what they mean as the sons or daughters of the parental desire. They remain trapped in the Paradise before the Fall, where everything is fixed at a place. The Fall itself is pushed forward into a mythical rather than hypothetical future which is in fact only the past replayed:

"When will you learn to read, Sébastien?"
"When I am eleven."
"Why at eleven?"
"My father learned when he was 11."

Therefore, in order not to begin to tell their own story, not to give themselves the means of reading it in books written by others, nonreading children remain good little believers. They fulfil their religious duties by keeping God in his place and worshiping his relics: the letters that only go by their names in the kind of spelling these children mistake for reading; the words that belong to the world of the fairies and whose meanings only exist under the gaze of the Mother, from which the child cannot be separated. Their God is himself a reader: he knows the meaning of their lives because he has read their destiny in his Big Book. The future is occluded by the heaviness of the myth, which prevents the subject from speculating, from moving forward in the quest for knowledge, from inventing what is still to come. What could one in fact gain by curiosity, by asking questions? Family secrets, which have been locked away in a dark crypt underpinning the family's psychic structure, are only discovered in the course of therapy sessions and are quite safe. The unconscious fantasy dictates that deciphering the code that opens the crypt would put the family at risk of implosion. When the child unconsciously positions himself as the crypt's illiterate gatekeeper, his academic failures and disorders become a privately encoded idiom, the family's own symptom. Sonia does not know that she was born between two deaths; Jonathan does not know that the name he cannot read on the fascinating model of a ship belongs to his uncle who committed suicide; another child does not know that the reason why his family abandoned him for several weeks as he entered first grade had to do with the death of his grandmother. The unreadable moves from the unspoken onto the book page. The silence is reproduced, like a forbidden appeal to the Symbolic.

What happened to little Sonia? If she returned to Portugal, was she able to "fall" outside the nostalgia that binds her and her parents to the mythic land of her birth and her mother tongue? Was she, thanks to her psychotherapy, able to confront the death-dealing position assigned to her in her mother's desire for a child between two "un-births"? Has she become a "hairdresser like mummy was before", so that she could remain daddy's Sleeping Beauty? Was she able to face the risk of no longer being "all-for-daddy", a daddy who himself was not in the know? Was she able to disrupt her search for beauty, attested to by her "object arrangements", in order to make place for another kind of order, for the *dé-lire* of symbolic differentiation and the arbitrariness of the linguistic code? Was she at last able to let herself read, situate herself as subject to the Symbolic, by renouncing the Big Magic Book of the unknown Monsieur who knew more than her own father?

The human subject's desire for jouissance stems from the regret represented by the myth of the maternal language, which is also associated with the myth of the Paradise and the world of the fairies. In this magic world, the Thing can be summoned by its sign; the desiring subject and the desirable object can be One; men and women can complete each other. As Marc-Léopold Lévy points out, the belief in magic, which remains a possibility for the child, reminds us that the jouissance aimed at by desire is always incestuous because it is trying to "return" to a world where the subject knows nothing of the frustrating arbitrariness of the signifier and the incest prohibition. He knows nothing of his own helplessness, of his absence from himself, of his alienation to the Symbolic order, where he can only be represented intermittently and always as a lack. The timeless world of the end of fairy tales is a dream solution to ward off the anxiety of a subject who has been cast, at the very instant of his birth, into the arena of others' desires, onto a map already drawn by the Symbolic, where the universal places of *I* and *You* await him. A unique object of parental desire, the subject is nevertheless part of the human species and, as a being both speaking and spoken, he must appropriate language in order to try and grasp the ungraspable object. In this way he will be able to create his *I* here and now, one that is mortal and marked by sexual difference but whose singular origin may be transformed into a story shared with others.

Notes

1 Pommier, G. (1993). *Naissance et renaissance de l'écriture*. Collection "Ecriture". Paris: P.U.F., p. 111 [Translated for this edition].
2 I would like to thank Dr Lionel Bailly, to whom this dream was recounted during a consultation at the Biopsychopathology Child and Adolescent Unit of the Sainte-Anne Hospital in Paris.
3 Sartre, J.-P. (2000). *Words*. Translated by Irene Clephane. London: Penguin Books, p. 28.
4 I will return to this ambivalence later.
5 Freud, S. (1909). "Analysis of a *Phobia* in *a Five-Year-Old Boy*". In *SE*, X, 3–141.
6 How does one therefore allow oneself to handle these venerable objects if not by becoming part of their sacredness? We should notice the repetition of the expression "cultural object" (*un bien culturel*) in Sartre's text. It appears just before he enters the

grandfather's study and here it is used about the child himself: "Fortunately, there was no lack of applause: whether they were listening to my gibberish or the Art of Fugue, adults wore the same smile of conspiratorial and mischievous relish. This shows what I really was: a cultural possession [*un bien culturel*]. I was impregnated by culture and I returned it to the family like a radiance, as pools in the evening give back the heat of the day" (Sartre, *Words*, p. 28).

7   "Our collocation 'holy dread' would often coincide in meaning with 'taboo'. Taboo restrictions are distinct from religious or moral prohibitions. They are not based upon any divine ordinance, but may be said to impose themselves on their own account. They differ from moral prohibitions in that they fall into no system that declares quite generally that certain abstinences must be observed and gives reasons for that necessity. Taboo prohibitions have no grounds and are of unknown origin. Though they are unintelligible to us, to those who are dominated by them they are taken as a matter of course." Freud, S. (1913). "Totem and Taboo". In *SE*, XIII, p. 17.

8   Sartre, J.-P. (2000). *Nausea*. Translated by Robert Baldick. London: Penguin Modern Classics, p. 10.

9   This theme is developed by Doubrovsky, S. (1982). "Phallotexte et gynotexte dans *La Nausée*: 'Feuillet sans date'". In Issacharoff, M. & Vilquin, J.-Cl. (Eds). *Sartre et la mise en signe*. Paris, Klincsieck: French Forum, pp. 31–55.

10   As a metaphor for Sartrian *essence*, their mineral nature represents Oneness while the Thing's existence finds a metonymic image in the organic swarming, the dampness.

11   For an illustration of this anxiety in the discourse of a male critic, see Chapter II, "How reading feminizes".

12   See Chapter II, "The reading eros".

13   Using Lacan's expression, I am going to call this experience *jouis-sens* (see Chapter II). Based on the work of a "master of reading", the French scholar Emile Faguet, I am going to try and situate *jouis-sens* as an effect of reading. I am also going to show that this subjective attitude or positioning is the basis of the novelistic adventure in Proust's *In Search of Lost Time* (see Chapter III, "*Dé-lire 1*").

14   What is a "position of jouissance"? The changes Roquentin undergoes in the scene of the rape in *Nausea* perfectly illustrate the ambivalence of the subject's psychic positioning in jouissance. This scene of a rape, where we no longer know who is raping and who is being raped, reveals the polymorphous nature of the fantasy of Sartre's hero's, who, suffering from terrible anxiety, initially identifies with the feminine, *capturing* position: "She felt this other flesh pushing into her own. I . . . there I . . . Raped. A soft, criminal desire to rape catches me from behind, gently behind the ears. . . ." (Sartre, *Nausea*, p. 146). Riddled with guilt, he then switches to the *forcing*, masculine position: "enter into the existence of another, into the red mucus . . . feel myself exist between these soft, wet lips" (p. 148). The capturing and the forcing positions, two expressions coined by Marc-Léopold Lévy, would then define two positions of jouissance, and of reading.

15   Chiantaretto, J.-F. (1995). *De l'Acte autobiographique: le psychanalyste et l'écriture autobiographique*. Paris: Editions Champ Vallon, p. 215.

16   For a more detailed discussion of this question through a reading of Marie Redonnet's story *Splendid Hotel*, see Chapter III, "*Dé-lire 2*".

17   This animism reminds us of the second scene of reading in the Introduction, taken from Maurice Blanchot's *Thomas the Obscure*.

18   All emphasis is mine.

19   Freud, S. (1919). "The 'Uncanny'". In *SE*, XVII, p. 222.

20   *Unheimlichkeit* provokes a "peculiar emotional effect", Freud tells us ("The 'Uncanny'", p. 226), due to the impression of insanity triggered by "doubts whether an apparently animate being is really alive; or conversely, whether a lifeless object might not be in fact animate" (p. 225).

21 We should add to this that the mother of young Sartre is more of a sister than a mother (and a fortiori another man's woman). Sartre is well aware of this: "There were three bedrooms in our house: my grandfather's, my grandmother's and the 'children's.' We were the 'children': both minors and both maintained . . . how could she have given birth to me?" (p. 16). In the family structure, where neither generations nor beds are in their proper place, the young mother is almost a twin, a mirror reflection. Does he not call her by her first name? Contrary to a father not only embodied but "designated" by the family discourse – and by the psychic structuring of everyone's place – Sartre's father seems completely "effaced". The nature of his attachment to the mother only exacerbates the feeling of strangeness when she "forgets about him".

22 Heine, *Die Götter im Exil*, cited by Freud, "The 'Uncanny'", p. 235.

23 Reading this passage, the reader quickly becomes aware that even for the adult Sartre, the monstrous, practically dead mother still remains an image impossible to bear. The narrative mentions the impression of having lost the mother only briefly, yet the fact that Sartre's autobiography ends practically at the moment the mother is about to remarry articulates this impossibility of imagining her loss all the more radically. The "young girl of my mornings" remains the most significant figure of the scene. For the adult narrator, it allows obstruction of the anxiety of *unheimlichkeit* which is about to reemerge. The young "sister" is the inverted image of Olympia and simultaneously her psychic ancestor, even though she is only reconstructed *a posteriori*. The lost time of the bathing and of the mother's tale, recaptured and written down here, preserves the belief in the "real mother" intact – one that is no longer present yet can always be called upon in a moment of desperation or of longing for an origin. Created after a catastrophe too devastating for the ego, she remains like a primitive and reassuring God. *From now on* and *forever* will then become the melancholic's coat of arms, wounded as he is by the loss of what was his native land: a place where the word became flesh, where things would speak of and by themselves. For further discussion of the myth of the mother tongue and the native land in the beliefs of nonreading children, see the later section of this chapter, "To read or not to be".

24 This idea is commonly found in children who are learning to speak. See Bonnet, C. & Tamine-Gardes, J. (1984). *Quand l'enfant parle du langage. Connaissance et conscience du langage chez l'enfant.* Paris: Pierre Mardaga.

25 We should understand this in the Lacanian sense of a logical relation (i.e. one that can be written, related by a signifier) between the masculine and the feminine positions of desire and jouissance. Lacan's formulation, "There is no sexual relationship," first appears in seminar XX, *Encore* (See Lacan, Jacques, Miller, Jacques-Alain & Fink. (1999). *On Feminine Sexuality, the Limits of Love and Knowledge: The Seminar of Jacques Lacan*, "Book XX, Encore." New York: W.W. Norton, p. 9, among others.)

26 The grandmother is here the only woman who has a relationship (of desire) with a man. As the grandfather's wife, her body is the site of the inscription of castration anxiety. The child knows he is not a completely satisfying object for the grandmother, while for both Karl and Anne-Marie he is a pure miracle. Before the reading scene and a little bit later we witness the loss of his little girl's locks. This reminds me of the Hebrew tradition described by Marc-Alain Ouaknin, where reading is preceded by "the age of three castrations – umbilical, oral and anal. The child inaugurates his own cultural autonomy, if we can put it this way. There is a ceremony of cutting the hair, which until now had been left to grow, an experience of loss . . . the hair represents numerous strands, like thin threads (ropes) in which one may always feel trapped. . . . It is a disengagement from the mother's body. The child attains his first freedom. In the course of this ceremony another inaugural event takes place: the child eats cakes made of honey, which have the shape of the alphabet. A sweet reading and an equally sweet entrance into the world of books, a sweet passage from the orality of nourishment to the orality

of reading." See Ouaknin, M.-A. (1994). *Bibliothérapie. Lire c'est guérir.* Paris: ©Le Seuil, pp. 294–295 [Translated for this edition].

27 From the Latin *ostensio* (to show).

28 In the next chapter we will see that this mythic book figures in the mythic constructions of certain nonreaders, where it represents a veritable theory of language that prevents them from decomposing language and bans them from accessing its graphematic constituents (letters or groups of letters representing a phoneme).

29 Lévy, M.-L. (2003). *Critique de la jouissance comme Une.* Toulouse: Erès [Translated for this edition with the author and publisher's kind permission].

30 I would like to thank Henri Schogt, professor emeritus at the University of Toronto, for this wonderful illustration of children's magical metalinguistic thinking.

31 This lack that will need to be produced afresh, given the human tendency to try to fill in the gap and reconstruct the undivided One in and through the incestuous jouissance of the native land (and magical thinking) – a maleficent, deadly tendency since it abolishes all desire. Writing allows some to produce a semblance at the very site of this gap, a *dis-reading* of the laws of the Symbolic (see Chapter III).

32 See Chapter II, "The reading eros".

33 Bobin, C. (1991). *Une petite robe de fête.* Paris: Editions Gallimard [Translated for this edition].

34 Lévy, M.-L. (2003). "De l'Origine de Dieu". In *Critique de la jouissance comme Une.* Toulouse: Erès, 105–130.

35 Melman, C. (1984). *Nouvelles Etudes sur l'hystérie.* Paris: Editions Joseph Clims [Translated and used for this edition with the copyright owner's, Erès Publishers, kind permission].

36 The English *to mean* has both the sense of "to signify" and "to want" and "to have in mind"; the French *ça veut dire* explicitly marks this double-entendre: "it wants" and "it says" simultaneously. This *vouloir-dire* is the marker of the symbolic Other's desire.

37 All names have been changed to protect the children's anonymity. My analysis was made possible thanks to the multidisciplinary team at the Biopsychology Child and Adolescent Unit at the Sainte-Anne Hospital in Paris. I would like to offer them my sincere thanks. All examples of case material come from the consultations of Maïté Auzanneau and Dr Lionel Bailly, the former Head of Service.

38 In Chapter III, "*Dé-lire* 4", I discuss the short story "The Torrent" by the Québécoise writer Anne Hébert, which depicts her own story of coming into writing.

39 This remains true even in the best of cases. Many of these children only draw amorphous forms or heads without bodies – mute, lost on the page, a few disordered strokes of a pencil.

40 During their first meeting with Maïté Auzanneau, who was then the consulting specialist in reading disorders at the Biopsychopathology Unit at Sainte-Anne, the children were given two prompts: (1) "Could you please draw your mother?" and (2) "Is she saying anything?" Arthur's mother ("That does not look at all like her, but I can't do better.") gives orders: "Brush your teeth!" Dimitri draws "Dimitri and Dad" (Dad was later added in a linked bubble). He explains: "She [the mother] wants to tell us something, and so she is calling us." Geoffroy's mother "Shouts like that: Geoffroy!" (a bubble spontaneously drawn by the child). These examples are mere illustrations; more extensive research must be done based on these drawings, including a comparative study with a same-age group of reading children, where the body of the mother generally appears more fragmented, more clearly differentiated and sexed. I would like to thank Maïté Auzanneau, as well as Christine Picard-Lepoire, my sister and a primary-school teacher in Le Havre (France), for giving me access to this material.

41 David, J. et al. (1994). "Les enfants non lecteurs, une population particulière?". In Préneron, C., Meljac, C. & Netchine, S. (Eds.). *Des enfants hors du lire.* Paris: Bayard, pp. 41–80 [All translated for this edition].

42 These criteria are based on the summary found in the Introduction to Kugler et al. (2000). "Les échecs en lecture respectent-ils la parité? (1ᵉ partie) Filles, garçons et lecture : vue d'ensemble sur les travaux récents", *Neuropsychiatrie de l'enfance et de l'adolescence*, 48, pp. 487–498.

43 Forty-four children were selected as meeting all of these criteria for nonreaders. Forty-three of them were boys (a second study was later conducted solely with girls). See Kugler et al. (2000), as well as Kugler et al. (2001). "Les échecs en lecture respectent-ils la parité? (2ᵉ partie) Filles et échecs et lecture: bilan de quinze ans d'expérience clinique", *Neuropsychiatrie de l'enfance et de l'adolescence*, 49, pp. 53–71 (" The failures in reading: do they respect gender parity? [part two]. Girls and failure in reading: what do we know after 15 years of clinical experience?")

44 See Kugler et al. (2000), p. 488.

45 Joubert, V.B. & Pecquet, F. "Les non-lecteurs à l'épreuve du Rorschach". *Les enfants hors du lire*, pp. 315–343. The section that follows is a revised version of a text published in the review *Tangences*, 54 (1977).

46 Freud, S. (1908). "On the Sexual Theories of Children". In *SE*, IX, pp. 205–226, quotation from pp. 212–213, 224–225.

47 In Lacanian terms, the repression of the signifier S1 induced by the Other then cannot occur and the metaphor (where S1 falls under the bar of the signifier) remains impossible.

48 Freud, S. (1909). "Family Romances". In *SE*, IX, p. 237.

49 "With his knowledge, independently obtained, that babies grow inside the mother's body, he would be on the right road to solving the problem on which he first tries out his powers of thinking. But his further progress is inhibited by a piece of ignorance which cannot be made good and by false theories which the state of his own sexuality imposes on him. These false sexual theories . . . all have one very curious characteristic. Although they go astray in a grotesque fashion, yet each one of them contains *a fragment of real truth*. . . . What is correct and hits the mark in such theories is to be explained *by their origin from the components of the sexual instinct* which are already stirring in the childish organism. For it is not owing to any arbitrary mental act or to chance impressions that those notions arise, but to the necessities of the child's psychosexual constitution; and this is why we can speak of sexual theories in children as being typical, and why we find the same mistaken beliefs in every child whose sexual life is accessible to us" (Freud, 1908, p. 214, my emphasis).

50 See Lévy, M.-L. (1996). "La Cigogne et le kabbaliste ou du comment et du pourquoi". In Picard, A.-M. (Ed.). *L'imaginaire de la théorie. Texte 17/18*. Toronto: University of Toronto Press, pp. 233–242.

51 Dom Juan or *The Feast with the Statue* is a play by Molière (1665).

52 Auzanneau, M. "Que faire pour sortir les non-lecteurs de leur état de non-lecteur?" *Des Enfants hors du lire*, 355–383, p. 376 [Translated for this edition].

53 McDougall, J. (1985). *Theatres of the Mind. Illusion and Truth on the Psychoanalytic Stage*. London: Basic Books.

54 Ferron, C. (1987). "Qu'est-ce que c'est que ça ?" *Quand lalangue fait symptôme. La psychanalyse d'enfant*, 3/4, pp. 105–124 [Translated for this edition with the author's kind permission]; "Enfants non-lecteurs en thérapie", *Perspectives psychiatriques*, 24/IV (1990), pp. 262–265; and Préneron, Salazar-Ortiz, & Kugler-Lambert, "Les conduits narratives: récits d'enfants non lecteurs". *Des enfants hors du lire*, p. 209.

Chapter II

The reading thing and the reading body

Reading is going towards something that is about to be.

(Italo Calvino)[1]

Reading as "acting out"

In 1986, a young French journalist, Elisabeth Barillé, published her first novel, *Body of a Girl*.[2] Its autodiegetic narration follows the sexual and romantic adventures of a bold and liberated young woman named Elisa. Her adventures revolve around a cat-and-mouse game with an ageing writer whose intentions towards Elisa remain unclear. As the slightly repetitive story of their missed encounters goes on, the reader expects the writer to eventually make the young woman his muse and thus overcome his writer's block. Yet the very opposite happens: the writing exercises he forces her to do, so as to transform her into the heroine of his future novel, in fact lead her to become a writer herself, with *Body of a Girl* the result of her literary efforts. The shortcomings of Barillé's novel are not the point here; instead, I would like to focus on the delicately painted scene of reading she has so helpfully included in her story.

Although Elisa had abandoned her diary and what she calls her "little pieces", the encounter with the writer mysteriously brings her back to writing. The moment when words again begin flowing from her pen reminds her of another jubilatory experience: "When, as the scene [of my story] became clear, the words came in a rush and I subdued them, I rediscovered the feeling of power which had seized me the evening I read like an adult for the first time" (Barillé, p. 55).

We immediately notice the seemingly contrasting impressions of the budding writer: first, "words come in a rush", then they are "subdued" and a "feeling of power" turns into a sensation of being "seized". This idea of dominating language, of having the power to say what she means, has to do with the gain in being provided by sublimation: it is the feeling of no longer being a subject to language, but a subject *through* language. In *Words*, Sartre offers us this wonderful metaphor:

> I had found my religion: nothing seemed more important to me than a book.
> I saw the library as a temple. Grandson of a priest, I lived *on the roof of*

the world, on the sixth floor, perched on the *highest branch of the Central Tree*. . . . When my mother took me to the Luxembourg Gardens . . . I lent my human rags to these lowly regions but my glorious substance never left its perch . . . I refused to come down; it was not that I wished to set myself up above men: I wanted to live in pure ether among the airy likenesses of Things.

(pp. 39–40, my emphasis)

This gain in being which the young Sartre derives from reading is an effect of subjectivation, of the production of the subject by the Symbolic. Sublimating the drive for mastery into a drive for knowledge transforms the "human rags" into a "glorious substance". But to get to the "roof of the world", the child must first repress the materiality of the letter: its *litterality* – which, as Lacan reminds us, echoes the English word "litter". Only on this condition does the signifier cease to be itself a thing and make space for the semblance of the signified, for the "airy likenesses of Things".

The moment of having "subdued words" is experienced by Elisa as an epiphany: her first genuine reading. She remembers exactly where she was in *20,000 Leagues under the Sea* when thing-presentation triumphed over word-representation.

Scene 4

I was ten years old. I devoured adventure yarns, travel stories. Alexandre Dumas, Paul Féval, Tabarly. Books for boys. "The Green Library."[3] "Fifteen Tales of . . ." All Jules Verne.

At nine o'clock in the evening I lit the candlestick, set in a lamp. The light brought out the contours of the room. The fold of the curtains lengthened into organ pipes. There I was in Captain Nemo's cabin. I was glancing through his ship's log by the warmth of the stove. I was pronouncing each word out loud, occasionally stopping to observe a diver moving cautiously forward over the sand, through the porthole. I was ten years old. I liked reading but at school I read poorly. My report was more specific. "Laboured reading. Must try harder." I kept trying. Every evening in bed I would pronounce the words "loudly and clearly", as my teacher recommended. I applied myself. I didn't skip over any difficult word; God knows there are enough of them in *20,000 Leagues under the Sea*. I had reached Chapter 18, page 184 in the 1928 Hachette edition, a school prize of my father.

It was a squid of colossal dimensions, being eight metres in length. It was watching with its enormous, unblinking, glaucous eyes. Its eight arms or rather feet, planted in its head, which have earned the name of cephalopod for these animals, were twice as large as its body and writhed like the hair of the Furies. The two hundred and fifty suckers, laid out on the inner face of the tentacles in the form of semi-spherical capsules, could be distinctly seen . . . Its variable colour which would change with an extreme rapidity according to the animal's irritation, went from being greyish-blue to red-dish brown.

Incredible! I read this passage in less than thirty seconds. I read without reading. The words capitulated from within. They revealed their meaning to me without my naming them. This was magic! Someone was reading for me! I thought I had swallowed another voice.

The strangest thing occurred the next day.

On waking up, I noticed that I had left the lamp on all night. I must have been sleeping restlessly; my nightshirt, hitched up around my waist, was all bunched up. What had prompted me to sit up against the padded bedhead, to take out a small, plastic mirror from the drawer of my night table, to place it between my parted thighs? I was looking inside my sex for the first time. I examined myself closely like a scientist hunched over his microscope, like the Canadian sailor who followed the unhurried ballet of the octopus though the portholes of the Nautilus.

My sex reminded me of the animal. The same reddish-brown, it was made not of suckers, but of numerous skins folded one over another like the convolutions of lambs' brains.

Moist, somewhat sticky, they had the smell of the sea.

Would I have had the courage to look between my thighs if an inner voice had not been revealed to me the previous night? I felt the strength which comes from a new secret. I knew I had been invested with a new power. I had a right to read words without speech, a right to look[4] at my sex without shame.

(Barillé, pp. 55–57)

The scene is composed as a triptych, each of the three panels telling the story of an *unheimlich* event. First, in the evening: "Incredible! I read this passage in less than thirty seconds. . . . This was magic! Someone was reading for me! I thought I had swallowed another voice." Second, at night: "On waking up, I noticed that I had left the lamp on all night. I must have been sleeping restlessly; my nightshirt, hitched up around my waist, was all bunched up." And finally, in the morning: "The strangest thing occurred the next day. What had prompted me to sit down . . . , to take out a small, plastic mirror . . . , to place it between my parted thighs?"

Although this motive force remains unknown to her, the narrator makes a link between the "magical reading" of her "inner voice" and the "strange" act that leads her to observe her sex. What had been repressed in this magical reading, only to return in the morning as Elisa's acting out? Have the drives, previously sublimated in reading ("I devour adventure stories"), regressed to the primal object of every fantasy, the sexual Thing? The oxymoron "reading without reading" conveys this double definition, never explained by the author, of the act of reading: a conjunction of two aspects that previously seemed impossible:

1   Sounding out each word: "I was pronouncing each word out loud . . . at school I read poorly. My report was more specific. 'Laboured reading. Must

try harder.' I kept trying. Every evening in bed I would pronounce the words 'loudly and clearly', as my teacher recommended. I applied myself. I didn't skip over any difficult word."

2   The pleasure of reading: "I devoured adventure yarns, travel stories. . . . At nine o'clock in the evening I lit the candlestick, set in a lamp. . . . There I was in Captain Nemo's cabin. I was glancing through his ship's log by the warmth of the stove . . . occasionally stopping to observe a diver moving cautiously forward over the sand, through the porthole."

The first kind of reading is summed up by one of Lacan's observations, which comes from a discussion of pre-Saussurean linguistics. "Taking the sign for an object", he says, "prevents us from grasping it as a signifier",[5] in other words as something that gives access to meaning. The impossibility of this double reading (of the sign as object *and* signifier) immediately points to the fantasmatic (fictionalizing) dimension that contaminates the narrator's "report", which, although presented as a true memory, is only invented after reading has become possible and serves primarily to reclaim a *droit de regard*[6] – the possibility to "look at one's sex without shame". That is its first goal. The report displays the exhibitionist qualities of this "body of a girl" and we should probably treat this scene with a little caution.

From the very beginning, Barillé gives the scene, in the original separated from the rest of the text by a blank space, an uncanny quality signifying an epistemological break – an initiation into the dimension of the Symbolic and the Unconscious. Like a guiding thread, showing us that we are indeed crossing over to another dimension, the light of the lamp illuminates both spaces. It transforms the room into a fictional scene: "At nine o'clock in the evening I lit the candlestick, set in a lamp. The light brought out the contours of the room. The fold of the curtains lengthened into organ pipes. There I was in Captain Nemo's cabin." Later, Elisa forgets to put it out – "On waking up, I noticed that I had left the lamp on all night" – suggesting that her "restless" sleep is a continuation of the conscious subject's "fading", of her loss of control over reality.

The burning lamp suggests an entrance into the Imaginary, opened up by the "magical act of reading" which has disturbed the subject's sleep and, on the following morning, prompted the acting out.[7] We are of course reminded of the incipit of Proust's *In Search of Lost Time*, where we see the opposite: the narrator puts out the candle, yet upon waking up believes it to be lit. He had fallen asleep over a book, and in his sleep the reading matter and the reading subject, words and things, all became muddled. The book's ghost-like characters came to life in his dreams, just as they do when the magical lamp projects their shadows onto his room's walls. But let's leave Marcel asleep and return to Barillé, trying to draw a few conclusions from what her writer's intuition tells us about the process of reading.

At first, the child's reading seems "laboured": she is moving from letter to letter with great difficulty, struggling to form words. Now and then, words conjure up a vision of the thing and the child's gaze momentarily loses itself in it, projecting the book's imaginary world onto the room's walls, which stand for the pages of the book. In the second moment, the child raises her eyes from the book and realizes that the room has been entirely transformed. The displacement is both metonymical – the closed space of the room surrounding the reading body is contaminated by the fictional scene of the submarine – and metaphorical: the soft folds of the curtain become organ pipes and the octopus calls forth the girl's genitals.

"Loudly and clearly": the Freudian *Lesen*

> . . . *the voice within your lips that had been swiftly and silently repeating all the words your eyes were reading . . . the frantic racing of my eyes and of my voice, which had followed after my eyes without making a sound, stopping only to catch its breath.*[8]

Reciting, sounding out, is a truly laborious job. The child's entire body is involved in deciphering the object-sign: first, tackling the individual visible elements (letters); then, once they have all been named separately, trying to assemble them to pronounce the entire word; and finally, in the best of cases, being able to see something behind them, something other than the letters' images.[9]

Before turning to the sublime body of the reader, let us first examine how Freud, before turning to interpreting dreams, conceived of reading. At that time, his interest focused on language disorders; his early conceptions are still relevant to the field of neurocognition. Drawing on the pathology of the aphasias, he defines a word as "the functional unit of speech", a "complex of images" or impressions, the "acoustic image", the "visual letter image", the sensory, "glosso-kinaesthetic" image of the speech organs, and, when we learn to write, the "cheiro-kinaesthetic image" received from the hand.[10] In speaking, repeating, spelling, reading or writing, these images enter into processes of association, with each circuit located in a specialized cortical centre.[11] Because Freud's thinking at the time relied on theories of phylogenesis and learning, he understood all of these sensory images, whether in relation to spoken, read or written language, as organized around the central acoustic image.[12]

We learn to speak by memorizing sound perceptions and reproducing, via repetition, the sound image perceived, until the kinaesthetic image (the muscular image of phonation) makes the copy resemble the original, the learner being able to simultaneously hear and feel himself speaking.

As we learn the alphabet, spelling associates the visual letter images with sounds that inevitably recall the sound images of words we already know.

The process of learning to read is even more complicated.

> We learn to read by linking up with each other, according to certain rules, a succession of word innervation impressions and kinaesthetic word impressions perceived in enunciating individual letters. As a result, new kinaesthetic word images originate, but as soon as they have been enunciated we detect from their sound images that both kinaesthetic and sound images so perceived have long been familiar to us, being identical with those used in speaking.

Next, we associate with those word images acquired by spelling the significance attached to the original word sounds. Now we read with understanding.
(Freud, 1953, pp. 74–75)

Because understanding written language requires that we start by reading
aloud, reading as such is a secondary process. Only phonation lets us establish
the cognitive links with words we have already learned in speech acquisition. The
child's "laboured" reading testifies to the fact that his or her entire body is dictat-
ing to the brain, struggling in a pantomime of remembering and slowly creating
new psycholinguistic habits. In this sense, learning to read is similar to learning
how to play a musical instrument.

Thirty years later, in *The Ego and the Id*, Freud returns to this argument when
he compares reading to the sign language used by the deaf. Here again, the read
word is seen as secondary.

The visual components of word-presentations are secondary, acquired through
reading, and may to begin with be left on one side; so may the motor images of
words, which, except with deaf-mutes, play the part of auxiliary indications. In
essence a word is after all the mnemic residue of a word that has been heard.[13]

In 1923, the Freudian *Lesen* therefore remains exactly what it was in 1891: an
act of deciphering, of connecting the acoustic signifier (the word presentation)
with the thing-presentation. Reading a word is still seeing a word that has previously been heard – "reading is a secondary elaboration of a word-presentation"
that uses "residues, and remains; it is one step further removed from the thing-
presentation; it is a tertiary 'elaboration' of the thing".[14] For Freud, the read word
would therefore lie at the end of a procedure we could formulate as:

Mnesic trace → thing-presentation → (sound) word-presentation
→ visualized representation
= representation (acquired by reading) of the word-presentation

In order to see (understand) what we are reading, we must follow these steps,
moving from the graphemic signifier (text) to the phonemic one (sound) – the
movement indicated by the second "reading" in Elisa's sentence, "I was reading
without reading", and then on to the signified. In Freudian terms:

The visual word image → the word sound image → the image of the thing-
presentation = understanding (i.e. meaning)

When we are reading aloud, the image of the written word and the image of the
thing may sometimes remain separate, which leads to noncomprehension.[15]

"Words . . . revealed their meaning to me without my naming them"

However, Freud also speaks of another kind of reading which can help us understand Elisa's oxymoron "I was reading without reading":

> If . . . I read a novel, which holds my interest, I overlook all misprints and it may happen that I retain nothing of the names of the persons figuring in the book except for some meaningless feature, or perhaps a recollection that they were long or short, and that they contained an unusual letter such as x or z.
>
> (Freud, 1953/1891, pp. 75–76)

The proper name is recognized instantly by its capital letter and syntactic context. In this case, we move directly from the hero's name (the image of the written word) to the visual image of the object (a man or a woman). In a novel, the proper name therefore functions as a pictogram. Does this mean we can sometimes skip the sound image? Freud suggests this is true: "In the case of the experienced reader the influence of the 'visual word image' makes itself felt, with the result that single words, especially proper names, can be read even without recourse to spelling" (p. 77).

Twice in Freud's text the influence of the visual word image is illustrated by the special case of reading proper names, which he calls "isolated words". By referring directly to a thing(presentation), these words operate a psychocognitive leap and in this way free themselves of the sound image. Today, we call this process "global" or "analogic" reading. It links the "face of the word" (representation of the word read) with the "thing", avoiding the need for the elementary linking of sounds, that is the representation of the pronounced word. As a little girl, Elisa experiences this leap as a "magical" moment – as if "someone" has been reading for her:

Word read → [word heard] → thing-presentation

This is the meaning of the first "reading" in Barillé's "I was reading without reading", which she then develops further: "Incredible! I read this passage in less than thirty seconds. . . . The words capitulated from within. They revealed their meaning to me without my pronouncing them. This was magic! Someone was reading for me! I thought I had swallowed another voice." The impersonal *someone* ["Someone was reading for me!"] conveys the moment of acting out that has seized the subject. A repressed element (the word heard) returns as an experience of the *unheimlich* (another voice is reading for me). "Reading without reading" therefore means that, as if by magic, the word directly summons the thing.

But how can we explain the effect this magical reading has on Elisa, causing her "restless" night and, on the next morning, provoking that autoerotic acting out?

Another voice: the book-thing

When reading, we no longer see what thought was there and because we regret that we no longer see what was before our eyes, we are desperately trying to search for it, to find it again, even to anticipate it. This being, as we have already understood, a series of movements – I would like to say motions – representing desire, imitating and repeating it. Endlessly.

(Jean-Michel Rey[16])

In *Totem and Taboo*, Freud speaks about the taboo of pronouncing proper names, which we often encounter in children. These, as he points out, behave like the "primitive peoples" in that they "are never ready to accept a similarity between two words as having no meaning; they consistently assume that if two things are called by similar-sounding names this must imply the existence of some deep-lying point of agreement between them". The same is true for the neurotic patients who refuse to write their names, lest they "surrender a part of [their] person".[17] Animism treats the written word as if it were indeed a thing. Unfortunately, neither Freud's ideas about proper names, which he expressed implicitly in 1891, nor his comments on the taboo from 1913 lead him to develop a specific theory of reading and its psychic effects. The French psychoanalyst Paul-Laurent Assoun, who tried to remedy this lack in "La lettre. Pour une métapsychologie du lire", remarks that Freud never makes a direct link between the read word and the thing: in his psychic topography, the written word is always only a visualisation of the word presentation. It can therefore only serve as a mediator between the sensory residues and consciousness, since the latter is, in a sense, topographically too far away from the former.

The word read still retains the acoustic word-presentation as its sensory residue, in the same way that thing-presentations remain sensory residues for word presentations. However, while the read word (which we should in fact understand as the visual representation, acquired by reading, of what are essentially verbal residues of word presentations) perpetuates these verbal residues by making them visible, its visibility is also a sensory quality that it shares with thing-presentations. Can we therefore argue, as Assoun indeed does, that the read word in a sense completes the circle, allowing the subject to replay the thing? In that case, the visibility of the read word might give consistency to the verbal residues that are too far removed from the thing – the thing that remains inaccessible and only exists in the psyche as traces. While the word cannot recall the thing, it can mimic it. Would this not be the reason why reading is a form of sublimation?

Freud only gives [reading] the function of transmitting and perpetuating these residues. However, we could suspect that there is a kind of archaic work going on, which is implicitly aware of the existence, within these residues, of a "remainder." This may explain to us that by putting word-presentations before our eyes, we are in a sense again facing the thing, even though it is filtered through the production of verbal scoria that is verbalization.

(Assoun, p. 115)

If, as Assoun suggests, the subject perceives the written word as a scoria or a residue of the thing (via the word pronounced), as something of the thing (an effect for a subject, which should therefore be called *lectum*), reading, as part of the conscious secondary process, becomes an activity allowing us to think, to "metaphorize" – to displace to another level of consciousness – and to sublimate our relationship to the object and its totality lost forever. The read word, therefore, in a sense replays the perception of the thing within the conscious secondary process. This is the exact definition of what I would like to call, with Barillé and Assoun, "the magical effect of reading". Could we go as far as to suggest that we can only "understand" (on the secondary level) what it is to perceive – that is to glimpse the representation of the thing (on the primary level) – because we can read?

The enormity of the thing in Elisa's text allows us to think further about the unconscious stakes of *Lesen*, before returning to Freud.

For Elisa, "genuine reading" occurs as she is struggling through a particular passage of Verne's *20,000 Leagues under the Sea*. It is a description of a monster: "colossal dimensions . . . enormous, unblinking, glaucous eyes . . . the hair of the Furies . . . suckers . . . variable colour . . . extreme rapidity . . . the animal's irritation . . . greyish blue to reddish brown". Through this detailed portrayal, the giant octopus, which would terrify us had it emerged like an uncanny apparition, is desecrated. The child's word-by-word reading follows the gradual dissection of the animal pursued by the text, that is by the spatial, and therefore also temporal, structuring produced by the signifying chain, for every piece of the octopus is a signifier. Here, we must keep in mind the true complexity of constructing the meaning of a single sentence, let alone of an entire text: the sentence "closes its signification only with its last term, each term being anticipated in the construction constituted by the other terms and, inversely, sealing their meaning by its retroactive effect" (Lacan, p. 805). Usually, a child needs time to become able to "close the loop" of signification and arrive at the thing presentation. When Elisa says, "words capitulated from within", what she means is that she did not have to embody them first. She did not have to taste them or let them into her head in order to bring up an image: the repression of the heard word occurred upon the appearance of the fictional monster, whose image arrived even before the sound of its name. This can only happen if a connection has been made between the representation of the read word and the thing presentation, bearing in mind that the latter is connected to mnesic traces and the unconscious material associated with them. From the word-for-word signification then emerges a meaning addressed to a specific subject, in this case a little girl: *Elle lisa!*[18] And it is precisely this ever-monstrous meaning that terrifies nonreading children – they must indeed know something about it, if they so strongly resist seeing what it intends to say.

This intention of meaning was already implied in the scene: it was projected onto the room's walls, transforming the curtains into organ pipes. Between the Real and the Imaginary, this fantasmatic projection outside the Symbolic is in a sense a metaphor of "pure" meaning awaiting signifiers. The child is immersed in it, abandoned to its *dé-lire*, as both the hidden face and the condition of reading – because the truth is that a book, any book, always speaks to and about oneself; in other words, it speaks about the Other. This is what Magritte's painting *The Submissive Reader* shows us – the unconscious knowledge that suddenly dawns on Elisa – the monster of the book is (like) myself.

Figured by the octopus, the book-thing has everything to do with the unconscious representation of *das Ding* – the maternal Thing, which for the little girl turns out to be somehow related to her "sex". Signification ("Words have revealed their meaning to me") puts the pieces of the octopus puzzle back together after they were "broken down" (as Freud might put it), dissected and named by the scientific gaze. It revives the mnesic traces of the thing, which become effects of meaning (for a particular subject). It is no longer Jules Verne or the sailor who is speaking but an Other who is both speaking (to me) and watching (me):[19] "Someone was reading for me! I thought I had swallowed another voice." There is an Other:

> What is most certain for the reader is that there is an Other speaking: not simply the author, but an Other whom the author allows to speak. Sheltered by this speech, we can have a conversation with our own most intimate Other. However, reading can also awake the repressed question of otherness. This strange state between sleep and wakefulness, between receptivity and hyper-vigilance, is what makes the act of reading a fantasmatic *Leistung* par excellence.
>
> (Assoun, p. 199)

"There are perhaps no days of our childhood that we lived as fully as the days we think we left behind without living at all: the days we spent with a favourite book," declares Proust to convey the ambiguity of this illusory activity (p. 3). As for Elisa, she "has a conversation with her most intimate Other" in the middle of the night ("the nightshirt hitched up around my waist, all bunched up") and on the following morning. The repressed Thing – the unconscious meaning (addressed to a particular subject) – replaces the previous fictional referent (the octopus), which it had acquired through reading, with a real and embodied one. Moving from fiction to real life and muddling the two together, the deferred acting out is itself a frame within a frame of the effect of reading and the novel. "What is writing?", asks Elisabeth Barillé on her website, and she answers: "It is spending one's life among fragile and irrational things, not saying either yes or no to reality."[20]

"When we are reading, the thing is there" – this is how Assoun sums up the thing, partly because of the shared sensory nature of the textual image and the mnesic trace of the thing, but also because of the subject's fantasy that can lodge itself in these "airy likenesses of Things".

In her scene of reading, Barillé has managed to depict the play of the unconscious in what resembles an epiphany – a sudden access to the Other's voice and gaze – the basis on which any future text will "make sense". By transforming the textual thing (the *lectum*) into a monstrous animal, she has offered us a metaphor, as Blanchot does in *Thomas the Obscure* (see the Introduction), of the "effect of the letter," that is the literary effect. In its different folds, the triple scene shows us a crucial fact, namely that reading has the "function of revisiting the primary repressed" (Assoun, p. 129), by allowing the neurotic, a notorious bookworm, to revel in the vice of fantasy while dodging the superego's surveillance.

Between evening (the access to thing presentations under the Other's watchful gaze) and morning (the encounter with the sexual Thing), "it is with images that captivate his Eros as a living individual that the subject manages to ensure his implication in the signifying sequence."[21] Without this subjective implication, which we have previously called a *dé-lire*, there is no genuine reading. The octopus appears behind the frame of the porthole. As Lacan suggests, the frame is an index of fantasy in which the object beckons the subject and simultaneously splits her in half. This splitting grants her a body now existing in language precisely because it has been "processed", like a corpse, by the signifying chain.[22] The scene can therefore be understood as a metapsychological account of its author's beginnings as a writer. The signifiers of the text cover her "body of a girl" like a veil, breaking it down and then putting it back together, in a book destined for the eyes of the Other. The ageing writer (whom Elisa is trying to shock), as well as the book's potential publisher (and we know she has succeeded), can certainly count themselves among the Other's many faces.

*

Soon we shall try to understand this ageing writer's psychological and narrative function for Elisa. How can a young female reader, uninhibitedly lost in her private pleasure, become terrifying? But before we find out, we must remedy the injustice we may have done to Freud. For although he failed to explicitly connect it to the letter's thingness and the visual word presentation, the founder of psychoanalysis did leave us a theory of the literary effect.

The reading eros

In a dream, it is not the man who sins – it is his dream.

(Stanislav Jerzy Lec[23])

There is in reading, at least at reading's point of departure, something vertiginous that resembles the movement by which, going against reason, we want to open onto life eyes already closed. This movement is linked to desire which, like inspiration, is a leap, an infinite leap: I want to read what is, however, not written.

(Maurice Blanchot[24])

In 1908, the founder of psychoanalysis, an avid reader, proposed the now familiar explanation for the pleasures we derive from literature.

> You will remember how I have said . . . that the day-dreamer carefully con-
> ceals his phantasies from other people because he feels he has reasons for
> being ashamed of them. . . . Such phantasies, when we learn them, repel us or
> at least leave us cold. But when a creative writer presents his plays to us or
> tells us what we are inclined to take to be his personal daydreams, we experi-
> ence a great pleasure, and one which probably arises from the confluence of
> many sources. How the writer accomplishes this is his innermost secret; the
> essential *ars poetica* lies in the technique of overcoming the feeling of repul-
> sion in us which is undoubtedly connected with the barriers that rise between
> each single *ego* and the *others*. We can guess two of the methods used by
> this technique. The writer softens the character of his egoistic daydreams
> by altering and disguising it, and he bribes us by the purely formal – that
> is, aesthetic – yield of pleasure which he offers us in the presentation of his
> phantasies. We give the name of an incentive bonus, or a *fore-pleasure*, to a
> yield of pleasure such as this, which is offered to us so as to make possible
> the release of still greater pleasure arising from deeper psychical sources. In
> my opinion, all the aesthetic pleasure which a creative writer affords us has
> the character of a fore-pleasure of this kind, and our actual enjoyment of an
> imaginative work proceeds from a liberation of tensions in our minds. It may
> even be that not a little of this effect is due to the writer's enabling us thence-
> forward to enjoy our own day-dreams without self-reproach or shame.[25]

Let us compare Freud's argument with several scenes from a short work written five years later by a French author who tries to approach the book-thing and "the unconscious factors in reading" (to recall Strachey's essay) from the position of the Master[26] – the literary critic. This turns out to be no small task. However, the author's candour, the way he sometimes lets the mask slip, can help us understand what, following Freud and Lacan, I will call the *jouis-sens*[27] of reading.

The equivalence between the sublimation of the destructive drives and the beginnings of intellectual development, established prior to Strachey (see our Introduction) by Freud and later by Melanie Klein, makes reading a mode of trans-formation of the sadistic components of the human psyche, which, during the first half of the twentieth century, had a direct effect on Western civilization. In this sense, the turn of the century, when the masses (including women) began to con-sume books and newspapers, is a key moment for understanding reading as an anthropological issue. Émile Faguet's *Art de Lire* will help us ask the following questions: How can the jouissance of the Other, with its "unconscious factors", be "translated" into the master's discourse and thus made into an object of knowledge when the critic's own body is caught up in its ebbs and flows? What episteme, what position should the (male) subject adopt to avoid falling prey to the Other? How can he remain distinct from that mass devouring romances right outside the university's walls? How can the drive for mastery at work in every reader be transformed into a drive for knowledge? And ultimately, how can we grasp "the reader", as a subjective position, through his act?

> Do you wish to learn how to read, just like one learns how to play the violin – in other words, to be able to play and enjoy playing as much as possible? This little book, which you are just beginning to read, is devoted precisely to this art. But what exactly is this art? Here, I believe, we may all find ourselves slightly at a loss. Since an art is defined by what it is trying to achieve, we should obviously ask ourselves why we read. Is it to educate ourselves? Is it to consider the quality of different works? Is it to enjoy them?[28]

Émile Faguet, a professor of French poetry at the Sorbonne Faculty of Arts who was elected to the Académie Française in 1900, was a regular contributor of the *Revue des Deux Mondes*, among others, and a lecturer popular with polite society. His book on the art of reading was published in Hachette's Collection des Muses in 1913. The exercise that the renowned scholar is asked to perform here resembles that of an art critic who analyzes a famous artwork in order to refine the tastes of art lovers or students by inviting them to observe the man of experience at work. But how can one teach others to "read well"? What skills, habits or guidelines are involved? How can reading become an object of reproducible knowledge?[29]

> Episteme . . . is a funny word . . . "putting oneself in the right position". . . . It is all about finding the position that makes it possible for knowledge to become the master's knowledge. The entire function of the episteme insofar as it is specified as transmissible knowledge – see Plato's dialogues – is always borrowed from the techniques [the know-how] of craftsmen, that is to say of serfs. It is a matter of extracting the essence of this knowledge in order for it to become the master's knowledge.[30]

Faguet is caught between the serf's know-how and the master reader's search for an ultimate truth. His legitimacy as a member of institutions of knowledge, the university and the Académie Française, together with his claimed legacy of great forefathers like Voltaire or Sainte-Beuve, command respect from the outset. Yet very quickly, this position of "reading master" proves uncomfortable. Because unless one is a pervert, how does one establish one's authority on the ways in which others obtain pleasure? The certified and certifying rhetoric of the professor and critic no longer has any use here. Why? Because the stakes inherent in the art of reading undermine the repression that is at the core of every institution – the repression of sexuality. For how can this constitutive efface-ment be respected when the scholar's search concerns, precisely, the forms of and reasons for pleasure? In order to establish a master's knowledge on the act of reading, Faguet must therefore "find the right position", and it is by adopting the stance and *savoir faire* of a craftsman ("reading slowly", "rereading", "how critics read" etc.[31]) that the nature of the act is revealed: reading has an effect on the soul, but also on the body.

Scene 5

The surprises we sometimes experience while reading works of fiction . . . also lead us to new discoveries. We are astonished and shocked; we say to ourselves: "But that can't be true!" But a certain *je-ne-sais-quoi* tells us that perhaps it is not as untrue as we may believe. We wonder about it and often end up thinking: "At the very least, it's not impossible." This is because a deep and unexplored part of our soul is half-revealed to us; thanks to this foreign help a part of our subconscious enters our consciousness and we see more deeply into ourselves than we had before.

Therefore if reading requires the habit of examining our conscience, it also instils it in us in turn. Whether we are beginners or already experienced read-ers, we do not compare fictional characters to people we know but to our-selves. This becomes a habit and we begin to read ourselves like a book,[32] or at least like a difficult manuscript.

(Faguet, pp. 28–29)

In reading, "a deep and unexplored part of our soul is half-revealed to us". The subject is half-said (*mi-dit*) by the signifier, as Lacan would say: "In this way lan-guage renews the jouissance it reveals and leads to the emergence of the fantasy that realizes a time. It only approaches the real in the measure of the discourse that reduces what is said to making a hole in its calculation."[33] Faguet's work tries to trace the movements of a passionately realist mind, one that is faced with the "shocks", the holes in knowledge procured by certain works of fiction. "But that can't be true! . . . At the very least, it's not impossible." Because it produces an effect of truth, this concession to the author's imagination involves two mutually opposing psychic agencies:

1   The strange thought is rejected by the consciousness.
2   A certain *je ne sais quoi* (*unbewusste*) questions the belief responsible for this rejection, therefore splitting the subject ("we question ourselves") into:

   –   the place of the (ideological) consciousness, and
   –   another space, where the thought in question would be "possible". Another scene? Another paradigm?

The original strangeness of the thought, which is inherent to its place of origin, shows itself in and through resistance: "At the very least, it's not impossible." Its extraneity dissolves into the "at the very least", which marks the hypothetical space of its potential acceptance: the "subconscious" figured as a kind of crypt – "a deep and unexplored part of our soul". The triggering of an emotion leads to self-questioning and eventually the integration of the disturbing thought: we recognize here the psychic movement of denial (Freud's *Verleugnung*) and its ensuing lifting: "That's impossible" → "At least, it's not impossible." → "In fact, it's about me!" The effect of reading has everything to do with the unconscious, and its analysis has everything to do with the process of working through with the integration of a rejected thought and with knowing a bit more about oneself. Using a metonymy,[34] Faguet likens the subconscious to a "difficult manuscript", so that, in a sense, the book allows the reader to analyze himself *like* a book. Let us go a step further. Because of their common nature, a sort of consubstantiality, the subconscious can be analyzed by the book, where the thingness of the letter reactualizes the Thing: "reading initiates us, insofar as her magic key opens the door deep inside us to the dwelling places we would not otherwise have known how to reach, its role in our life is a salutary one," says one of Faguet's contemporaries, who surely knew a thing or two about it.[35] This leads to the idea of an unconscious structured like a "text to be read", recalling Freud's analogy between the *unbewusste* and the *wunderblock*, the magic writing pad, a children's toy where writing is always on the verge of disappearing yet also remains accessible because, encrypted below the surface, the wax tablet preserves the memory of its traces.[36]

Faguet's argument obviously does not go as far as to postulate an "unconscious in the works", a portmanteau expression which indicates that a work of art both transmits the author's unconscious and reveals to the reader his own, as Freud suggested. However, the critic's guilelessness, which reduces the master's discourse to but a thin mask of the royal "we", does construe the hypotheses of a two-faced *subject of reading – a decipherer deciphered*[37] *– and of a dual recipient for the text* itself. As we have seen with Barillé and Assoun, there is indeed both (1) a text for the consciousness, that is a meaning [*signification*] to be deciphered (by any reasonable reader) – the Freudian *Lesen* and (2) a text for the unconscious, which makes sense (*sens*) insofar as it is addressed to a subject – the *lectum*.

With the help of psychoanalysis, I have previously described the reading subject as a subject *to* the signifier in the same way that we think of a "subject to a rule": a subject turned into an adjective, passivated. The same might be said about the subject to the letter, with Barillé's two instances of acting out ("Someone was reading for me" and "What prompted me to. . . .") showing us the *unbewusste* (the unbeknownst) at work in the effect of reading. Faguet does associate the reader's subordination with "examination of conscience", thus looking at the *après-coup* of reading through the prism of Christian self-knowledge. Nevertheless, the nodal tension he alludes to – "Therefore, although reading requires a capacity for introspection, it also instils it in us in turn" – suggests that the reader is bound by a double obligation: to "know himself" in order to be able to read, but also to read and thus to accept the existence of an "unexplored part of [his] soul". The moral outrage initially experienced by the master's superego therefore gives way to the humility of a sinner, of a man among others. Reading subjugates the master, puts him in his place: that of a "passivated" subject, a subject to the rule of the Symbolic. The reading body then reenacts this repositioning in the Real body. In the process of deciphering – as we have seen in Sartre's image of his reading mother, "a plaster statue" – the body schema is deactivated (one becomes insensitive to both heat and cold), leaving space for another, imaginary body curled up over the book. Rainer Maria Rilke describes this transformation as follows:

Bibliothèque Nationale

I am sitting here reading a poet. There are many people in the room, but they are inconspicuous; they are inside the books. Sometimes they move among the pages, like sleepers who are turning over between two dreams. Ah, how good it is being among people who are reading. Why aren't they always like this? You can go up to one of them and touch him lightly: he feels nothing. And if, as you get up, you happen to bump against the person sitting next to you and you apologize, he nods in the direction your voice is coming from, his face turns towards you and doesn't see you, and his hair is like the hair of someone sleeping. How good that feels.[38]

*

By putting Freud and Faguet side by side, the following table shows us that the critic's surprises and hesitations result from not only his theoretical insight but also from self-censorship, whether it is self-willed or not. The lacunae of Faguet's discourse are elucidated by Freud, who is less subject to inhibition; at the same time, Faguet's slightly affected style adds a measure of imaginary consistency to Freud's theorization.

In this table, we see that in Freud's account, the *uncanny* identified by Faguet becomes "pleasure", "jouissance" and "fantasy". What surprises and shocks us, "repels us", said Freud, is a daydream which the artist dares to unveil before us; "seeing" it leads to the conclusion of a fantasy resemblance between human beings, which psychoanalysis holds to be universal. Fiction therefore sheds light into the depths of our soul; knowledge (which is acquired and accepted without self-reproach because it is now seen as shared) "frees us" from our resistance to enjoying our fantasies. At the end of the twentieth century, the French writer Michel Butor described the effect of reading more simply, stressing the idea of a certain permeability to the other's enjoyment:

We could say that reading is a dream directed by the writer's words. It is a dream *we are led to dream*. But, obviously, the signs themselves do not

Table 2.1 Faguet-Freud: the *jouis-sens* of reading

FAGUET	Common Themes ≠ Differences	FREUD → Clarification
• *Surprises caused by* fiction	Encounter with the author's difference	• *The creative writer presents his plays to us or tells us what we are inclined to take to be his personal daydreams*
• *Lead us to* discoveries • *We are astonished and shocked.*	Questions about "effects"	• *We experience a great pleasure, and one which probably arises from the confluence of many sources.* • *How the writer accomplishes this* [?]
• *We say to ourselves:* "But that can't be true!"	First movement: Moral/ physical shock	• *A creative writer presents his plays to us . . . tells us . . . his personal daydreams* • *. . . repulsion*
• *A certain je-ne-sais-quoi tells us that perhaps it is not as untrue as we may believe; we wonder about it and often we end up thinking:* "At the very least it's not impossible".	A U-turn: A certain *je-ne-sais-quoi* leads us to lift the veil ≠ him = me?	• *We can guess two of the methods used by this technique. The writer softens the character of his egoistic daydreams by altering and disguising it.*
• *A deep and unexplored part of our soul is half-revealed to us* • *a part of our subconscious enters our consciousness* • *we see more deeply into ourselves than we had before*	The ego revealed/freed from the veil/fiction: The revelation of "our soul" (by means of jouissance)	• *the release of still greater pleasure* • *arising from deeper psychical sources*
• *we see more deeply into ourselves than we had before*	≠ does seeing/knowing it provide relief?	• *our actual enjoyment of an imaginative work proceeds from a liberation of tensions in our minds*
• *thanks to this foreign help*	How is this possible? The (initially rejected) *foreigner* does what I don't dare to do = express my fantasies	• *technique of overcoming the feeling of repulsion in us . . . connected with the barriers that rise between each single ego and the others* • [the writer] *bribes us by the . . . aesthetic yield of pleasure which he offers us in the presentation of his phantasies.*
• *Whether we are beginners or experienced readers, we do not compare fictional character to people we know but to ourselves. This becomes a habit* • *and we read ourselves like a book*	≠ fantasies are shared and recognized Reading = reading oneself ≠ new access to ourselves	• *The writer . . . enabling us thenceforward to enjoy our own day-dreams*
• *and we read ourselves like a book, or at least like a difficult manuscript*	Resistance (Faguet) ≠ freeing from guilt (Freud)	• *without self-reproach or shame*
SELF-KNOWLEDGE ("he is like me")	JOUIS-SENS	JOUISSANCE ("I am like him")

produce anything – we do. Usually without realizing it, we fashion the representation with words.[39]

We find the same idea in Proust:

> For it seemed to me that they would not be "my" readers but the readers of their own selves, my book being merely a sort of magnifying glass like those which the optician at Combray used to offer his customers – it would be my book, but with its help I would furnish them with the means of reading what lay inside themselves.[40]

> Nothing can result from the pure solitude of the lazy spirit, because that spirit is unable to set its creative activity in motion by itself, but even the loftiest conversation or the most insistent advice would not help it in the slightest either, because it cannot directly produce original activity. What is needed, therefore, is an intervention that occurs deep within ourselves while coming from someone else, the impulse of another mind that we receive in the bosom of solitude. As we have seen, this is precisely the definition of reading and fits nothing but reading.[41]

For both Proust and Faguet, reading facilitates self-analysis: the reader is a searcher of the soul, boldly confronting the unknown. For Freud, it is the "unpunished vice" that awakens fantasies and triggers neuroses. For Butor, it is a dream imposed on the reader: this psychic position echoes what is usually referred to as *jouissance* in the feminine position.

How reading feminizes

Scene 5 (continued)

> If the author touches us, let us not resist; let us follow this delightful guide, let us . . . be moved. It is true, we are no longer in possession of ourselves, but this is perhaps the very reason why we reached for a writer or a poet in the first place. This being possessed by fiction is something rather curious. It is a sort of intoxication, which is to say that we simultaneously undergo a loss and an expansion of our personality. It is a suggestive state. . . . [We] feel as if we were more potently, more . . . superbly alive than we normally are. This borrowed ego . . . is like a vase that is filled and delights in being filled; a vase that in receiving expands and enlarges. Our own soul envelops the foreign soul [of the character] it has taken in; it is penetrated and wonderfully enriched by it.
> (Faguet, pp. 22–23)

In retrospect, Faguet's contradictions, analyzed previously, seem to reveal his own resistance to the idea announced at the very beginning of his book, namely that the art of reading means obtaining *jouissance* like a woman. Was Barillé's powerful reclaiming of a "right to look without shame", which she linked to a "right to reading", also not a claim for the right to this Other *jouissance*?[42]

At the time when Freud, Faguet and Proust were writing, too much reading was considered harmful. "Life is not a reader because it has no sense of contemplation. Love, greed, hatred . . . lead us away from the idea of the book" (Faguet, 1912, p. 114). Marcel's grandmother scolds him every time she catches him reading: " 'That's no way to make him strong and active,' she would say sadly, 'especially that boy, who so needs to build up his endurance and will-power'" (Proust 1996/1913, p. 11). At the turn of the century, reading is a women's affair – it keeps men away from the action by which they are judged. Faguet reiterates this stereotype of reading as incompatible with masculinity in order to critique it: the reader, who has been rendered *passive*, neither acts nor engages in conversation, the main activity of the salon. It is therefore bold and very much against the spirit of the times that the author of *L'art de lire* confesses to the raptures induced by his passion.[43] The art of reading becomes a true art of enjoyment – an erotica. The reader is subjugated and enslaved by pleasure. He is told not to resist, to allow himself to sink into a "suggestive state" and in turn experience "intoxication", an expansion of being and a feeling of potency. The delicious reception of the other is a true dispossession of the self, with the reader turning into a vase that enjoys being filled and in doing so expands. He "reaches for a poet" and is "penetrated" by an other, a stranger who reveals to him his own hidden depths. Paradoxically, it is precisely because in succumbing to the author he adopts the position of feminine *jouissance* – whose "essence" Faguet is trying to draw out – that the reading craftsman can claim to have mastered the art of reading, to be able to say something about it and transmit it to others. Not a simple task for a university professor. "We must act wisely when dealing with even the most innocent passions because no passion is truly innocent. . . . Thus, each of us senses that there is indeed an art of reading and that if reading posed no danger at all, we wouldn't need an art to engage in it" (Faguet, p. 163). Having exposed himself to this danger by revealing the work's erotic aspects, the reader risks "becoming a woman", a passive and overpowered soul. The critic is obliged to reject this fantasy by putting things – and sexes – back where they belong: "Artists, like pretty women, are traps – we must arm ourselves" (p. 125). And so it is now the *author* who becomes a woman and a fatal seductress. And so, quite incongruously, feminizing the author allows Faguet to maintain virile potency on the receiver's side.

Scene 5 (continued)

Factory girls who read cheap novels can only react with the kind of immediate enthusiasm I have called self-abandonment. The secondary, non-immediate reaction only exists for those who are more mature and have a certain capacity of observation and memory; however, these readers experience a far more intense pleasure because they are able not only to abandon themselves, but also and especially to compare the novel to real life.

(Faguet, pp. 25–26)

"The entire function of the episteme, in so far as it is specified as transmissible knowledge . . . is always borrowed from the techniques of craftsmen, that is to say of serfs," Lacan had said.[44] By distinguishing between two different moments, which are marked by two different movements (divestment/repossession), Faguet appropriates the *savoir jouir* of "factory girls", serfs of their condition, in order to deliver his art of reading to men. His theorization therefore entails a denial which puts the blame on a radically different other, one who belongs to a different sex, age and sociocultural class. This allows him to say: "it's not me, it's her!"

However, we know that in fantasy, the positions are interchangeable. The theory's imaginary speaks volumes about its effects: at the beginning of the twentieth century, the "factory girls", who now know how to read and devour feuilletons and novels, unconsciously repeat, *ad infinitum*, these moments of giving in to pleasure. "They do not know what they are saying," Lacan says in *Écrits*, and Faguet implicitly agrees: "They do not know what they are reading." The factory girl of the fantasy has a clear epistemological function: she embodies the position of Hegel's and Lacan's serf, one who knows without knowing. While rhetorically she may be acting as a foil to the venerable master, psychologically her Other *jouissance* provokes envy (as with the young Sartre, seized by an uncanny mixture of horror and attraction before the grandmother's ecstasy; see Chapter I). Faguet, a great admirer of Nietzsche, cites the philosopher's more explicit account of the battle between the sexes, where the two positions of enjoyment become models for thinking about the relationship between the author and the reader. "To ask the artist to adapt to the spectator's or critic's viewpoint means asking him to diminish his creativity. This is similar to the difference between the sexes: we cannot ask the artist who gives to become a woman and to receive" (Nietzsche quoted in Faguet 1912, p. 113). "So far", Nietzsche continues, "our aesthetic has been a female aesthetic, in the sense that only the men who are receptive to art have articulated their experience of what is beautiful. This is a . . . necessary error." While something in art "overpowers" the subject, something in the process of reading "subjugates him", placing him in the feminine position. The passages Faguet chooses to cite reveal the psychic stakes of his "theorization" of reading: his resistance to the way the conscious body is made passive by the book-thing as an effect of the word that is read.

What is it that the critic observes and compares to real life? What ultimately constitutes the object of a theory that accounts for the pleasure we derive from reading? And, going further, what is *literariness*, the object of a theory of literature? If we want to avoid a similar kind of denial, how can we bring this *object* (the cause of desire) into a universalizing discourse which by definition negates the subject's existence[45] in order to make him an object of knowledge? For the author of *L'art de lire*:

1   The "instantaneous reaction" represents a position of a subject affected by *jouis-sens*. As an object of the other's fantasy, bound by the pleasure principle, the subject is unravelled ("at least, it is not impossible"), reading himself back to front and inside out (which reveals the "hidden depths" of his soul). This is exactly where the danger lies – this primary moment resembles a temporary delusion, where the subject is trapped in the Real of the Symbolic. This moment is then repressed: the movement of repossession reestablishes the connections between the Symbolic and the Imaginary, thus restoring a sense of reality.

2   The secondary movement is aimed at the production of knowledge. Memory and observation triumph over the effect of reading and its enjoyment. The subject regains control over the body that was abandoned to the (voice of the) Other. By "comparing a character to real life", the reader theorizes the effect of the thing and locates it in a series of conceptual objects: author, style, character, fiction or plot. Renewing his allegiance to the drive for mastery, which he makes into the reality principle, the reader becomes critical and believes himself freed from the subjection of the reading position (the terrible trap). In the critic's repossession, the *jouis-sens* of reading must be repressed so that the art of reading may be transmitted as an object of knowledge. The master's discourse makes it legible as a negation of an unbearable fantasy of feminization.

The very figure of the art of reading, the "young" female reader is seen as lacking both expertise and awareness. She represents a body affected by reading, one that is made to dream.[46] She is at the same time that body's refuse and its ideal.

"The penumbra of symbolic effectiveness"[47]

The imagination of the nineteenth century – the century of Freud and Faguet, but also of Proust and Rilke – transformed reading into a *locus classicus*, an icon of inner life which remains secret yet can be glimpsed from the outside.[48] In a century that valued action and social engagement, where the new paradigm ushered in by photographic voyeurism and scientific positivism came into full swing, intimacy preferred to remain hidden, or embodied by the *nature morte* forgotten in the corner of a drawing room or garden[49] – the female reader, isolated from the rest of the world.

Her motionless absorption in the book (a novel no doubt) allows the observer to transform her into a spectacle. However, while we are contemplating her tranquil pose, her neck and lost profile, the focal object of the image dissolves into a triangulation of gazes which puts it to flight. What exactly is this object? Is it the reading woman? Or is it the *lectum* – what is being read and produces pleasure, absorbing the subject body and soul? Or is it the Other scene of her "private theatre", suggested by her blurred gaze? Is the reading body, a figure of the Other *jouissance*, not a perfect effigy of the Freudian *Was-will-das-Weib*?[50]

Close to home yet miles away from the disappointing reality, the figure of the female reader leaves her body to the painter so that she may give her soul to the author, the other invisible man of the painting. A woman between two men, she silently embodies the effect of reading[51] – its secret mark, its clandestine espousal of fantasy. In the painting, this effect is shown by a process of *mise-en-abîme*: its centre, traversed by the reader's gaze, is a void. In the open book, the reader sees her idealized image in a fantastic mirror: "In every picture they paint for us, they seem to give us but a fleeting glimpse of a marvellous place unlike anywhere in the world, and we want them to make us penetrate its heart," Marcel Proust writes about reading.[52] Or as Léon says to Emma Bovary, nodding to her identification with the tormented heroines of her century:

> "What is better than to sit by one's fireside in the evening with a book, while the wind beats against the window and the lamp is burning?"
>
> "What, indeed?" she said, fixing her large black eyes wide open upon him.
>
> "One thinks of nothing," he continued; "the hours slip by. Motionless we traverse countries we fancy we see, and your thought, blending with the fiction, playing with the details, follows the outline of the adventures. It mingles with the characters, and it seems as if it were yourself palpitating beneath their costumes."
>
> "That's true! That's true!" she said.
>
> "Has it ever happened to you," Leon went on, "to come across some vague idea of your own, some dim image that comes back from afar, and as the completest expression of your own slightest sentiment?"
>
> "I have experienced it," she replied. . . . "I adore stories that rush breathlessly, that frighten one. I detest commonplace heroes and moderate sentiments, such as there are in nature."
>
> ". . . It is so sweet, amid all the disenchantments of life, to be able to dwell in thought upon noble characters, pure affections and pictures of happiness."[53]

The reading body, locked in the silent acting out, is the culturally acceptable figure of the hysteric. The "unpunished vice" is her exclusive right. Reading is a kind of self-hypnosis, a self-mothering of the melancholic hysteric (with Madame Bovary as its paradigmatic figure). And it undoubtedly falls into the category of what the nineteenth century poetically called "ladies' work" and which Breuer and Freud saw as encouraging the kind of daydreaming in their patients that was inseparable from their neuroses.[54]

Painters and novelists became interested in the "reading woman", the sitting odalisque lost in the words of another, at the very moment when Freud began to lie her down on the couch in order better to hear her speech and help her become the author of her own life. Those compulsive readers and embroiderers were therefore the first to begin to speak to him, and their desire for speech led Freud to give up on the hypnotic method. After all, did it not simply fuel their symptom, like reading did?

In paintings of female readers, the book is always a tool of revelation, a screen onto which her "secret garden" is projected – as if writing could re-present the subject. But isn't the reading woman, the figure of our subjugation to the Other's letter, also Sartre's "glorious substance" living in the pure ether of Things? When reading functions as sublimation, it represents the ego's structural melancholia, searching among the names of things for the traces of the lost object. This object is but the self of the mother's bath – of the time when the ego, the other and language were still One.

The female reader is a captivating figure since she represents the drives that have not yet been barred by the reality principle; the scene of reading is a transitional space, an intermediary zone between the inner psychic reality and the external world[55] ruled by the Other's desire. It is a metaphor of the still movement of a subject seeking her lost ego, her own evanescent form. The languid reader is ultimately the twin image of another figure of being, the novel's hero; the two come into existence almost simultaneously. In this sense, the reader is part of the novel's desire, which is to *dis-read* the subject – to free her from her subjection to the Other's law and language, from her castration. Completely taken by the book-thing, the female reader finds *jouissance* in her own abolition. Like in science fiction, where the robot (a creation of human technology) eventually turns against his creators, the *Lectrice* (who becomes the imaginary heroine of every Emma Bovary among us) embodies an impossible ideal – a human being able to obtain *jouissance* from the Other without desire or castration.

Literature is thus in a sense her *dé-lire* – a madness for which she does not have to pay her dues to the Symbolic that made her human. Is writing not going back in time, undoing the ego's "exile" that had been imposed by genuine reading? We create a hero in order to create a reader and a *jouis-sens* of the letter: "Let us see, Other Reader, if the book can succeed in drawing a true portrait of you, beginning with the frame and enclosing you from every side, establishing the outlines of your form,"[56] says the narrator of Italo Calvino's meta-novel, *If on a Winter's Night a Traveller.* The scenario is later elaborated further when the hero-author of the novel imagines that, as he is writing, his sentences are instantly being read by his beautiful neighbour, who is lying on her balcony with his book. He then changes his words to see her react to them. The fantasy reveals the *dé-lire* of literature: "I feel a throng of readers looking over my shoulder and seizing the words as they are set down on paper" (Calvino, p. 171). Likewise, Proust opens his novel with the figure of the child-reader that he was, a holographic illumination of the work as a whole. These words written to be read are a way of giving this child reader consistency, of bringing him back from his exile and making him the ultimate addressee of a work that wishes to recreate the memory of the *bain de mère* (the mother's bath);[57] with language thus again becoming the Good Fairy's magic formula, which always grants the object of desire.

Ultimately, does not everyone write, as Hélène Cixous puts it,[58] to save writing as a way of saving oneself, to allow the subject to bring something back to life – the ego's "thing",[59] the fine thread of meaning? Do we not write so that we can remain readers, abolished in the Other's jouissance?

"I can't wait to quench my thirst – for myself, for excitement, for words," Serge Doubrovsky says of his passion for writing. "I rush to find myself in my oasis; I need to drink from the fountain of my being."[60] And while he adds more prosaically that "autobiography is not a genre but a metaphysical remedy", we should extend this function to the novel as well. Its material, too, recreates the body that had been "broken down" in the process of learning how to read. "If the representation of the body must first endure repression", Gérard Pommier writes, "in order to re-emerge in the form of letters", as Elisabeth Barillé has shown us, "is writing not the only proof of this transformation, as well as a testimony to the body's existence?"[61]

Notes

1 Calvino, I. (1998). *If on a Winter's Night a Traveller*. Translated by William Weaver. London: Vintage, p. 72 (used with the kind permission of Penguin-Random House).
2 Barillé, E. (1989). *Body of a Girl*. Translated by Hubert Gibbs. London: Quartet Books. [Translation modified by KV.] The first book of a young writer (twenty-three years old, which, as the cover of the Folio edition points out, is also the age of the book's narrator) was one of the first unflinching portrayals of autoeroticism. This, together with its young heroine's misanthropy, caused quite a stir – the following discussion will perhaps show the reader why. Barillé has since published a number of books, mostly mainstream biographies: *Anaïs Nin masquée, si nue*, Robert Laffont, 1991; *Laure: la sainte de l'abîme*, Flammarion, 1997; *Lanvin*, Assouline, 1997; also *A ses pieds*, 2006, and *Petit éloge du sensible*, 2008, both published by Gallimard.
3 Translator's note: *La bibliothèque verte* is an imprint of the French publishing house Hachette intended for young boys (in parallel to the *Bibliothèque rose* for young girls). Launched in 1923, it originally published abridged versions of classic novels by Jules Verne or Alexandre Dumas, but it also included more modern authors such as Georges Bayard and Paul-Jacques Bonzon.
4 Translator's note: While retaining the connotation of the *gaze*, the English translation does not fully do justice to Barillé's double-sensed reclaiming of a *droit de regard*, which in legal French also means the right of access or inspection.
5 Lacan, J. (1970). "Radiophonie". *Scilicet*, 2–3, p. 56 [Translated for this edition].
6 See previous note.
7 Patrick Salvain's definition of an *acting out* can be helpful to us: "When a subject cannot recall an element that has been repressed, he may start acting without knowing what he is doing; in other words, the element returns in the form of action". This "act" is to be situated "on the border between real life and a scene of fiction". See "Acting out" in Kaufmann, P. (Ed.). (1993). *L'apport Freudien*, Paris: Bordas, p. 2 (Translated for this edition).
8 In the foreword to his translation of John Ruskin's *Sesame and Lilies*, published as Proust, M. & Ruskin, J. (2011). *On Reading* (1904). London: Hesperus, p. 6 and 15 (used with the kind permission of the publisher).
9 We may recall that reading aloud was also a requirement in medieval monasteries, which was meant to prevent monks from raising their heads from their work and

daydreaming or fantasizing about what they were reading – which of course did not prevent copyists from drawing their interpretative fantasies in the margins of manuscripts. The body was supposed to remain a "human rag", to use Sartre's expression, absorbed by the letter of the text, simply a mouthpiece for the Other, instead of the "glorious substance" living "in pure ether among the airy likenesses of Things".

10 Freud, S. (1953). *On Aphasia: A Critical Study* (1891). Translated by E. Stengel. New York: International Universities Press, Inc.

11 Here, Freud is taking sides in the dispute between functionalism and localization, when he questions what the latter saw as specific areas proper to speech disorders, as precisely isolated and impermeable cortical centres. Freud argued that lesions affecting these apparently localized centres provoked a whole variety of disorders and concluded, agreeing with Bastian, that speech centres react to damage as wholes by producing functional modifications (this idea was confirmed by later research). His hypothesis of a totality of the language field, which includes what was previously seen as independent centres, is supported by the fact that these centres border on other cortical centres that are also important for the speech function; in fact, they are situated between the terminations of the acoustic and optic nerves and the origins of the motor tracts for the muscles involved in speech articulating and arm movements. The speech apparatus is therefore shown to be "a continuous cortical area in the left hemisphere" (p. 102), which includes all these centres. Freud therefore only recognizes conduction aphasia as a condition (and no longer an aphasia caused by a central localized lesion). The model he proposes is more dynamic and more focused on speech functions. We cannot follow the path of his argument in detail here and will only examine the premises of his theory of speech and what he tells us about reading.

12 For example here: "(1) We learn to speak by associating a '*word sound image*' with an '*impression of word innervation.*' When we have spoken we are in possession of a '*kinaesthetic word image*', i.e. of the sensory impressions from the organs of speech. The motor aspect of the 'word' is therefore doubly determined. . . . (2) We learn the language of others by endeavouring to equate the sound image produced by ourselves as much as possible to the one which had served as the stimulus for the act of innervation of our speech muscles, i.e. we learn to '*repeat*'" (Freud, 1953, pp. 73–74, my emphasis).

13 Freud, S. (1923). "The Ego and the Id". In *SE*, XIX, p. 20.

14 Assoun, P.-L. (1993). "La lettre. Pour une métapsychologie du lire". In *Introduction à la métapsychologie Freudienne*. Paris: P.U.F., 114–134 [all following citations translated for this edition]. I refer the reader to Assoun's text, which resonates in the following discussion.

15 "Again, when I have to recite, whereby I have to pay special attention to the sound impressions of my words and to the intervals between them, I am in danger of caring too little about the meaning, and as soon as fatigue sets in I am reading in such a way that the listener can still understand, but I myself no longer know what I have been reading. It is clear from the analogy with our own behaviour that understanding becomes impossible once reading itself has become difficult. . . . [Therefore] reading aloud is not to be regarded as a different function from reading to oneself, except that it tends to distract attention from the sensory part of the reading process" (Freud, 1953, p. 76).

16 Rey, J.-M. (1982). "Petite préface à la lecture". *L'Ecrit du temps* (Spring 1982), pp. 65–68 [Translated for this edition and used with the P.U.F.'s kind permission]. Michel Picard's discussion of scopophilia in the process of reading is also interesting in this sense. Though the author does not make a direct link with the theory of the letter, it allows us to further develop the question of applying psychoanalysis to literature and its theorization. See Picard, M. (1986). *La lecture comme jeu*. Paris: Minuit, p. 61.

17 Freud, S. (1913). "Totem and Taboo". In *SE*, XIII, pp. 55–56.

18 Instead of *"elle lut"*, this could be a child's overgeneralization of the third person singular *a* ending of the French *passé simple* (simple past) used mostly in literary contexts.

19 In the Lacanian sense, the Other is the witness of the subject's jubilation when faced with the mirror image of his (future) ego. In other words, the Other is *presumed* to have witnessed this *jouissance* and therefore becomes the locus of being – which the subject has lost upon entering language, that is the Symbolic. From now on, the Other haunts the subject, like a custodian of the knowledge of his [lost] completeness.

20 Citation from Barillé's former website, http://www.elisabethbarille.com/, retrieved July 17, 2009.

21 Lacan, J. (2006). "In Memory of Ernest Jones: On His Theory of Symbolism". In *Écrits*. Translated by Bruce Fink. New York City: Norton, p. 595.

22 To paraphrase Lacan's argument; see Lacan, "Radiophonie", p. 61.

23 Cited in Malka, V. (2006). *Mots d'esprit de l'humour juif.* Paris: ©Le Seuil, p. 29 [Translated for this edition and used with the kind permission of the publisher].

24 Blanchot, M. (1989). *The Space of Literature*, p. 195. Translated by Ann Smock. By permission of the University of Nebraska Press. Originally published in French as *L'Espace littéraire*, copyright 1955 Editions Gallimard. English translation copyright 1982 University of Nebraska Press.

25 Freud, S. (1908). "Creative Writers and Day-Dreaming". In *SE*, IX, p. 152.

26 We should understand this term in the Lacanian sense: as the totalizing figure of power who ignores his own ignorance and division as a desiring subject, the unhappy victor of the Master/slave dialectic, based on which Lacan theorizes the Master's discourse as one of his four modalities of creating a social bond.

27 In Seminar XXIII, *Le Sinthome*, Lacan speaks about *jouis-sens* as a type of enjoyment inherent in language understood not as differential system of signs, but as a set of material (acoustic, graphic) signifiers which are fundamentally meaningless yet produce effects in the speaking being. See also Lacan, J. (1990). *Television*. Translated by Denis Hollier, Rosalind Krauss, and Annette Michelson. New York: W.W. Norton: "For these chains are not of meaning but of enjoyment (*jouis-sens*) which you can write as you wish, as is implied by the punning which is the law of the signifier" (p. 10).

28 Faguet, É. (1912). *L'art de lire.* Paris: Hachette (reprinted by © Armand Colin in 1992), p. 7 [All following citations translated for this edition with the kind permission of Armand Colin]. The "Collection des Muses", where the little book by the prominent critic was published, already included *The Art of Saying, The Art of Writing* and *The Art of Seeing*, and was later to add, among others, *The Art of Loving* and *The Art of Thinking*. In his text, Faguet "manages to be both subtle and brilliant. He knows how to explain things clearly and serves the right combination of light erudition and tasteful impressionism. He avoids both commonplace truths and an overtly theoretical approach. He has an eye for classification, for comparison and analysis, and manages to dissect the works and authors studied, only to present their common lines more clearly. He firmly defends the classical tradition (especially against the eighteenth century, which he considers of little interest) and strives to reveal the moral value of the foundational texts" (see Burgelin, C., "Émile Faguet". *L'Encyclopaedia Universalis* Available online at: http://www.universalis.fr/encyclopedie/T230805/FAGUET_E. htm; retrieved November 11, 2013 [Translated for this edition with the kind permission of publisher]). I would add that among Faguet's numerous works we also find a book on feminism, which is in fact relatively open-minded and indeed feminist for its time.

29 "'We read very little,' Voltaire said, 'and among those who wish to educate themselves, many read very badly.' . . . We indeed sense that knowing how to read is an art and that there is an art of reading. This is what Sainte-Beuve had in mind when he said: 'The critic is only a man who knows how to read and who teaches others how to read'" (Faguet, *L'art de lire*, p. 1).

30 Lacan, J. (2007). *The Seminar Book XVII, the Other Side of Psychoanalysis*. Translated by Russell Griegg. New York: Norton, p. 22.

31 Faguet's *L'art de lire* exists in the space between impressionist criticism and the *explication de texte*. His metaliterary stance represents a passage between the end of an era in which the author is still alive in his text, respectfully adored by his readers (or respectfully critiqued by the likes of Taine and Brunetière), and the age of "dead" authors, casualties in the war of textual interpretation. To focus on "reading" thus means committing an irreparable crime: the literary text takes on another function – that of a partial object separated from its author. Once detached, it is destined to become the foundation of a new discourse, making the reader the only master of the house.

32 See my later commentary on the scene of reading in Chapter III, "*Dé-lire 1*", scene 6.

33 Lacan, "Radiophonie", p. 98.

34 Rather than a metaphor, see the discussion later in the text.

35 Proust & Ruskin, *On Reading*, p. 27.

36 Freud, S. (1925). "A Note upon the 'Mystic Writing-Pad'". In *SE*, XIX, pp. 225–232.

37 Translator's note: The French expression refers to the Lumière brothers' short film *L'Arroseur arrosé* (*The Sprayed Sprinkler*), that is in the sense of "getting a taste of one's own medicine".

38 Rilke, R. M. (1929). *The Notebooks of Malte Laurids Brigge: A Novel*. Translated by Stephen Mitchell. New York: Random House, 1990, p. 38. See also the portrait of the man reading as a "cold stone", a closed "gestalt" in Sartre (1956). *Being and Nothingness*. Translated by Hazel E. Barnes. New York: Philosophical Library, p. 256.

39 As Michel Butor tells Luc Decaunes in *Clefs pour la lecture*. Paris: Seghers, 1976, p. 176 [Translated for this edition].

40 Proust, M. (1996). *In Search of Lost Time: Time Regained*. London: Vintage, p. 432, my emphasis.

41 Proust & Ruskin, *On Reading*, p. 26.

42 Lacan, J. (1995). *Séminaire XX, Encore* (1972–73). Paris: Seuil, p. 10. Now translated by Bruce Fink (1999) under the title of *On Feminine Sexuality, The Limits of Love and Knowledge 1972–1973, Encore. The Seminar of Jacques Lacan. Book XX*. New York: W.W. Norton, p. 3.

43 "If a man reads, it is a sign that he is not overtly ambitious; he is not tormented by the 'curse upon men and gods;' he is free of political passions, in which case he would only be reading newspapers; he does not like dining out, has no interest in being a builder . . . he does not mind staying put. He does not even enjoy the art of conversation. The frightful amount of time that people, especially in France, waste on rambling meaninglessly . . . would be enough to read a book a day, but instead prevents them from reading even just one a year" (Faguet, "Les Ennemis de la lecture" [The Enemies of Reading], *L'Art de lire*, p. 115).

44 Lacan, *The Seminar Book XVII, The Other Side of Psychoanalysis*, p. 21.

45 "There is no universal that does not have to contain itself with an existence that denies it." Lacan, "L'étourdit". *Scilicet*, pp. 5–51.

46 It must be reminded that this active passivity of "being made to" (*se faire faire* in French) is a definition of feminine jouissance, i.e. a psychic position that has nothing to do with the biological form of the body. See Chapter I "The book, between totem and taboo", note 13.

47 Lacan uses this slightly enigmatic expression in "The Mirror Stage as Formative of the *I* Function" (see Lacan, J. [2006]. *Écrits*. Translated by Bruce Fink. New York: Norton, p. 77) in reference to Claude Lévi-Strauss's paper "L'efficacité symbolique", published in *Revue d'histoire des religions* (January–March 1949). I am using it to describe the effect of reading on the subject, the way in which the visible materiality of language imposes an *aphanisis* on the ego and the body itself.

48 Beizer, J. (1993). "Reading Women: The Novel in the Text of Hysteria", *Compar(a)ison*, 1: p. 61: "We can think of that *locus classicus* of nineteenth-century painting, the woman reading before a window, as a graphic illustration of the ambiguous role attributed to the novel, for the hidden world enclosed in the book (or perhaps in the woman reading the book) is projected outwards, reflected by the landscape represented on the other side of the window: a world that ought perhaps to have remained secret, and yet comes to light."

49 See for example Adler, L. & Bollman, S. (2008). *Women Who Read Are Dangerous*. London: Merrell Publishers; see especially p. 117 in Peter Ilsted's *Girl Reading a Letter in an Interior* from 1908 and p. 103 in Peter Severin Kroyer's *Rosary (The Painter's. Wife in the Garden at Skagen)* from 1893. I refer the reader to this beautiful book for some of the many images of female readers in Western painting and specifically in nineteenth-century painting. However, Laure Adler's slightly ideological introduction, which seeks to portray female readers as "women dangerous to men", seems somewhat reductive because it does not distinguish between work and leisure, between knowledge and daydreaming, between the object relation and its scientific transmission or the autoerotism involved in reading fiction. The danger, if there is any, lies in the very position of a reader.

50 See *The Reader* by Jean-Jacques Henner (1880–1890), *The Reading Girl* by Théodore Roussel (1886–1887), *Young Woman Reading* by Lovis Corinth (1888) or Vincent Van Gogh's *L'Arlésienne* (1888), all in Adler & Bollman, pp. 89, 95, 97, 100, respectively.

51 The reader played a similar role in the eponymous book (and the film) by the literary critic Raymond Jean, *La Lectrice* (1987), Paris: Éditions J'ai Lu, 1998. It is no accident that a critic uses the eroticized body of his fictional reader in order to say what his theory cannot express.

52 Proust & Ruskin, *On Reading*, p. 23.

53 Flaubert, G. (1994). *Madame Bovary*. Translated by Eleanor Marx-Aveling. London: Wordsworth Editions, p. 63.

54 See for example Breuer, J. & Freud, S. (1893). "On the Psychical Mechanism of Hysterical Phenomena". In *SE*, II, p. 12.

55 Winnicott, W. D. (1971). *Playing and Reality*. London: Routledge, p. 3. See also Picard, *La lecture comme jeu*.

56 Calvino, *If on a Winter's Night a Traveller*, pp. 141–142.

57 See Chapter I, scene 3.

58 Hassoun, P., Maillet, C., & Rabant, C. (1988). "Entretien avec Hélène Cixous". *Patio 10*, pp. 61–67.

59 Chapter III, scene 7.

60 Doubrovsky, S. (1989). *Le livre brisé*. Paris: Grasset, coll. "Le Livre de poche", p. 327 [Translated for this edition].

61 Pommier, G. (1993). *Naissance et renaissance de l'écriture*. Collection "Ecriture". Paris: P.U.F., p. 111, p. 102.

Chapter III

Dé-lire – the poets' dream

> *Seafarers are lucky. To determine their "position", they only need to state their latitude and longitude.*
>
> (Catherine Millet)[1]

DÉ-LIRE I: THE BOOK, BEING'S NATIVE LAND

What, then, is literature? In the Introduction, I used the fantasmatic scene of reading from Blanchot's *Thomas the Obscure* to illustrate the book's effect on the reader as an instance of madness. We see the same stroke of the Real in Magritte's painting *The Submissive Reader.* Through the hallucinatory image of reading as a form of delusion, both Magritte and Blanchot ask "What is literature?" – a question that in Blanchot's case runs through the entire body of his work. With *Thomas the Obscure*, the literary reader is situated where meaning and its jouissance are given flesh – he remains a body strained between his act of reading (his wish to decipher) and the resistance he needs to mount against the inevitable imprint of the letter, against *jouis-sens.*[2] This conflict, depicted by Blanchot as a *deliration*, is a good rendition of the literary effect: the psychic *travail*[3] performed by the reader, his fantasmatic struggle with the Other's desire. It is in fact this very enigma – the madness named "Thomas the Obscure" – that the present book aims at uncovering.

Between psychoanalysis and literature, our question can therefore be restated as follows: How to stage the hold of the letter on the subject, and hence the subject's resistances and delusions, as the very birthplace of literature? If we understand literature as both the *reception* of traces (the effect of the Other's text) and their *production* (writing) which strives to preserve the being of things, can we dare the equation: Writing = *Dé-lire*? Writers do tell us about the works, the *travail* they put their fantasy through; about the psychic stakes and the price they must pay for their "choice" of writing as a mode of sublimation. In this final chapter, their illustrations of this process will continue drawing connections between the reading body's affections, its symptoms and drives, and the Symbolic order and the ego's Imaginary. By paying close attention to their *dé-lire*, their denial or dismantling of the Symbolic, we shall bring to light their moving attempts at making sense. By transforming the irreducible distance between the subject's "living body" and Blanchot's "anonymous shapes of words", they open up a space of inscription. Are their attempts but the labour of believers? It seems, indeed, that the act of writing entails a strange reverting to a time before reading, a time when one knew nothing about it. It is undoubtedly this position of not knowing – the denial of our symbolic castration – to which we owe the unending pleasures of literature being's *terra incognita*.

Proust's child reader

Scene 6

For a long time, I went to bed early. Sometimes, my candle scarcely out, my eyes would close so quickly that I did not have time to say to myself: "I'm falling asleep." And, half an hour later, the thought that it was time to try to sleep would wake me; I wanted to put down the book I thought I still had in my hands and blow out my light. I had not ceased while sleeping to form reflections on what I had just read, but these reflections had taken a rather peculiar turn; it seemed to me that I myself was what the book was talking about: a church, a quartet, the rivalry between Francois I and Charles V. This belief lived on for a few seconds after my waking; it did not shock my reason but lay heavy like scales on my eyes and kept them from realizing that the candlestick was no longer lit. Then it began to grow unintelligible to me, as after a metempsychosis do the thoughts of an earlier existence; the subject of the book detached itself from me, I was free to apply myself to it or not; immediately I recovered my sight and I was amazed to find a darkness around me soft and restful for my eyes, but perhaps even more so for my mind, to which it appeared a thing without cause, incomprehensible, a thing truly dark. I would ask myself what time it might be; I could hear the whistling of the trains which, remote or nearby, like the signing of a bird in a forest, plotting the distances, described to me the extent of the deserted countryside where the traveller hastens towards the nearest station; and the little road he is following will be engraved on his memory by the excitement he owes to new places, to unaccustomed activities, to the recent conversation and the farewells under the unfamiliar lamp that follow him still through the silence of the night, to the imminent sweetness of his return.

I would rest my cheeks tenderly against the lovely cheeks of the pillow, which, full and fresh, are like the cheeks of our childhood. I would strike a match to look at my watch. Nearly midnight. This is the hour when the sick man who has been obliged to go off on a journey and has had to sleep in an unfamiliar hotel, wakened by an attack, is cheered to see a ray of light under the door. How fortunate, it's already morning! In a moment the servants will be up, he will be able to ring, someone will come to help him. The hope of being relieved gives him the courage to suffer. In fact he thought he heard footsteps; the steps approach, then recede. And the ray of light that was under his door has disappeared. It is midnight; they have just turned off the gas; the last servant has gone and he will have to suffer the whole night through without remedy.[4]

Reading as a form of acting out can provide the neurotic, and also the melancholic, with a space of play. This may sometimes prove dangerous, namely when the ego, caught between subjectivity and objectivity and easily pervaded by the Other's names – names of heroes, names of things – discovers its own radical lack of consistency.

"[It] seemed to me that I myself was what the book was talking about": Proust's literary subject comes into being in the figure of a child, oscillating between wakefulness and sleep, between dreaming and awakening. Like the Freudian child, the future poet who blurs the lines between play and reality,[5] Proust's subject, too, initially finds himself in a place of transition: between the pleasure principle and the reality principle, between the inner world inhabited by the book-thing and the outer world which has faded away and can no longer be perceived. Between the "unintelligible belief" of being what he is reading and the "incomprehensible darkness" of the visible, the child of the future book comes into existence in an *unheimlich* non-place (not quite yet a transitional space). Once he has gone to bed early and is left alone in the dark, between sleep and wakefulness, he is literally lost from sight and the ego is no longer able to draw its consistency from the other's gaze. The child suffers from reading as if it were an illness – like the sick man, seeing the light under the door, he is confused about what time it is. The associative twists in the mind of the little sleeping reader, who has become possessed by the book's words, are ruled by two transient figures: the traveller and the dying man. Both can be seen as parables of reading, insofar as it means searching for oneself in another place, where Being could regain its lost consistency, and the realization, upon awakening, of the futility of his quest.

The Traveller is a figure suspended between exile and the desire for return, torn between the "excitement he owes to new places, to unaccustomed activities, to the recent conversation . . . under the unfamiliar lamp" and the "imminent sweetness of his return" to a reality of habits and familiar (*heimlich*) surroundings. The Sick Man, on the other hand, is caught up between suffering and relief, which are associated, respectively, with the night's solitude and with the moment of awakening, when another person might come to his rescue. The patient's mistaking of the artificial light for daylight is put in parallel with the reading child's confusion between being lost in the kindly light of the dream (where I am what [I] am reading) and the shock of waking up in the dark (Where am I? Who am I?). "[And] when I woke in the middle of the night, since I did not know where I was, I did not even understand in the first moment who I was" (p. 9). Sleep overcomes him as he is reading and leads him to that "marvellous site, different from the rest of the world", which is also the realm of the dream.

The two figures metaphorically associated with the reader stand for literature itself, in so far as its deliration opens a path towards the Unconscious. In this way, Proust's experiment methodically (metanarratively) links the effect of reading to the unconscious imaginary; the latter becomes readable thanks to a kind of natural continuity, a consubstantiality with the book and with what is read in the book. Proust represents this passage first as the state of being half asleep; then through the child's fragile ego, which has not yet separated itself from the other; and finally as a movement of displacement which releases memories by lifting the cloak of self-censorship. This non-space of literary play, of the search for the self which upon awakening is always again lost, allows for the expression of traumas and fantasies. By depicting this psychic position – of the reader opening himself up to the Other without self-censorship or anxiety – at the very beginning of his text, Proust opens up a space for free associations because the scene of reading paves the way for "unintentional reminiscences", if not for the Unconscious. The figure of the sleeping reader then enables the narrator to quickly introduce the first fantasy:

> Sometimes, as Eve was born from one of Adam's ribs, a woman was born during my sleep from a cramped position of my thigh. . . . My body, which felt in hers my own warmth, tried to return to itself inside her.
>
> (p. 8)

Here, the dreaming body of the reader is seized in a torus of self-contained jouissance, reminding us of what Faguet described as the body's oscillation between languor and repossession (Scene 5), or what we saw in Elisa's appropriation of the "sailor's gaze" directed at the octopus-female sex (Scene 4). Who is penetrated by whom? We see the same anamorphosis and doubling here, between the subject, the dream and the fantasy revealed by reading.

Being what I read: the ego, as a reflection of the social superego and its force of censorship, has been temporarily suspended and effaced. *Being what I write* can then become its project and Chevalier Golo's figure, projected by the magic lantern onto the walls of the child's bedroom, its embodiment. The reading subject, "in its essence . . . supernatural" and accommodating "every obstacle, every hindersome object that he encountered by taking it as his skeleton and absorbing it into himself", becomes the subject of writing. Does Proust's description of the literary effect not remind us of the scene in Elisa's bedroom inhabited by the *lectum*?

> . . . a magic lantern [which] replaced the opacity of the walls with impalpable iridescences, supernatural multicoloured apparitions, where legends were depicted as in a wavering, momentary stained-glass window . . . this intrusion of [the past, of] mystery and beauty into a room I had at last filled with myself to the point of paying no more attention to the room than to that self.
>
> (Proust, pp. 14–15)

Finding itself in unintelligible darkness, confused, its perceptive and topo-graphical bearings lost, the ego sees its "original features . . . decomposed" (p. 15). By staging the metempsychosis of a child lost in the dark, by projecting Golo's "astral body" (p. 15) onto the walls, the novel's opening lines undercut the sub-ject's narcissistic certainty in order to rethink literature as such. The literary act is conceived as the ego's passivation, its becoming the repository for the Other's projections: "None of us constitutes a material whole," the narrator tells us, "our social personality is a creation of the minds of others" (p. 22). Since the ego's consistency relies on external visible objects,[6] the search for the lost self necessar-ily entails a process of disbelief and a destabilizing of what remains of the ego's ideological foundations. This may mean putting the hero's consistency at risk (as we see in the opening phrases and in the wished-for androgyny of the dream), in order to then rebuild him at his discretion as a mass of words, a mass from which an image of the self can be carved out – a space separate from the Mother, whose completeness has at last begun to crumble.

Like a hologram of the entire literary project to come, the slumberous scene of reading which opens the search deterritorializes its narrator and, at the same time, contains the Imaginary, safeguarding the book and its future symbolic trajectory: better to believe oneself a literary character than to be left alone in the dark. In his ambivalence, Proust's reading child is a foreshadowing of what the novel por-trays, in its hundreds of pages, as a bodily struggle between the subject and the letter. It depicts a paradox: on the one hand, the price due to the Symbolic in order to transform the Thing into a literary work; on the other, the illusion that such work, composed of letters, might ultimately be able to make up for the subject's castration, for the breaching of the body as a condition of writing. This mirroring of the entire work in the figure of the reading child, terrified by the "truly dark" real outside the book, is in itself a metapsychology of reading as a form of exile. We can therefore look at writing as a way of undoing this exile. The letter lends itself perfectly to this task since it is a memory of the thing.

The ego, an effect of reading?

Scene 7

Doing away with humbug and telling the truth: that is one of the aims I have pursued most stubbornly throughout all my books. This obstinacy has its roots in my childhood: I hated what my sister and I used to call "silliness" – a way of smothering life and its joys under prejudice, set habits, pretence and empty phrases. Early in my defence [against this oppression] I relied upon my own self-awareness: when I was very small the mystery of its first appearance, its evident and yet disputed sovereignty, and the scandal of its future extinction haunted me, and they have an important place in my books. Somewhat later, when I was about fourteen, I identified myself with Louisa May Alcott's Jo and with George Eliot's Maggie; I longed to assume that imaginary dimension which made these story-book heroines and the writer who projected herself into them so fascinating, and to assume it before an audience. I did not begin by writing a novel about an apprenticeship to life, because between the ages of twenty and thirty I was detached from my past. But later I did try to recount my life, endowing my experience with an artistic necessity. . . . I wanted to make myself exist for others by conveying, as directly as I could, the taste of my own life: I have more or less succeeded.[7]

Here, Simone de Beauvoir gives us a poetic definition of the ego – "a taste of my own life", "my own self-awareness: when I was very small the mystery of its first appearance, its evident and yet disputed sovereignty, and the scandal of its future extinction" – and connects the origin of her desire to write to its vacillations and megalomania. As the agency responsible for our sense of identity, the ego is captured by the mirror image and remains alienated in the specular ideal. Searching for the unity it perceived through misrecognition and by negating its own illusion,[8] what Lacan calls "the little master",[9] is constituted "in its nucleus by a series of alienating identifications" (*Écrits*, p. 347), for which the subject pays the price of his own repressed desire (*Écrits*, p. 633). Thus, if this little master "knows a bit about [his desire]", it is indeed only a little bit.

De Beauvoir's autobiographical acting out is enticed by a similar lure, an effect of reading: to try to give herself the same firm determination the novel gives to its heroines, so that their glorious image transforms the "deplorable" contingence of her own existence into a necessity. "A man in all the truth of nature", Rousseau promises to himself, "and this man is to be myself!"[10] The "self" is invented as a pious wish, an object of desire and a possible effect of writing. If only letters could give it the ideal shape of an object! The novel provides a structure to this ideal because, as Freud tells us, its hero is "His Majesty the Ego". Like in our daydreams, the literary hero, to whom "nothing can happen",[11] is the focus of all desires; his name on the page mimics identity, wilfully ignoring the "scandal of [his] future extinction". Nothing can challenge his (linguistic) survival; no fear can disturb the inescapable syntax of his desire. The magic of the name creates an effect of thingness, generating imaginary consistency, which in combination with the plot structures the genre, giving to what Freud called the "egocentric story" (p. 149) its ontological function. Hagiography's twin, the canonical form of the novel as a medium, is the lovechild of historiography and the romantic expression of individualized desire; its message is philosophical, anthropological and therapeutic. It figures the ideal of a subject striving for self-knowledge through a text and a narrative that are his own "cause". The reader who sees his ego reflected in the novel as he would in the mirror image derives an equal amount of pleasure from it: "[when] I identified myself with Louisa May Alcott's Jo . . . I longed to assume that imaginary dimension which made these story-book heroines and the writer who projected herself into them so fascinating, and to assume it before an audience." The novel produces a *semblance* – the illusion of a possible equivalence between the subject and the unary trait represented by the letter of the name.

Whether the hero is destined to win or lose is beside the point. A being will have existed – a future perfect, which, thanks to the *jouis-sense* it conveys, could very well be the motto of the novel's reader, in essence a neurotic.

The heroine of *All Said and Done*, who "wanted to make [her]self exist for others by conveying, as directly as [she] could, the taste of [her] own life" tells us that she has "more or less succeeded". For Simone de Beauvoir, the word retains its pre-Saussurian transparency and performative magic, and the novel retains its prestructuralist ontological function. This magic thinking has an effect on the real. Confiding in Claude Lanzmann, de Beauvoir says:

Scene 7 (continued)

... when my sister and I talk, there are indeed things *she* remembers, that *I* cannot recall because they have not been noted down, registered, it is as if they no longer exist. There is no question about that. Writing embalms the past, but leaves it slightly frozen, mummified. I no longer have very warm or vivid memories of what happened to me in the past. Or they are warm and vivid when, for example, I read myself a little and through this reading I bring them back to life. But in general, memories do not come back to me spontaneously.[12]

"[Through reading] I bring the thing back to life." Lacan writes, "The letter [. . .] produces all its truth effects in man" (*Écrits*, p. 424). Both formulations illustrate the belief operative on the two sides of the book – namely, that the truth effect comes from the magic of the book's Thing. What, on the other hand, has *not* been transformed, jotted down and published (that is to say, read) is dead to memory: "[I] cannot 'bring back to life'" what was not written down; it is as if it "no longer existed". The ego is here a desire for an image that, through rereading, has become its own myth, something slightly frozen, mummified, embalmed. Because of her little word-schemes, the autobiographer reading her own text is thus in danger of thinking herself a master illusionist, while in reality she is a mere play thing in the hands of the letter.

De Beauvoir's desire for independence, which mimics Rousseau's original project (offering the reader the true face of the "self"), points at the limits of the human subject's struggle to bend the signifier to his will: that of using writing to save face, to acquire a measure of consistency.

With my distant hand I count the pages that remain. They will do. This exercise book is my life, this big child's exercise book, it has taken me a long time to resign myself to that. And yet I shall not throw it away. For I want to put down in it, for the last time, those I have called to my help, but ill, so that they did not understand, so that they may cease with me. Now rest.[13]

"I, truth, speak," Lacan says (*Écrits*, p. 340). And also: "At the outset, subjectivity has no relation to the Real, but rather to a syntax which is engendered by the signifying mark there" (p. 38). We are forced to produce the Symbolic in order to weave the Real and the subject together. We could say: I, truth, read. "Read this sentence. Truth is always in the sentences," the French writer Christine Angot tells the reader in *La Peur du lendemain*.[14] The effect of continuity and consistency created by writing, by the trace left on the page, can be a great help for a subject that is "uncomfortable in his own skin". Bit by bit, between the words, the ego can start believing in itself. Malone, Mal *alone*, Mal *one:* at the end of the book, words, called to the rescue by Beckett's metahero, die together with the letters of the ultimate word, *moi*, without having created any true sense of reality. What Beckett shows is the vanity of all attempts at producing, through writing, an identity between being and the Thing of the novel. *Moi*, the final word, is only the absence of the void made present, a signifier that intrinsically and eternally "materializes the instance of death":[15] Now rest.

In the same way, Rousseau perceives a yawning gap between the word and its effect of thingness: the gap of the unknowable, of the Real, which reveals the delusion of representation. "I may have supposed to be true what I knew could have been so."[16] With the help of this syntactic loop at the beginning of his autobiography, Rousseau does his best to fill in the gap by writing "despite the impossible". By creating verisimilitude as an effect of reading, he tries to produce a semblance.

A doubt thus arises at the very beginning of the confessional contract – of "showing [a man] in all the truth of nature" – because "nature", in order to be shown, must first be written. Truth, insofar as it is announced by the *I*, is only a supposition; constructing the ego as a text means patiently connecting the "bits and pieces" of knowledge together, of mending the ego with the help of the *I*'s syntax. A second magic formula connects the syntax of desire to the truth effect of the letter: "And if I have sometimes used some indifferent ornamentation, this has only ever been to fill a void occasioned by my lack of memory" (Rousseau, p. 5). This "indifferent ornamentation" reminds us of Barthes's "useless detail",[17] insofar as it also functions as a quilting point, stitching together language and the ego (a "supposed" entity) through the writing of an *I*. The effect of the Real produces an effect of subjectivity, which in Rousseau transmits the ego's command to writing: it is forbidden not to know. Filling the void with ornaments means producing "fictions" which deny not only that the impossibility of Being plays a role in the constitution of the biographical logic, but that it is in fact its unconscious cause.

The letter, a piece of the body

It is precisely because the question of being is structurally inherent to writing that, in *Nausea*, Sartre chooses to demolish the beliefs and illusions of being's completeness through the existential torment of his hero, the biographer Roquentin. While trying to write a book about the life of a certain Marquis de Rollebon, Roquentin undergoes a brutal transformation, a loss of belief. This is followed by an *Aufhebung*, when he realizes that the thing cannot be reduced to its name and that all writing is necessarily an illusion.

> The Marquis was present: pending the moment when I should have finally installed him in historical existence, I was lending him my life. I could feel him like a slight glow in the pit of my stomach. . . . Monsieur de Rollebon was my partner: he needed me in order to be and I needed him in order not to feel my being. . . . I no longer saw my hand writing letters on the paper, nor even the sentence I had written – . . . I saw the Marquis . . . he had freed me from myself.[18]

The name Rollebon (*le bon rôle* – the good role) has become an ego ideal thanks to the consistency of its letters. Its essence was purely an effect of the name, of the visual word presentation. Mistaking himself for the thing of his book, the subject is lost in the streets of *Bouville* (Mudville), wandering aimlessly like a phantom without any desires or plans. Then, one day:

> "Care had been taken to spread the most sinister rumours. . . ." I had thought out this sentence, to begin with it had been a little of myself. Now it was engraved in the paper, it was lining up against me. I no longer recognized it. I couldn't even think it out again. It was there, in front of me; it would have been useless for me to look at it for some sign of its origin. Anybody else could have written it.
>
> (p. 139)

The letters have "lined up" against the ego, which can no longer find its bearings. Since all continuity and consubstantiality between the text and the self have vanished, the character, the avatar of this magic belief, also loses his substance, his *raison d'être*. While before ". . . he weighed heavily on my heart and I felt full up. Now nothing remained of him. No more anything remained, in those traces of dry ink, of the memory of their brilliance . . . noiselessly, Monsieur de Rollebon had returned to his nothingness" (p. 140). The pronoun *he* appears as a sign of absence, of the hero as the pure effect of reading: "His task was to perform [*représenter*]. He stood in front of me and had taken possession of my life in order to perform [*représenter*] his life for me. . . . I no longer existed in myself, but in him" (p. 143). In the moment of crisis, language becomes autonomous and it is no longer possible to identify with Rollebon's name: the word is not the thing! No word can express being – the Real escapes us, producing anxiety because behind things "there is nothing" (p. 140). "In their place *something* remains in the warm room, something I don't want to see" (p. 142, original emphasis). Like a soul that has been lost out there, "existence, liberated, released [of the thing now] surges over me". "I exist," Roquentin exclaims, writing down in his journal: *I exist*. This moment, which psychoanalysis would call a working-through, seems to restate the Freudian *Wo Es war, soll Ich werden*: in the place of the book-thing, the subject can now speak of himself as an *I* and entrust his adventures to the "adventure of language".[19] To say *I* is to appropriate language – to inhabit it as an individual caught up in the universal implied by the deictic. In order to mould it, to make it express one's singularity, the subject must first become aware of his own incompleteness and lack.

> My thought is *me*. . . . I exist by what I think. . . . It is I, *it is I* who pull myself from the nothingness to which I aspire. . . .
> My saliva is sugary, my body is warm; I feel insipid. My penknife is on the table. I open it. . . . I jab the knife into the palm. . . . It is bleeding. . . . I look with a feeling of satisfaction at the white paper, where, across the lines I wrote a little while ago, there is this little pool of blood which has at last stopped being me. Four lines on a white paper, a splash of blood, together that makes a beautiful memory. I must write underneath it: "That day I gave up writing my book about the Marquis de Rollebon."
>
> (Sartre, *Nausea*, pp. 145–146)

The new (philosophical) subject is a subject to renouncement; his adventure tells the story of his encounter with the lure of the letter. He will have to pay his dues, his pound of flesh, to the Symbolic. As subject of writing, his story only really starts with a cut. The body which informs the ego and the hand as the writing tool are marked by what we should read as the initial letter of a new kind of writing; the wound is the castrating blow of the Symbolic and its law. The little pool of blood on white paper, with the added legend ("I gave up"), shows that there is no being except for the speaking being (*parlêtre*). Roquentin can no longer mistake himself for his words. *"Wo Es war, soll Ich werden"*: Where the Thing was, wrapped up in its name, the letter *I* now appears as the cut in the body, granting the subject access to symbolic castration.

Christine Angot knows a thing or two about this "blood pact" at the origin of writing.

> Excuse me? Did I hear you right? I thought you said, "Is this autobiographic or what?" If they ask you, just say you don't know. What is this obsession? An artist and her private life are like a postpartum woman and her child. What ties them together is secret. You can look at the child, but you do not lift the mother's gown to see if she's covered in blood. Can you imagine anything more insensitive? I mean, what is that about?[20]

What is it then? A little pool of blood as evidence of the secret link between what is being written and the splitting of the body,[21] the "breaking down", in Freud's terms, of the body of the mother.

In Angot's text, Roquentin's wounded hand, the ambivalent metonymy of the writing subject, bleeding as he signs his work, becomes the sex of a "postpartum woman" hidden under her gown. The source of truth is thus linked to the sexual

Thing. For both Sartre and Angot, the bodily reference serves to highlight the need of giving up the ego's omnipotence in order to produce something that is of oneself yet no longer oneself – letters, which have fallen away from the mother's body. Angot formulates this using a feminine corporal imaginary: "Fortunately, literature has a universal vocation. For my next book, I will have to be excised, perhaps infibulated; pieces of my flesh, of my sex, will be left to dry in the sun."[22] As a synecdoche of letters, these "pieces of flesh" show the writer's need to endure the signifier's breaching of the body's imaginary completeness before she can appropriate language through the semblance of writing, thus gaining access to the law and desire. This is the definition of writing as a mode of sublimation, of which the French writer Marie Redonnet will now give us a splendid illustration.

DÉ-LIRE 2: DELETING THE NAME OF THE FATHER

> *The poet knows. . . . If he does not become a hero and a creator of language for other men, or a priest, or a father, he condemns himself to the powerlessness of maternal identification in feminine jouissance. These are the stakes inherent in writing.*
>
> (E. Lemoine Luccioni)[23]

Scene 8

The Splendid is not what it used to be since grandmother died. The lavatories always need unblocking. The wall-paper is peeling off the walls because of the damp. The Hôtel Splendid is built over an underground lake. It's grandmother's fault. No one had ever built a hotel on the edge of the swamp. . . . I inherited the Hôtel Splendid. But in exchange, I owe an allowance to my sisters. They chose to come and live at the hotel instead of taking the allowance. Here they are housed, fed and served. Maybe I should not have agreed to this arrangement.[24]

Scene 9

The roof of the church finally collapsed. The father said nothing. He lost interest in the church long ago, when it closed. It has been closed for as long as I can remember. The father does not have enough money to have the roof repaired anyway. Since the church is closed, what difference does it make? . . . It is very old, it just barely holds together. Forever Valley is no longer a parish or a village, it is only a hamlet. . . . The valley below drew in the inhabitants of Forever Valley little by little. . . . I was raised by the father. . . . The father must have raised me so I can look after him in his old age. He doesn't want to end up in the rest home. The home is his obsession.[25]

Redonnet's triptych, *Hotel Splendid* (HS), *Forever Valley* (FV) and *Rose Melie Rose*,[26] was published in the late 1980s. Each of the three novels can be read in a trice and seemingly rewritten forever. This effect is no doubt caused by the child-like simplicity of Redonnet's phrasing. The tone resembles a young girl's diary, or perhaps a difficult and shy transcription of oral speech. Yet the simplicity quickly becomes disconcerting because the speaking subject appears to be standing on the edge of an abyss. There is a constant threat that the writing will cease – that it will become impossible. It seems like an enormous undertaking: the female narrators have so much to say in such a short time; they are so afraid of words that at any given moment they might simply choose to fall silent and abandon their arduous task of transcription. The three short novels must therefore be read very quickly, so that, as with Proust's magic lantern, we can glimpse the strained silhouettes of their female characters whose tenuous connection with the Symbolic reduces them to mere outlines of human figures struggling to exist in the world.

Redonnet's tales may not look like much, but what they illustrate are the conditions of possibility of a subject's narcissistic survival and the complex stakes of her access to the Symbolic. Each of the novels represents a different stage of this process, with the first two panels of the triptych staging its premises: (1) effacing the name of the father, leaving a blank space from which the subject's primary trace can emerge; and (2) the invention of the first letter of a new alphabet, which inscribes the place of the subject now freed from the grip of the Other. Similarly to Barillé's scene of reading (Scene 4), Redonnet's parables have no doubt been inspired by her own experience of becoming a writer.

These excerpts show us that the novels' heroines are tied to their places of residence by very peculiar contracts. These have been decided on by the Other – the grandmother (*HS*) and the father (*FV*). Puppets in the hands of a destiny against which they have no desire to rebel (or they lack the psychical means to do so), the narrators of the first two books are forever bound to these spaces, which are paradoxically highly unstable. The humidity of a swamp continuously gnaws away at the foundations of the Hotel Splendid, threatening to swallow it up completely. Forever Valley is a dilapidated hamlet slowly being drained of its population; eventually it is engulfed by a reservoir. There is nothing "splendid", nothing "forever lasting" about these places, except for their names – precarious names which the subjects will endeavour to safeguard and hijack. Saving writing is a way to save ourselves.

Indeed, the two narrators seem to belong to their birthplaces, body and soul. The hotel and the hamlet represent nests they have never left. Their naivety as to what is happening to them stems from this native bond[27] with their surroundings. The first narrator will not leave. She becomes consubstantial with her habitat (as an animal becomes part of its environment). She remains alone in her sinking building, like a sea captain whose uncompromising sense of duty dictates him to perish under his ship, or in this case, under the hotel's blinking name: Splendid, Splendid, Splendid.

The second narrator, uprooted from her native village, which now lies at the bottom of an artificial lake, chooses to die of anaemia and boredom in the "valley below".

Their geographic movements (essential to the story) resemble a circuit rather than a progression: there is no accumulation of knowledge, no initiation. We are not in a *Bildungsroman*. Propelled by their life drives, the women are struggling not to be destroyed by the perverse contracts they have been locked into by their ancestors, and which they suffer without flinching.

> I inherited the Hôtel Splendid. But in exchange, I owe an allowance to my sisters. They chose to come and live at the hotel instead of taking the allowance. Here they are housed, fed and served. Maybe I should not have agreed to this arrangement
>
> (*HS*, pp. 3–4)

> The father must have raised me so I can look after him in his old age. He doesn't want to end up in the rest home. The home is his obsession
>
> (*FV*, pp. 3–4)

The stories follow their circular movements, resembling those of a domestic animal bound to its body's labour: in the first case, the compulsory, endless and thankless tasks of the housekeeper and the nurse, who seems to be living in a kind of eternal menopause; in the second case, the automatic and joyless gestures of the prostitute, a prepubescent girl, who is never going to be fully developed. Bound by necessity and duty, Redonnet's febrile females struggle not to fade back into the native landscapes from which they originate. There is only one way of escaping the universe of the Other (i.e. escaping psychosis), and that is to focus on one's project. The latter consists in trying to preserve the Symbolic function so that the desiring human subject may survive (a desire that will only appear clearly in the third and final novel, *Rose Melie Rose).* This is accomplished in two different steps.

Splendid splendid splendid splendid

Scene 8 (continued)

> Grandmother thought big. Hotel Splendid is written in big capital letters above the roof, and also above the front door, twice so you can see it better. Grandmother thought it took two signs to announce the Hotel Splendid from far away, *two blinking signs, she was firm about that.* They are the only neon signs in the region. The electricity bill is high, but that is the last thing I will let the hotel do without. Without the neon lights blinking in the night, the Splendid would no longer be the Splendid. . . . *By night, you might almost think the Splendid was new. There is no danger of getting lost in the swamp at night thanks to the signs.*
>
> (*HS*, pp. 23–24; my emphasis)

Despite the efforts of the prospectors, engineers and construction workers, the railway project never becomes a reality. The swamp prevents any attempts at leaving a mark on it. Only the hotel's neon sign punctuates its unstable centre: an attachment point, the start of a lifeline, the zero of a future signifying chain, but also a vanishing point where the nondimensional landscape leaks away, foiling any meaning-making attempts of the reader-traveller. The boundless maternal space of the swamp tries to reabsorb the (naïve) subject; it threatens to dissolve her in primordial indifferentiation, in a deadly incest foreclosing all existence: "The embankment [where they fell] was swallowed up. Grandmother and my sisters belong to the swamp" (*HS*, p. 112). In order to "escape", the narrator therefore needs a vessel able to resist this fusional capture. Thanks to the knowledge transmitted by the grandmother, the swamp has become a marked territory: "The Splendid has a unique view of the swamp. . . . Thanks to grandmother's enterprising spirit, this is the only swamp with a hotel in the entire region" (p. 113). The "hotel" structures the boundless universe around a point of origin, the future space of the subject. Saving the hotel therefore means not only preserving the *punctus* that transforms the maternal space into an adaptable, habitable place, but also making it the "you are here" of any map, with the material support of a sign. Signs play a key role in Redonnet's work. They are allegories of the letter's function for the human being – the striking presence of the Splendid's neon sign is indeed the only human trace in the primordial chaos of the swamp. Shining in the dark of the night, the sign can be interpreted as a proof of the subject's existence, but also as a desperate S.O.S. or a white flag waved before the enemy – the archaic real, the maternal Thing, which threatens to annihilate and engulf everything. The neon marks the point of departure indispensable to any future geometrization of the void, which was previously initiated by the grandmother. The subject of *Hotel Splendid* has no other function but to preserve and protect the building that serves as a material support to the neon message: 1 0 1 0 1 0 – a representation, if there ever was any, of the intermittent character of reading, of the fragile thingness of the read word.

Nevertheless, the final scene of the book does stage a kind of exit, a moving away from the flashing of the object-sign and the paralysis of its autistic reading.

Scene 8 (continued)

The signs are working again, but only halfway. I only turn them on at night. When night falls and I turn them on, only one word is lit up, the second one, Splendid. That word stands out against the sky. Travelers cannot help but see it. But since the word Hotel isn't lit up, the travellers cannot know that the Splendid is a hotel. That explains why there are fewer and fewer guests. . . . In the evening, I stand at the window. The Splendid with its half-lit signs is reflected in the snow. The letters are leaning, like the hotel. You might think you were on a boat. . . . The Splendid is visible from everywhere in the swamp. Its signs shine at night, they are visible from a great distance. There are two . . . spots in the sky and on the snow. They are the reflection of the Splendid signs.

(pp. 112–113)

In this final post-cataclysmic image, the broken sign represents the unreadable. It no longer informs (no *lectio* is possible) because it no longer refers to anything. The letters have become mere spots. They are now also doing a lot more work – or a lot less:

1   "Grandmother thought it took two signs to announce the Hotel Splendid from far away." In the beginning, the neon is a sign-object that is inseparable from the hotel: it questions, shows and names. This means that if the word *hotel* stops working, there will be no more clients.

2   The erasure of the building's function – what exactly is "splendid" over there? – transcends the nominalism of the ancestor's project because the part of the sign that no longer works was what designated the thing itself. The sign becomes a pure signifier, a string of letters without a referent. The deserted hotel under the blinking sign is therefore an illustration of the *Lesen* now functioning as *lectum* (a sign *for* a subject), creating a potential space for metaphor and therefore for literature.

The "breakdown" makes *lectio* impossible, thus staging the fundamental instability of writing, yet the author, who certainly knows something about the Unconscious, also shows us the *dé-lire* inherent in the subject's access to literature. Redonnet is a pen name; the writer's family name is Hospitalier. Like *hôtel*, the French word *hôpital* comes from the Latin *hospitalis domus*, "a place to receive guests", in other words the foreign, the Other. She shows us that the subject must bring the signified under the bar of the sacred signifier, the Name-of-the-Father (which shone in the middle of the swamp and bound her to her residence), in order for the Splendid to become something other than a hotel. The word *hotel* having been erased, the occupant can start "thinking she were" ("*se croire*") on a boat, between heaven and earth. The bright spots of light which the signifier *Splendid* reflects on the sky and the snow-covered earth join the transcendental Other to the white page where the author's name can be traced. "The signifier *originates* from the effacement of the trace," Lacan said.[28]

Forever Valley restages the question of the signifiers of the Name-of-the-Father through the peculiar relationship between its young female narrator and "*the father*", whose generic character is implied by the use of the exophoric. The father is in fact in charge of the young woman's education, and at the same time the priest and patriarch of the village.

X: the first letter of a new alphabet

Scene 9 (continued)

I wondered for a long time whether or not I should tell the father about my personal project. . . . I need his consent. . . . I told him I wanted to look for the dead. . . . The father seems to look at me differently now that I have told him about my project. He must have thought I could come up with my own project. *He was disappointed that I never learned to read.* But I don't need to know how to read to look for the dead.

(FV, pp. 12–13, my emphasis)

It will be a pit of exactly the same dimensions as the first pit. *I want there to be symmetry* between the front and the back of the church. *I am not really digging at random* after all, I am digging on each side of the church, at the four points of the compass. *That is as good a plan* as any other. It didn't occur to me at first, but now I see it clearly.

(FV, p. 67, my emphasis)

You have to have solid legs to look for the dead.

(FV, p. 19)

It's easy for me to dig now. I have been digging for four weeks, so I am in shape. I don't have any trouble lifting the shovel anymore.

(FV, p. 82)

Contrary to *Hotel Splendid*, the rock of Forever Valley is immediately given as a territory: an organized, marked out and named space. A "father" pretends to still be running the place, but he is sliding into paralysis and impotence. Almost all inhabitants have left because the village is soon to be submerged by a reservoir. What is thus at stake for the protagonist is to transform the father's territory – to divert his dilapidating institutions, with their agents either dead or dying and their monuments crumbling. "Mayor was mostly an honorary title", since "there was not much to preside over" (*FV*, p. 5). The narrator will transform this deserted place into a space of play. Her "project" – something impossible to envisage for the heroine of *HS*, whose task was only to preserve – consists of digging pits to "look for the dead" (perhaps those who were submerged by the swamp surrounding *HS* hotel).

Like in *Hotel Splendid*, the signs in *Forever Valley* are only relics of writing. They no longer name the object to which they are attached. Thus the Town Hall-School houses a dancehall and a brothel. The institutions formerly ruled by "the father" and the mayor have been taken over by the mayor's wife, Massi, the director of the dancehall, and by the narrator, who is trying to transform what is left of the church and its garden. By asking Massi to educate his protégée, to initiate her to "dancing" – a euphemism for prostitution which the protagonist endures impassively and relates in a matter-of-fact way – "the father" participates in her degradation, which is a consequence of the disintegration of his law. This effacement, the desertion of the village and the father's "agony", allow the protagonist to conceive of her strange "project". We observe its conception in real time by following the story, since the narrator's thoughts, naïve and hesitant, are offered to us directly, like in a logbook and without any psychological or historical explanation.

What is this *project?*

First of all, the first-person narrator wishes to bury the dead, like Redonnet herself: "I started by writing the first important word on the page, and that word was: the Dead. This inaugural word then gave birth to my writing," the author said in one of her interviews.[29] This is no doubt because this desire marks precisely the origin and the unconscious structural function of writing and its necessity for the subject, as Michel de Certeau tells us in *The Writing of History*:

> On the one hand, writing plays the role of a burial rite . . . it exorcises death by inserting it into discourse. On the other hand, it possesses a symbolizing function; it allows [one] to situate oneself by giving oneself a past through language, and it thus opens to the present a space of its own. "To mark" a past is to make a place for the dead, but also to redistribute the space of possibility, to negatively determine what is there to be *done*, and as a consequence to use narrativity that buries the dead as a way of establishing a place for the living.[30]

The desire of the narrator in *Forever Valley* therefore reenacts the founding act of the writing of history.

Her work pays off – the pound of flesh has not been paid in vain. The unexpected happens; while looking for "the dead", she unearths what lies deep under the surface.

Scene 9 (continued)

> I ran into mud all of a sudden. I knew I would hit the sludge again if I continued. . . . it is exactly like the second pit. . . . *There is a sort of vein of sludge running across the garden deep down, from east to west.* . . . The subsoil of the garden is made up of the ridge of rock in one direction and the vein of sludge in the other. There is no way I could have known. . . . The four walls of the church collapsed at the same time. . . . There is nothing but a pile of stones where it used to stand. . . . *I straightened up* [*j'ai mis de l'ordre*] the pile of stones. It is almost in the centre of the four pits.
>
> (*FV*, pp. 86–87; my emphasis)

In Redonnet's metaphorical village, the Symbolic (the father's law) has been radically undermined; the planning and mapping of the land has fallen into disuse. Below the hamlet lies the undifferentiated "sludge", the swamp of *Hotel Splendid*, the original magma that has now again begun to seep out. In order to record her movements through this territory, to leave a trace, the subject must confront this undifferentiated mass and struggle, with her own body, to form a border against the void of the Thing. Only then will she be able to exist for a while and avoid dissolution in the maternal magma. The next step is to reorganize the symbolic territory of the paternal institutions. The centre of Forever Valley, marked only by the ruins of the Old World (the world of "the father's" desire and jouissance), is transformed by the protagonist's labour and unflinching resolve. An unforeseen geology comes to light; a new map is drawn. By digging the pits and marking the four compass points on the ground – "the fashioning of the signifier and the introduction of a gap or a hole in the real is identical,"[31] Lacan argues – the narrator accomplishes two important things at once. First, she inscribes the realm of "the father" in the universal human order. Second, she undertakes an archaeology of what lies beneath (questioning the past) in order to invent a primitive historiography that would put the dead where they belong and thus, as de Certeau has explained, establish a place for the living. She will neither expose the dead of a lost civilization, nor establish a genealogy (this only happens in the third novel, *Rose Melie Rose*). However, unbeknownst to her, the project is gradually transformed: it becomes a monument to the dead and, at the same time, a primitive letter.

The nameless narrator – at first an archaeologist, then a geologist – creates a geography by barring the maternal Thing (the swamp in *HS*) with the paternal rock (*FV*) and marking their intersection with the pile of stones from the church. In this way, Redonnet shows us the origin of a "work" of writing. This creation

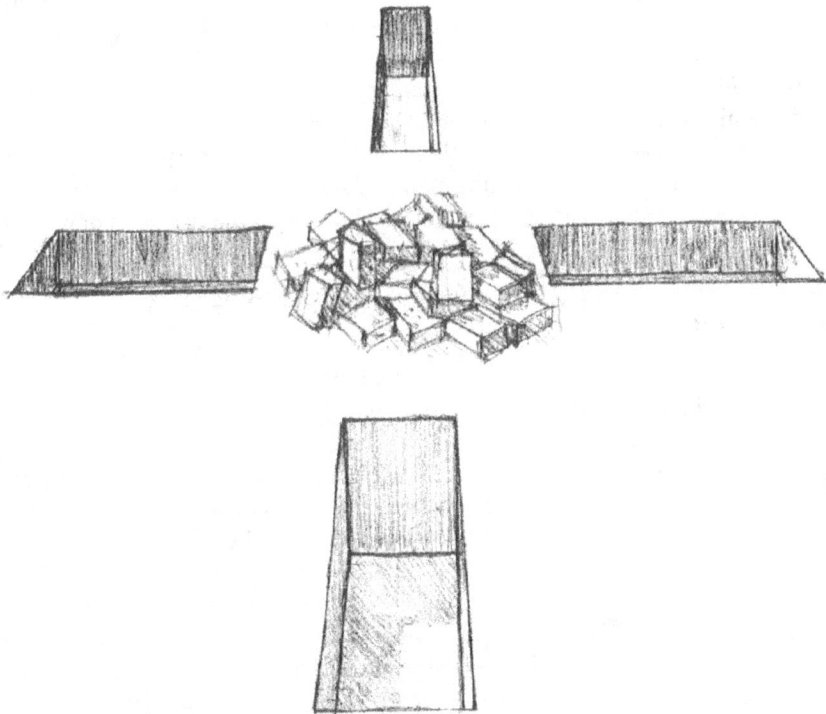

Figure 3.1 X : the first letter of a new alphabet
© Didier Drillien

of a new object in the world is also a sublimation, since the object materializes a singular desire and represses the shifting grounds of the maternal Thing, but also transforms the "father's monument" into the first letter of a future history.

If, in the end, the narrator of *Forever Valley* buries her father, dead before the project is finished, in the first pit; this is because his death in fact marks one of the project's limits. Alain Juranville's commentary on the question of writing can be helpful to us here: "Writing . . . leads the human being beyond his condition as a subject and into the imaginary identification with the symbolic Other, with the father as non-living. In the production of a work as a process of sublimation this identification must be endured."[32] Redonnet's first words, which inaugurated her writing, were "the Dead". This inscription of what would become the first letter of a future text is a metaphor of what the author knows about her own choice of writing as a mode of existence.[33]

In the third pit, which lies to the south, the narrator of *Forever Valley* buries Bob, the probationary officer who was her favourite client. She then finishes her work by filling in the two other pits, which were full of sludge, with the stones from the church. "The stones from the church are the best thing for filling in empty pits. . . . *You would never guess* there used to be a church in the rectory garden" (*FV*, p. 95).[34] A new object is created and a new order of things established. The father's territory has changed beyond recognition: its reorganization constitutes an epistemological break for the subject, a task performed by the body. As Lacan says in *The Ethics of Psychoanalysis*, the signifier is "fashioned by man, and probably more by his hands than by his spirit".[35] The subject's titanic work enables her to invent a new chain of signifiers, including the cross (the illiterate person's letter X), which by functioning as the signifier zero represses the maternal Thing, turns the father into a dead father and designates the position of the future subject of writing.

Writing: the body's labour against the precarity of the letter

The "personal project" of Redonnet's female narrators is first and foremost a work of the body – a labour to manage death. The first two panels of the triptych stage this work through the physical relationship to the ancestor's deserted spaces, to the gift of old and apparently useless things. Physically handling the Real – unblocking, cleaning, digging in the garden – allows these women to create an empty space so that things can be moved about, like in a Gem Puzzle. The body's movement transforms the landscape into a locus in which the elaboration of knowledge, essential to the future existence of a human subject, is possible; this knowledge is both geographical (horizontal) and geological (vertical). Whether the movements of the Sisyphean housecleaner, repeated over and over, or the thankless and morbid task of the gravedigger, the aim of the narrators' personal projects is to leave behind a trace. In this landscape the body bleeds and signs, reenacting the primary creation of the symbol – the original *archè* of the autograph – and at the same time making the subject exist. The holes that are either preserved (unblocked pipes, *HS*) or dug (*FV*) mark the subject's struggle to put desire – and humanity – back into motion. We have seen that unblocking and plugging, the efforts to make sure that the hotel (the house-ship) does not succumb to the swamp of indifference, are ways of preserving the name as a message addressed to an other in the middle of the desert. They are also means of transforming the sign into a signifier, by deleting some of its letters, the letters of the Name-of-the-Father. What saves Redonnet's project from a deep melancholia is precisely this belief in the therapeutic powers of the Symbolic (visualized through writing). Preserving the stubbornly upright signifier as the support of a subject waiting to exist; marking the landscape with a centre, in order to establish a topography of what lies below the father's garden, while discovering the archaic Thing that seeps from beneath – these are the two stages, two necessary rites of passage, on the way to existence.

From *Hotel Splendid* to *Forever Valley*, the body of each of the two narrators is first of all a space of movement, a hollow. It is sterile and solitary yet stubborn, because it has been set in motion, so that at least the Symbolic can remain alive, and humanity, though disappearing, can leave a trace. Thanks to the signifier's emergence on the edge of the Thing, the subject therefore begins to separate herself from her place of origin. However, what the signifier gives form to is, precisely, a void – a crucial stage in the process of sublimation. The signifier, destined to be repressed, marks out its place as the place of effacement.

Scene 9 (continued)

The water has a dark colour because of the mountains reflected in it. Everything gets mixed up inside my head when I look at the water in the reservoir and tell myself that down on the bottom there is the hamlet, there is the garden which is a cemetery, there is the father's grave and Bob's grave. . . . I spend hours looking at the water. No matter how much I look, I can never see the bottom. . . . Forever Valley is completely submerged now. To think that there used to be nothing but rock at Forever Valley, except for the rectory garden, and now there is nothing but water.

(FV, p. 101)

The final place of the subject is on the edge of the void, a void which is to be her destiny: in the frame formed by the window of the hotel, isolated against the white swamp, on the edge of the reservoir that has erased their birthplaces and the traces of writing, the narrators exist against all odds. From these edges and dams, they manage to perceive at least a reflection of the ungraspable Real.

The subject's coming to reading (and later to writing) is structurally preconditioned by this precarious signifier, which in and through its absence designates the void of negation. Redonnet is a paradoxical writer: she shows us that the signifier is not a sign that communicates; she teaches us the kind of disbelief necessary to reverse its totemization. "All art", Lacan writes in *The Ethics of*

Psychoanalysis, "is characterized by a certain mode of organization around this emptiness . . . [while] religion in all its forms consists of avoiding this emptiness" (pp. 129–130).

Redonnet's wonderful short novels restage the very process of individuation, represented as the subject's gaining access to desire, an access which is precon-ditioned by a knowledge about lack and its inscription as a void by means of the body's labour. The word *hotel*, effaced as the Name-of-the-Father, and the inscrip-tion of the first letter of a new alphabet in the field of the Other, give us an idea of how this process can be accomplished. It is a movement from victimhood – perishing in the maternal magma (not yet "broken down"), caught in a frozen and endless reading of the Name-of-the-Father shining above the maternal landscape – to agency, and the accomplishment of a life's project.

DÉ-LIRE 3: WRITING TO DIS-READ THE NEED FOR SEPARATION

> *This grave is a source. This stone listens and answers.*
>
> (Helène Cixous[36])

> *Books are carnivores. They feed on flesh, on tears, they rub shoulders with death, they drink from the cemetery, this is all familiar, I have built my work on my father, I received his remains as a dowry: his teeth, his skin, his letters, a fortune in terror and impossible consolation.*[37]

In her book *Dedans*[38] (*Inside*), which won her the prestigious Prix Médicis in 1969, Helène Cixous tells the story of an ageless and sexless subject confronted with the death of a beloved father. As the story continues, the narrator glimpses a possibility of putting the dead body inside the grave, so that she can be reborn as an individual subject. The book is the father's grave, but also the founding stone of a monument built in his memory by the writer's entire oeuvre.

As the reverse side of Redonnet's narrators, the little girl in Cixous' autofiction dreams of finding words that could restore [*redonner*] a body to the dead father so that writing may bring a subject into existence. The challenge which the poet accepts, the "commitment" she makes in 1969, is to go on existing despite the horror of having lost, at the age of ten, her real father.

> I made a commitment and promised myself to stick to it – through writing – this was thirty years ago – but it's not an achievement – there wasn't anything heroic about it – to sign and make a commitment – or to go mad. I had no choice: going mad is a form of suffering nobody would choose. . . .
>
> Also, at that moment, I signed with your hand. . . .[39]

She says this to her father, who has become the sublime body of words, her ulti-mate interlocutor.

To write or to "go mad" [*folir*] indicates that the writing project is in fact trying to "(re)make a body because a body has been lost".[40] On the edge of madness,
Dedans, Cixous' first book,[41] describes this commitment to writing as an attempt
to put the dead body inside the grave, to sublimate it and turn it into a poetic body,
giving the daughter a language.

> *Dedans* was necessarily written within the father, in seeking him right up to
> death and revenant (coming back, ghostly). There is something simple and
> mysterious in the origin of writing: "I" am in the father I carry within me, he
> haunts me, I live him. There is a rapport between the father and language, the
> father and the "symbolic".[42]

Ever since, Cixous has described her writing as a process of *vécrire* – of producing a textual body to be read and of immersing herself in the sea of words in
order to *dis-read* the unbearable Real.

In this sense, *Dedans* tells the story of this *dé-lire,* this unravelling of what
knowledge, the coming to reading, had constructed: as a literary character,
the father becomes the writer's imaginary child. At the risk of becoming like the
father, corpsified in the jouissance of madness, the subject of enunciation will
have to extricate herself from this textual body, the site of her rebirth into the
world of speaking, living beings.[43] By transforming the secret father of the book
into a master of words, a treasurer of signifiers, the melancholic subject will be
able to read backwards, to *dis-read* the signs of death on the father's body and
change them into letters – remains, teeth, skin . . . letters, as she writes in the passage cited – and then use these letters to write, to become, "adrift between terror
and impossible consolation", a subject to writing. As the living language of the
poem, *vécrire* becomes a true religion of the dead Father.

Almost thirty years later, the father's old letters, written when he was a young
physician in love with his wife, strangely befall her, the daughter finds them
impossible to read: the danger is that of a radical loss of belief.

Let us first see how writing happens in the name of the father.

Father's voice in the words

Scene 10

How many millions of millions of particles were you, my love? Are those
able to hear still alive? I have something to tell you, before the last centres
explode, please just wait a moment, I am waiting for us to be alone, just wait,
I am begging you, do not go away just now, the form of my father, the ear
sister of my mouth, if you could hold on until now, just wait a bit more, my
love, you've got all death before you, just wait, wait for me, at least a while.

(*Dedans,* pp. 88–89)

Wait for me, listen to me. . . . The beauty and tenderness of the words addressed
to the father, the daughter's demand for love and her appeal to his knowledge

are among the most moving passages in the book. They are vital: since the father died before he could reveal the secret of language, he must be transformed into an interlocutor who will walk the daughter through the passage to the Symbolic. The coming to writing therefore becomes the daughter's appropriation of this place of the Other – the place of the father as the master of words, the almighty enunciator of the first and later of all possible signifiers. The psychological game of *Dedans* consists of giving him everything in order to get something back.[44]

> *Scene 10 (continued)*
>
> [My father] had fallen silent, without an explanation, and he lay still and quietly on the bed. So I secretly summoned him. . . .
>
> My secret father and I had a . . . happy conversation, but we were whispering so as not to go against the necessity of the real. I strained to understand his words; they were all new to me. . . . From his mumbling I could only grasp the tenderest sounds I've ever heard, breathing such fire into my body that I took it to be that kind of joy that enables humans to fly. Were my father's words made from that wind that can carry you away and whose name I didn't know? I took a leap.
>
> (*Dedans*, p. 31)

With these words breathed into her, a visible representation of the words she hears, the writer will begin to make marks on the page. The (imagined) father names the world, gives his daughter the words of the body like sensual presents.[45] These magic words are a treasure bound to the father's voice, gaze and touch. Pronouncing and reading them will become equivalent to bringing the father back to life; just like Marcel's Combray remained alive in his madeleine, the father's tender caresses are preserved in the written words.

The father's gaze in the letters of God's name

So as to keep this secret father (dead and revenant) all to herself, the daughter must first appropriate him. The little girl writing the father must prove to herself that she is indeed the only one who really knows him – as he was the only one to really know her.

> *Scene 10 (continued)*
>
> Was it him? He was motionless, I was running, I wasn't getting any closer to him, I kept going, still he was in front of me. Perhaps he was in my eyes, or perhaps I was only an image he had left behind, attached to him by a gaze?
>
> (*Dedans*, p. 34)

The "gaze" links them together – like in the Lacanian mirror, it is what creates the connection: the adult recognizing the child in the reflection becomes an ideal, constructed *a posteriori* as possessing knowledge regarding the completeness of being, completeness which the subject glimpsed yet lost as soon as speech began to name. The "witness" is invested with jouissance by virtue of supposedly having had access to the subject's truth. *Dedans* is trying to return to this gaze: if only he could look at her once more, answer her call once more, if only he could restore to her this lost completeness. The demand is articulated in the following passage:

Scene 10 (continued)

He stretched himself out, filling the horizon and yet I couldn't get any closer to him. Slowly I quit wanting to come close, he had grown too large. I could recognize him, I gazed on him, but. . . .

I started calling, trying out all the names: "You! Hey you!" I yelled. "Man! Hello! Man."

"Daddy!" I sobbed and sobbed.

God! God! I screamed, throwing the word like a stone into the dark waters where it ricocheted, Dieu, Dieu, Dieu, Di.

Then he stopped and turned around and I saw him: the face of God was a hand.

(*Dedans*, pp. 34–35)

She is looking for the word, the name that will support her claim, namely that he is still her father looking at her. The point is to make him see, to make him visible, All-One, complete like a thing, so that he can do the same to her. In this nightmarish scene, the gaze that is desired is barred, forbidden by the hand of God. The subject remains alone with the dead father struck down by fate: "He was no longer holding me . . . nobody here knew" (p. 36). The imaginary father having disappeared as an ideal, the subject risks dissolving into the chaos "at the centre of the world, a yawning gap of disorder and noise" (p. 36) because she believes that no one will ever recognize or know her. The trick is then to transform the figure of God [*Dieu*] into *Di* – in other words, to turn the imaginary father, the all-powerful Ideal, into one who can be named, who can be symbolized by a fragment of the name of God. The fragment denotes the word spoken, *di, dit*, as well as the premise of an injunction, of an address and a demand for answer – *Dis!* (Say!) – in an attempt to *dis-read*, to unravel the dead father.

The father's answer is silence – a secret sign, the very enigma of primordial writing.

The primordial letter on the father's body

Towards the end of the book, we suddenly encounter an immigration officer who asks the narrator-heroine to identify herself and state the reason for her being there. The fragmented account shows us the (imaginary) father and the daughter (of writing) recognizing each other.

Scene 10 (continued)

When were you born? Where were you born? What is the reason of your visit? . . . I was born two hundred years ago in Westphalia . . . six hundred years ago in Palestine . . . and since then, once or twice here and there . . . (I escaped, I was scared of dying – or of being born; I thought: over there, nothing and no one exists anymore, you can get there, you can find; me? No, not me, but who knows, a trace.) Never; once, when I was very young, I believed; I wanted to, I sought to; twice, with him; he was there, I recognized him, he had all the signs. A star shone between his breasts. A laugh glimmered between his eyelashes. . . .

(*Dedans*, pp. 149–150)

The fragile ego, unable to answer the questions of the immigration officer, remembers a time and a place where it knew that it was the self-identical One. "Me? No, not me, but who knows? A trace." As an optical illusion, the ego is only a trace, and unless it has a name (which it receives from the other) it can easily be effaced. Remembering this scene therefore means recovering a belief founded on the symbolic identification with a complex sign.

The scene resembles a primordial fantasy. The identity of the "suspended" subject seems to arise from the moment of recognition based on an association: "he was there, I recognized him, he had all the signs. A star shone between his breasts. A laugh glimmered between his eyelashes."[46] "All the signs" equal a mark on the body and a gaze full of emotion. But what exactly is recognized? The father's star has already appeared in the story: the narrator presents it as the father's emblem only his daughter was able to see; this secret knowledge is then displayed as a mark of her own distinction.

Scene 10 (continued)

I KNEW HIM, better than his own mother, better than his wife. I will not tell anyone that it was me who saw it first, the little mark in the form of a star, which the cousins discovered on his belly.

(*Dedans*, p. 43)

Just like the archaeologist marks the treasure he has discovered, the mark makes the father forever her own, as if he was a work of art. In this scene (which takes place at a border, on her way into exile), the glimmering gaze and the remembered star return the father to his daughter, simultaneously inscribing her as the author of this discovery or deciphering. Becoming the addressee of these signs, their reader, the recipient of the vector of meaning, leads the subject to postulate herself as fathered, as repairable, as One.

The gaze and the star both identify and separate her from the father: as unary traits they produce and are of the father (in the sense of a partitive). Their conjunction – the starry gaze of love, the gazing eye of the star – arrest the ego's headlong flight into the "yawning centre of the world" (p. 36). By becoming signs for the subject, they situate her as the endpoint of a vector now structuring the world. What is recognized is the place this has opened for the subject of the Symbolic, the reader of signs. By falling away from the paternal body, the gaze and the star are subtracted from the father's monolithic form, the All-One, the Totem. The father figure is thus divided into, on the one hand, the bearer of signs, a parchment of primitive writing and, on the other, the privileged interlocutor whose consent is sought so as to make his gaze "glimmer" again. His gaze does not die: now and forever, it remains a sign for the daughter. The secret father therefore restores to the subject some of what she had lost by being abandoned by the real father. The star and the gaze, which are both the father's traits and his objects, come to plug in the gaping hole of absence and love and save the subject from dereliction. They are gifts, keys to unlock the dreams to be written. The star, the gaze and then there's also Oran, of course. And that will suffice to transform the world.

O R : letters or let her be

The star is a primordial trace – not yet a pictogram, not yet a signifier (which only acquires a value through its difference and negativity). It is a kind of unary trait[47] which historically (i.e. in the history of the subject, here represented as the subject of writing) comes prior to the intervention of another sign, which founds the future signifying chain: Oran, the name of the capital of the fatherland.

> I lost myself often within the city of my birth. It was a veiled woman. It was a signifier. It was Oran. . . . The first of my treasures was the name of my native city which was Oran. It was my first lesson. I had heard the name Oran and through Oran I discovered the secret of language. . . . Then I lost Oran. Then I discovered it, white, gold, and dust for eternity in my memory and I never went back. In order to keep it. It became my writing. Like my father. It became a magic door opening into the other world.[48]

"The city of my birth . . . was a signifier. It became my writing. Like my father." Oran is invested by the writer as the very place where the Imaginary meets the Symbolic; they both join with the Real of the loss. This is because the name must be seen as well as heard: it is both a password to access the Symbolic (*Oran* comes before *I*[49]) and a place where the body is born, formed around the treasure of the orange grain ("the mystery of the fruit", ibid, p. 2), also the mystery of the star as a seed of identity: I am (in) the star which is (on) the body of my father who is (in) Oran.

This word-thing (ORAN) is a (Lacanian) Name-of-the-father, the first word read and written in the Cixousian mythology. ORAN is where the subject enters the Symbolic, the primordial signifier, which engenders the chain of writing. It initiates a play of differences based on a deleted star,[50] which marks the centre of Oran

(O R ✿ N) and whose effacement simultaneously creates it. In this way, the text turns the father's body into a thing; it is read and buried, and by writing his name the daughter enters the world of the living. Cixous becomes a reader by the function of the letter as the symbolic father's sign on the body. Its effacement – repression – figures the subject's future destiny as a subject to writing: the endless graphic deformations of Cixous' later books (*Or-An*, *Hors-En*) turn the name into a synecdoche of all others, the expression a wishful thinking: that these word-things may continue to flesh out the subject's body and being.

Cixous' work therefore rewrites O R ✿ N indefinitely, under the gaze of the shining black star, the immutable sign of the ego ideal founded upon the father's love. The final configuration of the different figures of the father that appear in the book is no longer a form that can be seen as a Whole – an obscure, threatening and faceless shape – but instead bears a sign written by a God, who is the result of the same creative gesture. The star drawn on the flesh is the mark of the birth of "a father-for-myself", who will make the daughter a reader of the world and of its poets.

Father's letters or the prohibited reading

Written thirty years after *Dedans*, *Or, les Lettres de mon père* (with the double meaning of the word "letters") tells the story of a terrifying moment when a box[51] with the word BEBECONFORT written on it suddenly arrives at the narrator's door. It contains hundreds of letters written by the father, the one from before – a man in love with his young wife before his daughter was even born. The father who emerges from these letters is the Oedipal father, thus bringing down the construction of *Dedans*, in which his little fairy, the reader in love with the letters of her secret father's name, was living happily ever after: "I am quivering between two fathers," she says (*Or*, p. 34). "For forty years, I've lived with my own personal father reserved for me recreated decomposed rebuilt by me. And suddenly I wake up exiled from my familiar desert. Finished. This is an enormous and threatening event" (pp. 32–33). By the end of the book, the question remains whether to read or not to read the father's real letters, but the work of the unconscious is now acknowledged. Something has been loosened but not released.

> Is the new doctor [the father] going to efface my previous father, wiping the black background of the painting with a piece of cloth? And turn to me, with a merry voice, his eyes gleaming: It's me! It hits my eyes, my ears, I would rec-ognize him, he would be the real one, and my inner father would have always been the other, modestly stepping back into the shadows, taking my dreams and his X-rays away with him, the back door closing behind him silently.
>
> (*Or*, p. 196)

Reading the letters would represent a risk: the veil, which has covered the corpse, transmuting it into a sublime body, would be lifted, laying bare the father's lack, his desire of an other – the mother, who would in turn have to be hated as a rival, something that (still) seems unthinkable. An unfaithful father, not all for the subject, writing with his own hand. Like little Poulou standing before his reading mother (see Chapter I, "The subject to the letter"), the child is struck by an aphanisis, projected outside herself, outside the image of the "myself for you/you for myself" (*toi-par-moi/moi-par-toi*). In this existence, the subject sees herself as lacking, as an incomplete remainder.[52] *Or, les Lettres de mon père* tells us how a feared catastrophe has been avoided – the death of the subject of writing, a death which is in fact only a figure of separation, of the cut: "I was begging him to stay alive as a shadow instead of the doctor to leave a piece of himself with us mute lying on the narrow bed to whom I could come recite the monologue of my life he would not speak, speaking could open a cavity" (p. 180).

Years after *Dedans*, *Or* still keeps writing alive in the name of the prince: "Now I am alone with my dead relatives. I have always thought that I would eventually end up never reading these letters" (p. 198). To not cease not reading the name of the father at the end of each letter means not to lose one's faith, the religion of the dead Father, the source of words, the puppet master of the scribbling hand. The father–daughter alliance, consumed by nonreading, finally finds its metaphor in the transformation of the letters into the daughter's engagement rings. The *dé-lire* of the father's letters enables Cixous to go on writing. The name of the father remains the Thing of the book, kept alive by this flight and metempsychosis. Helène remains Cixous, her father's father through her oeuvre; her jouissance fashioned as a reading of the hieroglyphs traced along the page of the prince's sleeping body.

But what about the mother, the prince's wife and widow?

Writing, a "magical incest"

> Convinced that I am, you see, that in one way or another I cause damage or harm or injury to the being on which I am scribbling.[53]

> *Mutter, Kann ich trennen?* Tears: *Tränen*[54]

> (Helène Cixous)

Where and how does the character of the mother emerge? We still remember our shock halfway through *Dedans*, when, screaming in capital letters, the following sentence appears: "BECAUSE I HATE HER, MY MOTHER IS NO MORE."

Writing seems thus founded on a murderous desire, the typography evoking a wishful thinking, the magic underpinning of writing.[55] This commanding pronouncement edges the poet's writing to come with the "impossible, and yet" proper to sublimation. The coming to writing, as Marie Redonnet has shown us in *Hotel Splendid*, replays what in the coming to reading had compelled the subject to separate from the fusional magma of the maternal body and language, appealing to the Name-of-the-Father for support. When writing is asked to rebuild that "something of the body" which has been lost during an experience of grief or trauma, there is a risk that it becomes the very site of resistance to this separation. Knowingly, because she is sensitive to the Freudian cause, Cixous stages the poet's *dé-lire*: the belief that words can restore the wholeness of the maternal body and reverse its "breaking down",[56] a precondition for the subject's entrance into the Symbolic. As we have just seen, for Cixous, the Symbolic is supported by the imaginary construction of an ideal father, the whisperer of words.

In 1999, Cixous decided to make a book of her mother, Eve. However, the letter was first inscribed on the parchment of the dead body of the father, the secret lover of the little girl's fairy tale. How can one then use this magical writing to "invent" the excluded third party, the place of the mother? With the violence of an acting out that spares the daughter from madness, wasn't writing born from a death wish against the mother, from the vital necessity of her erasure?

Naming the book (initially called *Ma terre*, "*My Land*") after the mother's native city, Osnabrück, is therefore a figure of exorcism or denial. How can the mother be approached (once the father has been made into an "oeuvre") without stirring up the hatred we witnessed in *Dedans*? And, given that she was still alive, how to ignore the possibility that she might actually read the book? After 150 pages of what seems a form of resistance (the book is 230 pages long) the subject of writing finally "dares" an approach:

Scene 11

It's a book without an event. The event is Eve.
  I must make sure the book has enough water, I thought.
  You would have to think of a way to silently slip into her room in the morning, when she was asleep . . . our bodies roused by a violent hatred. . . . It was in 1950. The fire burned everything in its way . . . I think that I'm not telling the story very well because everything in this scene should be so pure, we should remain suspended in the silence of an abandoned synagogue and not have to give an account of it. So you would move carefully and quietly. The bed seems to have been large, it was the parents' bed. . . . In its corner, at the feet, you quietly placed a carefully folded piece of paper, also quite big, so as not to disappear in the folds of the sheets. The paper said: I'd like you to die. You couldn't have done anything worse. However, something in the very fact of giving the hellfire the form of five words meant taking – this was a strange and improbable impression – by who knows what kind of little unknown magic proper to writing, the edge off, or worse, take away the force, and as if the core or indeed the truth of this hatred. Yes, at the very moment of the act, with the sensibility and incompetence proper to childhood, you had the painful feeling that by this deposition in signs in paw prints in drawings you were distancing yourself from the astral splendour of this hatred, a coldness was slipping in, and even worse – as if a semblance took hold of the violence and howling of the wolf. You got the feeling or indeed you felt. This scene

could have taken place more than once. But no repetition could suppress the explosion of the act. It was necessary that it took place. In the morning, you were woken up by the thirst for action. . . .[57]

Reading this scene, the reader oscillates between fascination and perplexity. Is it a childhood memory? ("It was in 1950. . . . I feel as if I am not telling the story very well . . . The bed seems to have been large.") Still, the metanarrative interventions – "It's a book without an event. . . . I must make sure the book has enough water, I thought. . . . You would need to think . . . everything in this scene should be so pure" – and the modalities of enunciation – "So you would move carefully and quietly . . . this scene could have taken place" – give the account the vagueness of a reconstituted memory or a literary scene. Before this terrifying speech, which dares to announce the child's matricidal wish, the subject of writing carries on cunningly disguised. A false bluff? Cixous, who is no stranger to the questions of the unconscious, half says [*mi-dit*] how writing connects the Symbolic with the violence of the Imaginary, the arbitrariness of the sign with the abhorrence of the maternal Thing, in what she later calls a "magical incest" (p. 165). What is really being read and written?

Scene 11 (continued)

The idea is to detach die [*meures*] from the body of the sentence. To cut it out, to put die aside and so out of sight. Die alone is very beautiful; isolated, die shines die in itself gradually becomes, before our eyes which never leave it, a new unknown word, the word die is blinking, what could it mean one die two dies three dies is rolling quietly, glimmering like honey, a little pot of dies my brother says. Enough childishness. Time to attack the absent saint.

(Cixous, p. 154)

For the child whose thinking still carries the traces of magic, the word summons the thing; when she learns how to read, the word becomes a series of letters to be formed properly, and these letters eventually only represent themselves. However, the poet's writing rediscovers the magic language of childhood, undermining the rules of syntax and punctuation. The child highjacks the word *meures*, first making it into a weapon against the reading mother and then into a polyphonic toy that can be separated from its intention. The word *meures* shines like the anonymous mark of a desire without a subject. In French, the magical *meures* is a subjunctive which virtualizes action; even though when isolated from the phrase it comes to resemble an order (*meures*! die!) that one does not dare to fully issue. The additional "e" separating the subjunctive *meures* from the imperative *meurs* remains in place (like a seme[58]) and represents the phantom of the subject and the trace of her desire, like the unique imprint left by the first engravers in their pictograms – their trademark. An isolated subjunctive, seemingly inoffensive in the hands of children, *meures* expresses the imaginary matricide at work in the advent of the letter: "It was essential that the scene took place," the narrator says about this act of writing; this scene "could have taken place more than once". The French subjunctive ("*Il fallait qu'il ait eu lieu*") and then the past conditional ("*Cette scène aurait pu se passer plus d'une fois*") do not empty the scene of its reality, but on the contrary fill it with additional value – it becomes the foundational myth of the writer's coming to writing and her realization of her own power. It represents the demand to the Symbolic formulated by the anguished subject. The writer does not want to, and indeed cannot, "tell the story".

Why then is it so essential that the mother should die?

The teller of autofiction does have an explanation: in the bloody conflict of the family romance, the mother has been victorious. "We see her lying in her place, across the bed . . . imagine the offense and the torment cutting deeply into the membranes of the brain and flooding the docile regions of morality and amorous sensibility with blood" (p. 153). Before the mother's body, sleeping on the large parental bed, the little female Oedipus, orphaned and inconsolable, has created an infantile theory of her loss, which could be formulated as follows: "She is still there: he is no longer there" (p. 152). The colon between the two statements acts as a quilting point, a signifier (in the Lacanian sense) which stops the sliding of meaning and serves as a point of suture between reality – life or death; presence or absence – and fantasy (she or he). The magic of writing makes the punctuation mark the place represented by a disappeared representation: "Where it was . . . I can come into being by disappearing from my statement [*dit*]," runs Lacan's reformulation of Freud's *Wo Es war, soll Ich werden* (*Écrits*, p. 801). Like a hieroglyph of the primitive scene ("we see her lying down in her place"), these two points, one over the other, transform the unthinkable loss, a "torment demanding to end", into a formula that makes sense.

> Put these two facts together, a lightning strikes, a thunder destroys the calmness of the mind. Admit, admit: the father is dead, the mother is still alive, we could even think: the father is dead the mother is alive, she is alive he is dead.
>
> (Cixous, pp. 152–153)

In other words, she is alive because he is dead: the mother in lieu of the father. We see the signified (which consciousness struggles to accept) sutured by the quilting point in both parts of the sentence "strike" and "destroy" like a "lightning" or "thunder". Punctuation allows language to write the "truth of being" – a pause in the subject's pulsing between two signifiers. Cixous writes it as: "he dead she asleep" (*il mort elle dort*) (p. 153), without any punctuation at all. Indeed, why her and not him when there is only one letter of difference (m/d) between the two? By writing the fantasy outside the laws of grammar (*mort* – dead becoming an adjective-verb), the (Oedipal) father's inconceivable death finds a cause that can be written. But what kind of *Causa* is this cause hiding?

What else is this scene of writing telling us – the scene that, we remember, the writer would have liked to have been so "pure" that there would be no need to "give an account" of it and would instead be received by the reader "in the silence of an abandoned synagogue"?

Scene 11 (continued)

We see her lying in her place, across the bed, it's hard to believe that she's asleep, he dead she asleep a vision burning in the mind, imagine the offense and the torment cutting deeply into the membranes of the brain and flooding the docile regions of morality and amorous sensibility with blood. You no longer see anything but a sticky cloth. One needs to have lived through this scene. I myself have not lived through it personally, but I was subject to its electrocution by a germinal contagion. When the poisoned finger penetrates between the lobes, you understand that, engendered by a mad aberrant mental indignation, deadly wish arises which refuses all thought, discernment and judgement, which simply wants wants wants wants wants that you die. . . . You would take a sheet of graph paper. With the intoxication quickly spread by the necessity in your veins you would write exactly: I would like you to die. The sentence breathes the truth of a being. . . . It cannot be made up.

(Cixous, p. 153)

How should the analyst-reader, who is here asked to remain silent, react to this hateful cry, to this madness? The "abandoned synagogue" is a metaphor for the desecration striking the venerable body of the sleeping mother – the "absent saint" – and liberating the writer's speech. The book becomes a call; it represents itself as a demand to the Symbolic.

She said nothing to me. She didn't give me any other names. She did not take me in her language . . . it was I who called to her . . . I begged her, eyes glued to her lips ready to exhale, I begged her: Mommy, smile. Save me from this darkness, turn on the light. . . . [S]he herself never knew in what field of agony I was walking aimlessly throughout this life, in which she was Mommy and I was only struggling to be. . . .

Mommy doesn't paint me. I have a body with legs and branches of arms but face there is none. Mommy doesn't account for me. . . . She doesn't give me an image. I walk raw down the street. . . . Call me my angel, my love, call me my little duckling.

I would also like my pearl my piece of silk my coffee-grain . . . call me my darling and I'm yours.

(*Osnabrück*, pp. 162–163, 170–171).

"I am without a trace," the poet will also say (p. 179). By tracing the subjunctive *meures* and addressing it to the mother, the child demands to cross over to the side of human beings, where speech is possible, where there is no need to howl like a wolf out of fear or pain. The message folded and slipped into the parental bed scribbles on the sleeping body "in signs in paw prints in drawings", in order not to kill it and hence kill oneself, to annihilate oneself completely. The child who puts the "word-note" [*mot*] in the mother's bed is an "agent" of the adult's unconscious, a literary agent.[59] Cixous's *Osnabrück* is trying to accomplish the same matricide, the same impossible separation, as this "folded note": "Will you let me, mother," the subject begs at the end of the book, "will you let me separate myself? [*Mutter, Kann ich trennen*. Tears: Tränen.] Mother, can I separate myself. Repair and then separate, repair in order to separate can I mother, can I separate" (p. 219). Trying to issue the same call to the Symbolic in order (not to) separate oneself, to do "as if", the "folded message" is a synecdoche of the work of sublimation and its irreducible fantasmatic dimension. It belongs to the magical thinking that seeks to "repair", to pretend that, rather than being purely arbitrary, the signifier has a fixed meaning. In this way the child is trying to avoid falling under the law of castration; the law then returns in the Real of the body in the form of a hallucination, in what the narrator calls "an accident". "We're at a conference. My right hand was suddenly detached . . ." (p. 175). Two pages after, this experience is interpreted through the following graphic composition: "and for thirty years I have written and not written with my right hand only to give the tremor something to do [Or so that she dies]" (p. 158).

Therefore:

> I cannot write about my mother who is alive . . . writing about her means stamping on her body while she is asleep . . . if she was dead it would be a bit different, the dead allow us to put them to bed on paper, but the idea of putting my mother to bed makes me want to die. . . .
>
> Every time my thought would approach her body it was to declare very strongly I am not going to do that I must not do that and I saw the monument of my father grow larger, Eve naked Georges more and more covered.
>
> (p. 161)

> Me too, I thought, if my mother had died young, I might have been condemned to become a successor [a doctor like the father], instead of being the scene of my plague, I might have been untouched and clear of an unconscious, an apple from before God, and clean of any lettering.
>
> (p. 218)

Both the literary child and the subject of *Osnabrück* act out in order (not) to stop suffering from what the author calls, in capital letters, her "MAGICAL INCEST" (p. 165), the jouissance of "astral splendour", a mixture of hatred and fascination for the maternal body. "I want you to die in order not to feel the poisonous finger between the lobes, cutting through the membranes of the brain", both delusional metaphors of a primordial coitus between the mother, the daughter and writing,[60] where the writer, masked by a "sticky cloth" of the folded message, of the page, stages her own conception ("What jouissance almost disappearing with mommy. . . ." p. 190) by telling the story. The writing of her hatred – from "BECAUSE I HATE HER MY MOTHER IS NO MORE" in *Dedans* to "that you die" in *Osnabrück* – has not been enough to separate the subject from the fantasmatic mother. The subject knows that "there are too many threads in this story some of them spinning life, some of them spinning death, you cannot get out of them without doing some cutting, you betray because of loyalty" (p. 218). Eventually, she becomes aware that: "I cannot write this book. Neither begin nor finish. Not yet" (p. 230). The book tells the story of an obligation to write and, at the same time, the failure of writing as a mode of sublimation. "Where It was [*ça était*] . . . I can come into being by disappearing from my statement [*dit*]", said Lacan. To use Spinoza's words,[61] in order to become the "adequate cause" of his emotions, the subject must transform his passions (his suffering and pain) into action. Cixous' need for writing carries within itself this painful impossibility and therefore also its poetic illegibility, the suffering subject becoming the very *Causa* of her writing and project – hence the great empathy felt for her by her students, and especially by her female readership.

To tell the familial tale, Cixous dips her quill in her unconscious, helping us think through the complicated entanglements between literature, the choice of literature as a mode of sublimation, the singular rapport to (maternal) language and its *dé-lire* as an appeal to the Other – the universal, grammatical Other, who marks my abolition as an incestuous *moi-par-toi* – and a simultaneous refusal of his law. Either madness or writing? The child as the helpless object of maternal jouissance, subjected to her family romance, is a figure of incompleteness, of the project of being and therefore often the embodiment of literature itself.

DÉ-LIRE 4: THE LITERARY ADVENTURE: AN IMPOSSIBLE MATRICIDE[62]

> *Oh mother, I hate you! And I have not even yet explored the field of your devastation within me!*
>
> (Anne Hébert[63])

To believe Anne Hébert's evil tale "The Torrent", written in 1945 and published some twenty years later, we must first perform the complicated operation of suspending disbelief – Can a mad child really tell his own story? – something we must do in every account of madness written by the madman himself.

The story of François Perrault tries to form an edge around a gaping hole of an unknowable, unthinkable acting out: the murder of his mother. The tale follows the account of what François knows about himself; the hero's anamnesis is indispensable to his survival and his very existence. It is presented to us in the form of an inner monologue delivered by a man who is roughly thirty-seven years old; it is a story of a suffering conscience, struggling to make sense out of nonsense.

Throughout her literary career, the darkness of Anne Hébert's poetry and novels, which were read and appreciated in both her native Canada and in Europe,[64] continued to supply postwar Quebec literature with many archetypal figures of evil: the mad child, the monstrous mother, the incestuous and diabolical father engaging in orgiastic Sabbaths, perverse murderers and vampires, to name but a few. Did these monstrous figures allow her to say something about the tyrannical grip of religious morality? Hébert's writing and the work of those who followed in her footsteps probably offered a catharsis, an exorcism against what was perceived as a possession of the soul. It seems that the mad child of "The Torrent", though longing for identity and the freedom to think and desire, somehow became the begetter of a whole body of literature, a literary father called upon to extirpate, displace and sublimate the no-longer-tenable imagoes and ideals. Hébert's novella marks the beginning of this process. In her story, the advent of literature is represented by its opposite – a failure of sublimation, a deliration that fails to result in either individual or collective adventure. In this way, it offers the reader a fictionalized view into the troubled metapsychology of the hero of a Quebec novel still to be written.

Between helplessness and incipient power, the figure of the child is ambivalence personified: either a religious fanatic devoted to his unthinkable grief or, like Redonnet's young narrators, a little soldier of the Symbolic. Derrida's *puissé-je* (would that I might)[65] comes to mind as an image of this state of being and of the multiple and problematic functions fulfilled by the child in our imagination. Between the "what can I?" (*que puis-je?*) of the *fatum* and Hamlet's backshifting modal[66] "if I could" (*si je pouvais*), the child of "The Torrent" is trying to move away from the jouissance of satisfying the Other and towards the virtuality of a (yet) inadmissible desire. *Je puissè*, with its modified spelling, the subjunctive form of the French verb *pouvoir*, cannot be written in the indicative form as an assertion. This impossibility gives voice to the Other scene of unconscious desire, the royal road to which, prior to literature, was the dream. Would that I might kill her: how fortunate that Perceval, the great hero of chivalry, did it for me so that *I* may go on existing, beyond the horror. At least for some time. Thus, at the dawn of the new postwar era, Quebec has an archetype of the subject in becoming. The child, a figure split between objectification and subjectivation, is pinned down by the discourse and will of the maternal Other, indeed of all others, and nevertheless is driven by the life and desire that beats within him.

Adventure, or the time beyond the mother

Upon starting Hébert's "The Torrent", my first reaction was: enough with the psychology! Leave us some mystery and darkness! Give us a bit of delirium! Then,

I thought I understood: the narrator, François, is a straight-A student, who, despite his madness, can recount his story in a writerly style. Later, in the second part of the book, this strangely fortuitous writing, this *I* dictated to the writer-typist, will transport him beyond his story, which is that of a child crushed and tormented by a perverse mother, a Québécoise version of Bazin's *Folcoche*.[67] Had the story been told by an omniscient narrator, had François remained pinned down by an implacable *he*, there would have been no chance of redemption – the subject would have been denied all transcendence. This *I* – which is also the *I* of "I am writing this", which is what irritates and puzzles us (How can he analyze himself so well? Whose couch did he end up on?) – makes "The Torrent" a work about art as a (desire for) salvation. The novella will help us complete our argument, showing us how reading and its mode of magical thinking leads to *dé-lire*, in other words, to literature.

Let us start from the end, where the different layers of the narrative come together. Because the narration is autodiegetic (told by the hero), the end of the anamnesis marks both the end of the story and the fictional death of the subject of the statement. The madman throws himself into the torrent, without a shadow of a doubt:[68] "I deliver myself to my own end. I absorb myself into myself; and I am nothing. . . . I want to lose myself in *my own adventure. My sole and fearful wealth*" (pp. 46–47, my emphasis). The torrent becomes a figurative place, designating, at the same time, the "adventure" (a life of terror accompanied by the torrent), the anamnesis (the inner monologue to which I owe my survival) and the textual space before the reader's eyes: I finish with the closing of this text,[69] with its final word.

Already on page nine, the narration's prolepses and anticipations construct the hero's future: "There was another reason, which I only discovered *much later. I have said* that my mother worked without stopping. . . . *The other day*, I found a little notebook that had belonged to her in the shed" (p. 9, my emphasis).

The story itself depicts a world with no space for play and no time to think or dream. The obsessional and insane mother's control over her child is as complete as God's reign over the mother. The narrative can therefore only work towards the prospect of a *would-be*, a potential of being, towards the meaning-making process enabled by the thread of reading. Only from this would-be can a subject think and play, can the terrible story be transformed and an artwork (an oeuvre) completed. The prolepsis ("which I only discovered much later") designates the production of the incipient subject through the story he tells; writing as a process is not represented here. Its suspense traces the desire in the narrative; it allows the reader to catch her breath while these hard and dreary lives, heavily laden with silence, are being fashioned. The reader foreknows the child's escape. She is waiting. It does not take long.

The slave's first action has to represent a *no* to the master; it symbolizes a desire to be somewhere else, to see oneself differently by catching sight of another face – such is the boy's simple intention. But what springs out of this belated mirror stage is human monstrosity: a frightening bogeyman (imago of the future François) appears by the side of the only road running close to the mother's territory, a personified road.

Scene 12

I wanted to cry, for the road was bare and forlorn in the sunlight. Unvarying, soulless, dead. Where were the processions I had imagined I would discover? Over this ground had passed *feet other than my mother's or my own*. Where were those footsteps now? In what direction had they gone? They had *not left a mark*. Surely the road must have died.

(Hébert, p. 11, my emphasis)

In fact, the child encounters the exact opposite: the road's incarnation, its living spirit. And the spirit speaks. He reveals to François the origin of the world: the fault and the Name. "Do you know any stories? No, eh? Well, I know some. . . ." (p. 12) says the tramp, who blocks the child's path before unknowingly divulging the secret origin of all stories: the mother has a first name; she is a woman! The mother's naming by this *ersatz* absent lover, this Dionysian "routard,"[70] borderline werewolf, is the condition *sine qua non* of the "aventure"[71] of what is to come: the hero-child's separation from the mother, his coming to existence as the sole purpose of the story being told. The mother's name is in fact the signifier of her sin, of her outlawed desire: "So you left the village because of the youngster, eh? . . . Big Claudine! Not over-shy [*avenante*][72] in those days" (pp. 12–13). In one bold sentence, the devilish stranger sums up the *curriculum vitae*[73] of the *avenante* Claudine, thus toppling, in a flash, the unforgiving figure, the all-powerful Great Mother, the Ruler of Time. Her tumbling into historical time makes her human, that is to say lacking and desiring. The fact that she has come from somewhere along this road opens up a gap between *she* and *I.*

Scene 12 (continued)

I was frightened and aching all over; nevertheless, I felt an inexplicable curiosity and attraction. I understood obscurely that what was to follow would be as awesome as what had just happened. My senses, dulled . . . were awakening. I was living through an impressive and terrifying adventure.

(p. 13)

Here and in this way, the child, who has been "deprived of the world" in the name of a "will higher than my own" (p. 7), is reborn as the hero of his own tragedy. The intervention of the Roadman propels him onto the path of History, the timeline of *adventure*, of becoming, outside the world saturated with the mother's signifiers. Without this fragile faith in a beyond, there is no possibility of a talking cure, no desire to make sense for oneself. But the hero's feeling of "living through an impressive and terrifying adventure" should also be understood as a sign of writing's self-awareness: the fictional road maps out the adventure of the reading to come.

When the child escapes off screen, outside the mother's grasp, he cannot find the traces he was looking for (he is not yet ready to read the world), but the mother's name that has been heard becomes a founding signifier of a salutary "beyond". The signifier pronounced by the stranger's raspy voice immediately rematerializes in the student's textbook. The scene of reading will once again actualize the unconscious stakes of the relation to the mother and the Symbolic.

Scene 12 *(continued)*

My school books had belonged to my mother when she was young. That evening, under the pretext of preparing my things for school, I examined these books one by one, looking avidly at the name inscribed on the fly-leaf of each volume. "Claudine Perrault" . . . Claudine; beautiful Claudine, big Claudine.

The letters of her first name danced before my eyes, twisting into fantastic shapes like flames. It had never before struck me that my mother's name was Claudine. Now it seemed strange to me, painful. I could no longer tell whether I was reading this name or whether a voice close to my ear was pronouncing it, a railing and demoniac voice, the breath touching my cheek.

My mother came in. She neither brightened the atmosphere nor reassured me in my depression. On the contrary, her presence gave weight to the supernatural quality of the scene. The only spot of light in the dark kitchen was projected from the lamp[74] onto the book that I was holding open. My mother's hand moved quickly within this luminous circle. She seized the book; at one moment the "Claudine", written in a lofty and wilful hand, seemed to draw all of the light to itself; then it disappeared and in its place, in the same haughty handwriting, was "François," "François," in fresh ink, and "Perrault" in the old. Thus, in this narrow light, in the space of a few minutes, the long hands played, and sealed my destiny. All my books were thus dealt with. My mother's words hammered in my head: "you are my son. You are a continuation of me."

(pp. 15–16)

Like a counter stamp, the writing in François' book is a destiny tattooed on the child himself. At first, the letters of the mother's name are not entirely symbolic (in the sense of being arbitrary representations of sounds). They are filled with a particular affect that stirs the child; they seem consubstantial with the mother's person. They are "lofty" like her. They are pictograms carrying the substance still formed by the mother–child dyad. However, the "drawling" voice of the Roadman, the excluded third who introduces the name "Claudine" into the child's world, makes its signifier resonate even further, loading it with desire. The "beautiful, big Claudine" can now become the heroine of the child's family romance; she was the object of a desire from which the child himself originates. By designating this desire, the daemon's voice invents a place of origin, an unknown place – the place of the subject of enunciation. From this locus of desire, the child is now able to *read*, with equal yearning, both the mother's name and her body, "breaking it down," separating it from language and the symbolic law to which she, too, now appears as subject. That is what François finds so funny and what Claudine would like to undo by "entering the scene," by transforming the damage done – her delegitimization (and decompletion) – into action. By deleting her given name, as one deletes a bad memory, she tries to reassert control. However, the family name remains untouchable. PERRAULT, the end of this short line of writing, which only consists of two signifiers (the mother's given name and the father's surname), becomes a paradigm because although for Claudine the gesture has a metaphorical value (setting her score with the past), it simultaneously inscribes both the mother and the son as subjects to the Symbolic, to the Name-of-the-Father. PERRAULT squares the mother's account and simultaneously opens up the son's: the latter's name, now written on the first page of the textbook, in fact prefigures his status as a storyteller, as the author of his life's story.[75] By writing down, in her "lofty" hand, the son's name instead of hers, Claudine is trying, as if by magic, to establish François' place as an extension of herself. But she is wrong: their places are incompatible because the signifier introduces a play of difference – a signifier is where others are not. Was there a glimpse, in the short interval between the deleted CLAUDINE and the newly written FRANÇOIS, of a void, of a possible space beyond the mother where one might write and read oneself?[76] Or does the mother's gesture prefigure, within the fictional framework, her own abolishment by the son, a kind of homophonic and metaphorical *palimpsest?*

"My dreadful wealth"

As a concrete outcome of the child's sudden desire to go look somewhere else, it therefore becomes possible to put his story, the one we are now reading, into words and to make sense of his uncertain existence ruled by the mother's crises. The feeling of adventure centres on the idea of another time and space where he could be: "Deep within me, however, I experienced at times a formidable, and unknown wealth whose slumbering presence astonished and troubled me" (p. 16, translation modified).[77] This *unknown* power is sensed again precisely when he is forced to think about literature.

Scene 12 (continued)

I considered the structure of a classical tragedy, or of a poem, to be a mechanism of principles and recipes bound together only by the author's will. However, once or twice, I was touched with Grace, and perceived that the tragedy or poem depended solely on its own inner necessity, a condition of any work of art.

Such revelations touched me painfully. In an instant, I could measure the emptiness of my existence. I had a presentiment of despair. Then, I would stiffen my resolve, and absorb whole pages of chemical formulae.

(p. 17)

A certain *je ne sais quoi* slips through the charts and grids of principles, recipes and formulae – the foundation of religious dogmas and science alike – and disturbs the boy's obsessional regime, the result of the mother's control and her admonitions against softness and giving in. An unconscious desire revealed by the Thing of the book? François quickly recovers. But his "stiffened resolve" and the "profound disenchantment" he feels towards the school prizes he has won too easily, but also his subsequent refusal to pursue his studies, are a direct consequence of this moment of suspicion and doubt. What he measures in the tragedy and the poem is his own emptiness. To "measure the emptiness of my existence" is to measure the void, to apprehend its limits. The knowledge of the unconscious imparted by literature, with its *jouis-sens*,[78] has taken effect. The literary work, the Thing of the book, divides the subject, seizing him where he did not know he was.[79] Having grasped its own splitting, the ego then tries to undo this effect by absorbing chemical formulas as a kind of antidote. The mother's rigid principles (which also function as formulas) have made lack and desire inconceivable. The Grace that touches François by means of the poem is therefore the ego's aphanisis, a moment of effacement during which it is confronted, in an instant, with the law that creates transcendence and that stands as the third term between him and his mother. The ego glimpses the autonomy of the Symbolic, and this new state of submission brings with it its own jouissance – that of meaning, at last divined. The literary work performs two paradoxical operations at the same time: it charts out human destiny as what needs to be produced in and through words, and in doing so it opens up a space of freedom for self-creation. It stages the human desire to be, a desire that stems from being a speaking being. To the hero of "The Torrent", this is and continues to be simply unbearable. For him, this space of freedom is the roaring pit of the mother's arbitrary law and of the hatred it necessarily incites in him; Claudine's signifiers have been engraved in the tables of a merciless law by the will of a cruel God. And in the writing of that God, the reader will find no inner necessity, no interpretation and no space for play.

The child's idea of the existence of a space outside the mother's perverse law and panopticon arises more concretely because of the silence imposed by his deafness. In a fit of rage following the son's second act of "free" will (the first was his escape towards the road) – his refusal to return to school (p. 20) and become "her" priest (i.e. to devote himself to the worship of the mother's signifiers) – big Claudine throws herself at François and beats him with a set of keys. He loses consciousness and later awakens deaf.[80] Cast into this indifferentiation, the eye begins to see and scheme, to divide the world into images, soon-to-be imagoes of his solitary and suffering soul: "I would remain for hours contemplating an insect" (p. 22). Shielded from the maddening noise of the mother's speech – she stops speaking to him altogether anyway – he discovers a world he can make his own, and he subjects himself to it: "I had never possessed the world, but there was a change now: part of the world possessed me. The stretch of water, mountains and secret hollows came to me with a sovereign touch" (p. 21). This "sovereign touch" should also be understood as an effect of the resemblance and contiguity between the outside, previously named and marked by the mother's vociferous signifiers, and the chaotic inner space of the ego, constantly on the edge of destruction.[81] The landscape gives the deaf child material for images, semblances (in the Lacanian sense) and identifications: his own signifieds[82] waiting to be written.

Initially, he regresses into a world outside language, a presymbolic world. The space beyond the mother, where a subject could come to be, takes the shape of a landscape with the torrent as its vanishing point, figuring the unimpeded power of the drive.[83] It is thus first through a geography[84] that the child finds material for self-representation.

> The water had hollowed out the stone. The rock on which I stood jutted out over the water like a terrace. *I visualized the creek beneath, dark, opaque, fringed with foam. False peace, profound darkness. The reserves of fear.*
>
> (pp. 23–24, my emphasis)

The landscape gives shape to what was previously intuited as the "wealth" of an Other place, the *unbewusste.* The creek on the edge of the torrent, down beneath, is its first image – the initial topography of the new François. What the boy realizes is essentially that *there is an Other beneath me*, a place of terrifying desire and formidable hatred. Dreams are born in this magical cave – tales made of images, rebuses without head or tail. By locating, via fantasy, the crypt of his soul bordered by the torrent, François builds himself a secret hideaway, a stash of personal imaginary, a cave that is full of "wealth" despite the terror that lies behind the door. Immediately, a question appears.

> When I returned to my pallet on the floor of my room, I was not really separated from the torrent. Falling asleep, I could hear its roar, which had become an integral part of my self, the image of my impetuous fever. *The elements of a dream. Or of something to be undertaken? I sensed that there would soon emerge from my torment the monstrous visage of either the one or the other.*
>
> (p. 24, my emphasis)

Here again, the prolepsis points out the project to come ("I sensed that there would soon emerge . . .") that is accomplished through the narration itself, tying together its object (an inkling of another scene) and the enunciation (the production of this scene). François' intuition can be seen as a synecdoche of the entire novella – the "monstrous visage [emerging from my torment]" sets up the Imaginary, Real and Symbolic, the three dimensions of the human subject searching for meaning. His torment calls for a form resembling him (a character's face) which could express the monstrous and delirious nature of all singularity. By taking on a recognizable shape, he is no longer monstrous.[85] This taking on a form means that one has already overcome the torment by means of a distance that has been produced: the subject prevails thanks to the form given to the monster. Here, Hébert offers us a concise expression for the unconscious at work in every writer, for what makes the act of symbolization an obligation.

For the subject of "The Torrent", the image of the dark creek is the first step towards self-representation and meaning. It allows the Real (the unthinkable monster within) to be circumscribed as a place before it is inscribed in the singular delirium of the dream and the fantasy (and transcribed in the universal language of the literary work). The very possibility of the anamnesis that we are listening to, of the account that we are reading, is constructed in the story as a series of quilting points, where the statement and the enunciation refer to each other, knotting together the Real, Imaginary and Symbolic in the terrorized child's hope of saving himself through speech.

The ego's projection into an elsewhere (a space to exist) happens in three steps:

- First, the hint of a Time beyond the mother, created by the (third person's) announcement of her name and history, opens up a space for the adventure of the subject's own destiny. Meaning appears as a direction shown by the road bordering the mother's territory and situated, through the erasure of the mother's name from the book, in the intermittent place of the signifier on a page.
- Second, the inkling of an Other inner space – rich and monstrous, rich in monstrosity, separate – is precisely what is conveyed by the poem and the tragedy, as well as "imaginarized" (given a form) by the dark creek. Meaning is to be drawn out of the crypt; it is the dread obscuring a hatred that cannot be fully assumed.
- Third, armed with the road as a figure of destiny, with the palimpsest of the mother's body as a surface for the writing project and with the creek as the lair of the monstrous unconscious, the subject first makes the torrent into the image of his rage and desire. Only then can its inner landscape be revealed in a dream and transmitted to others through narration.

By recounting these moments of grace and doubt, by lifting the veil of the maternal signifiers and the Law and discourse of mastery they construct, the subject of the anamnesis scatters his story with little white pebbles that trace the child's journey towards a potential space of invention. These moments of suspicion transform the time to come into a destiny, a space for the narrator to dwell in – and the child will live just long enough to become its dweller and storyteller. *Enough* indeed: the permission to inhabit this potential place beyond the mother's law is conditioned by a horrifying act, which the adult storyteller is unable to recognize as his own. His guilt prevents him from truly ruling this space, and thus from accomplishing his life's work. Because of a gap in representation, his act cannot be *made sense of*; it cannot become one of the pebbles in his path. It is precisely this impossibility that ultimately makes the story in a scream followed by silence, in which the subject disappears. This is the dread intuited by the child and presently experienced by the narrator, the statement and the enunciation forming a Mobius strip: the future points at an impossible present which itself is but a recurrence of the past. Because the son was not able to "break down" the mother, the hole in the torus is the missing knowledge of her destruction – an unthinkable, irreparable act.

The unthinkable inscription, or writing as killing

Because he cannot confront his unconscious desire, François is driven to acting out. The time of the anamnesis catches up with the story precisely at the point when the hero loses consciousness and unconsciously commits an act of which he wants to know nothing.

Scene 12 (continued)

Yet I broke through the limits of this dead space. I opened my eyes to the luminous morning.

(p. 26)

. . . I remember being deafened. . . . And then, there was a blank that since that time, I have worried over trying to fill in. And when I sense the possible approach of the dreadful light in my memory, I struggle to be free of it, and I attach myself desperately to the darkness, however troubling, however menacing it may be.

(p. 25)

. . . material proof of the crime. I myself have searched for twenty years. A certain dulled part of my memory which is sealed up.

(p. 44)

The historical time that previously organized the child's story and adventures fades into a present terrorized by the repetition of what remains unthinkable yet from now on never ceases to insist: "The inhuman circle, the circle of my thoughts unending, the material of my eternal life" (p. 25). Having followed the road so far, at the end of the first part we suddenly realize that it only leads towards the dark creek, from which there is no escape, and where the narrator is left broken and helpless. We have reached François' unconscious. His speech is a symptom, not a talking cure. There is no longer any meaning, any outside or projection. In a flash, his act destroys not only the causal force of his account – the incipient subject created through the figure of a child to be saved – but also the reader's hope for a plan of revenge fully borne by the subject, a sort of catharsis that would put the hero in control of his destiny, the narrator of the story and the writer of his coming to writing. The terror that is gradually conveyed by the story, that was felt to be the hidden cause of the tragedy and the poem and later was located in the darkness of the creek, is given a reason here and, for the reader, a referent: the mother is stomped to death by a horse, the untameable Perceval, a majestic incarnation of the torrent of hatred bubbling on the edge of the creek.[86] In the encounter with Perceval, who defies the mother without guilt, the child enjoys this defiant *no* like a "feast" (p. 23). By putting a limit to the mother's omnipotence, by castrating her, the horse opens up a surprising potential of "passion", another name for the adventure of existence. In a moment of psychotic decompensation, François gives in to his own jouissance, incestuous and full of hate, becoming one with the untamed Perceval.[87] This "evil" channelled by the torrent that gives it direction, embodied and made consistent by Perceval, is the force that causes the "immense" mother to be now "lying flat", like a toppled statue, "slain" like a dragon or a God.

A mother has been killed . . . in the name of the Symbolic

> The horse had been set free. He had made his terrible gallop through the world. An evil passage for anyone who had been in his way. Then I saw my mother, lying flat and still. I looked at her. . . . She was immense, covered with blood and stamped with hoof-prints.
>
> (p. 26)

The immensity of Big Claudine's body offers itself as a surface of writing. She has been toppled, stretched out, stamped. Who was the daring writer? A fantasmatic scene unfolds, similar to Freud's "A child being beaten." A MOTHER HAS BEEN KILLED. HER BODY HAS BEEN WRITTEN ON. The final (and fatal) stage of François' liberation has been completed without a conscious subject, by crushing the maternal body and leaving on it the mark of the beast – a horse called Perceval.

"(Ah, Perceval, who were you, then?)", François asks in parentheses (p. 37). What is this name? Where did it come from? It appears in the Perrault family and in the story without a warning (p. 22), like those mysterious characters, strangers from nowhere, heroes of legends, whose timely arrival transforms them into improbable instruments of revenge: Oedipus arriving in Thebes; Perceval, the knight in Chrétien de Troyes' romance, appearing just at the right time, before the decisive Battle of Belrepeire.[88] Within Claudine's rigorist universe, the horse's name seems quite incongruous. It is a fantasy. It comes from another dimension, from a language unknown to the Perrault family – the language of literature. It ties together the realism of François' wretched tale with the author's future adventure of writing. On the level of the statement, Perceval is an instrument of vengeance; on the level of enunciation he is the intertextual signifier of a desire for the Novel. A dagger and a stylus, he holds the thread of the adventure and the red thread of desire. And his name is not just any name.[89] Who, then, is Perceval?

Perceval, the young and naïve hero of *Perceval, The Story of the Grail*, has become enchanted by the knights' shining armour and feels an overwhelming desire to become one of them, to take to the road in search of adventures and beautiful damsels in distress. He is the exact opposite of the repulsive tramp of "The Torrent", whose adventure only leads him to the ditch by the road and who feels no sympathy for the "attractive Claudine". Perceval convinces his mother to let him go; she falls to the ground and immediately dies of grief. François, too, kills his mother by necessity, by the sheer force of his desire to exist. What is Perceval looking for? Where do his adventures lead him? Mysteriously and unwittingly, he seems to be on a quest to rehabilitate the figure of the dead father, who has suffered a peculiar wound "in the groin". Perceval fails to recognize a test that would have restored to the Fisher King (who has suffered the same wound) his former glory and wealth; he fails to ask this *ersatz* father, fallen and castrated, the right question at the right moment, and he is therefore condemned to wander aimlessly for years, devoid of love and glory. At last, his quest ends when he finds the Symbolic Father in his encounter with the Church. By transforming the dead father into a divinized Father, he is freed of his guilt; by the same token, he seals the fate of knighthood, putting an end to its pagan erring. *Les non-dupes* (those that are not duped by their unconscious) err, Lacan joked.

And in the beginning Perceval is indeed a dupe. He has no words of his own and can only parrot his mother's advice or remain speechless when mocked for his naivety. This means he cannot ask any questions; he isn't at all curious. He seems entirely dependent on preestablished formulas, on his excessive desire to be a knight. His accidental moment of glory results from a series of *faux pas* caused by his passion of ignorance (and his paralyzing Oedipus complex). By a blind, overzealous obedience to a rule, he does not dare question the strange things he witnessed as so many metaphors of the secret of his origin (the scene associates the father's identity with sexual symbols). Then, once he has understood that his silence before the Fisher King (see line 3004) was a bungled action, he is struck by enormous guilt. The reader may find it excessive – after all, Perceval *hasn't done anything*! However, it is unconscious guilt,[90] and the clue lies in the wound shared by the father and the King – a wound between the legs.[91] The guilt felt towards the father (whom Perceval failed to save) is mixed in with castration anxiety. The quest for the Holy Grail is thus a search for the phallus, for the imaginary representative of the "at-least-one-who-would-not-be-concerned-by-castration". Instead, Perceval finds God.

As for François, he dethrones God from the very same place, obliterating him as a possible recourse at the very moment that he kills the mother. The world he leaves behind is godless, empty of value or meaning. Although we could rewrite the name of (Claudine's) father, PERRAULT, as PÈRE-HAUT ("Father above"), to the son this transcendence remains an empty sign. The foreclosure of the Name-of-the-Father is the cause of François' paranoid psychosis – a psychosis whose delirium consists in a *dé-lire*, an attempt at reading meaning into the scheme of things rather than into the scheme of words. This is because the origin of the Symbolic and its syntagmatic structure are no longer supported by the signifier One, of which the Name-of-the-Father is the first representative, and this foreclosure produces both an excess and a lack of meaning.

"Each person bears within himself an unknown crime, a draining wound, which he expiates."[92] In Chrétien de Troyes' romance, Perceval's unfinished quest concerns a secret crime in a cursed family, of which he, as the youngest son, remains completely unaware. Was it a sexual crime, an incest disrupting the generational order and preventing the salvific speech from emerging? The adventure of Perceval's quest traces the son's symbolic journey through the territory of the family Imaginary. Hence the name of the horse in Hébert's story, the writer of the primordial letter: it comes from what Freud calls the *family romance*. In "The Torrent", Chrétien's Perceval, whose name is revealed to him during his first exploit, thus represents the name of the secret to be disclosed – the secret of one's origins, the search for which is staged by the family romance. This is the ultimate meaning of the letter printed on Claudine's body – it is a cypher, a name of the father, which cannot be deciphered for lack of the right words, because the subject has failed to reach the universal position of the reader. Perceval the knight was unable to name the father otherwise than by giving him the name of God. The mystery of his crime and his aimless wandering therefore continue to represent, simultaneously and paradoxically, the son's desire to both know and not to know. And because of his inability to ask the right question at the right moment, a question both accursed *and* salvific, François, like Perceval, is doomed to endlessly wander upon the maternal earth. The question he does not dare to ask is: Who is PERRAULT? Who is my father? He only attempts the meek "(Ah! Perceval, who were you then?)", cloaked between protective parentheses, thus letting the Other off the hook and leaving the question unanswered. François is only able to tell his impossible tale by producing a litany of substitute questions spelling his failed quest:[93] "I am the offspring of evil", he says eventually, "the son of big Claudine. . . . What do I have left to renounce? Unless it be myself, and my own drama?" (p. 46).

To secure at least a minimum of existence, François fulfils his subjective destiny – to topple the phallic statue like the totem of a religion that drives its disciples to extinction.[94] But his act is not his own. Instead, he liberates the guileless Perceval and entrusts him with the unbearable task. PERCEVAL – in other words, Oedipus – is the image of lethal power and utter defencelessness. He is an extension of the unconscious and of the child's own hand, of his hatred, of his desire to escape and of his destiny as an incestuous son.[95]

Literature, or the failure of *père-version*

Using his hoofs as a pen, Perceval, the horse, traces a primordial letter, imprisoning its blind reader in an infinite quest: his guilt is endless, with no chance of penance. As a child, he could not return the mother's gaze; now he cannot read her corpse, which bears the mark of the Other. There is no signified available that could efface the horror of his act and the desire it betrays: "I believe in the present. I raise my eyes, and see the open door of the stable. I know of the blood there, and of the woman stretched out on the ground with the marks of rage and death upon her" (p. 27). The scene of reading will remain blanched by the impression of an excessive, forbidden jouissance, a bodily contact with "the Angel": "The impression of an abyss, an abyss of space and time, where I fell down a void, succeeded the tempest" (pp. 25–26). The story comes to a halt. There is no signifier, only a space where meaning has spilled outside language, shocking, without an address. "There was nobody there," Lol V. Stein would have said. The narrator's road is barred by a tattooed corpse which cannot be "broken down" and therefore remains illegible. Because the mother's body is still a Whole tainted with hate, the subject will not be able to read (himself). The anamnesis can only provide a kind of meta-narrative constructed in the *après-coup*, where it cancels itself out. The hero is submerged in a present that makes all action unthinkable. The mother's territory becomes a no man's land.

> I have now no points of reference. . . . I am dissolved in time. . . . Anguish alone distinguishes me from the dead symbols.
>
> (p. 26)

This anxiety, born out of an encounter with pure meaning – without signifiers, without an object, without even a salutary deliration – now becomes the "subject" of the story: hence the second and truly agonizing part of "The Torrent" (pp. 26–47). The anamnesis and the adventure have in fact produced a semblance. The hero does not owe his freedom to action, but to an unconscious act. Who then is the subject of action? Only a metanarrator, struggling with his subjectivity, monstrous by definition. How does one give a human form to this monstrous face of the work, given that it begins with the terrible damage to the mother's body, a damage which, like a 0 awaiting a 1, represents the first letter-stamp, the first signifier of a subject of writing? The narrator occupies this impossible position in the very place of being, of the unleashed rage of the symptom; in the place where *it* does not think,[96] where he cannot write about himself any longer.

> But what is the use of discussing the reasons for my gestures, my compulsions? I am not free. . . . [And sleep is] a descent into the deepest gulf of the subconscious, where I can neither play nor defend myself, even as feebly as when I am awake.
>
> (p. 35)

The subject is the subject of the unconscious *in the works*. The hero is no longer the master in his own house, a position he could only claim during the anamnesis, while he was trying to reconstruct his reasons and traumas. Ironically, he was only in control while telling us about the horrors of his childhood. Back then he was at least a subject – a subject to the mother – but now the story of his legend is ruled by anxiety and hatred. Yet he keeps going, despite everything, by fits and starts, sinking ever deeper into uncertainty. In the name of this *face of the work*,[97] he manages to give at least some consistency to the hero; the latter takes on the shape of a man – through perversion. As one of the benefits of the discourse about oneself, desire will at last emerge, terrible yet predictable, looking for a prey: to kill an (other) woman, to kill the woman in the mother so that the mother may live again.

> My head is silence. I analyse the fragments. I reshape my unhappiness. I complete it. I clarify it. I take it up where I had left it. My investigation is both lucid and methodical. Little by little, it corroborates what my imagination, or my instinct, had led me to suppose.
>
> I admire my detachment; I marvel at it.
>
> I cannot remember ever having felt such calm. . . It disquiets me. With what increased fury will the next assault of inner tumult come upon me? Will this pause indeed bring a sweetness to my life?
>
> The desire for a woman has come back to me in the desert. No, it is not a promise of sweetness. It is as unpitying as everything else within me, a desire *to possess and destroy the body and soul of a woman*, and to watch the woman play her role in my own destruction.
>
> (p. 28)

For François the man, this is now the only possible course of action. The "new" desire stems from a sadistic, perverse fantasy, giving the *I* a scene where he can imagine an object to be destroyed, so as not to die himself, or not just yet. By saving the son from a complete structural collapse, this *liveable* reality briefly staged by perversion protects the man as well, giving him just enough time to finish the story. Before he merges with the torrent, François the man therefore resorts to perversion as the last recourse and out of defiance. However, his act of defiance is to be carried out in the mother's house, a place still ruled by the signifiers of her law and jouissance.

To François the reader, the character of Amica immediately seems to condense the primary features of the figures inhabiting his own psychic landscape (the ego, the superego and the ego ideal). She is adventurous and nomadic. She is a woman like the mother and has the same feline grace and gaze; she is dark like Perceval, wild like the torrent; she is desire and guilt, calculation and reprobation. As both gaze and knowledge, she embodies the big Other's conscience[98] and the mother's femininity; she is fascinating and repulsive enough to kill. Or perhaps, enough to write? Something surprising happens, with an uncanny, calming effect on François' insane and morbid world: we could call it a new *discourse*. It only lasts a paragraph, but its vision and style are strikingly different from what precedes and follows it.

Scene 13

The shawls and skirts in which she drapes herself seem to be held only by the moving clasp of her hands, that tighten or loosen according to the whim of her movements, now lively, now relaxed. A cascade of folds slips from her hands and reappears further down in serried waves. The interplay of folds and hands, in one hand, a knot of folds clasped at her breast, the glistening silk stretched taut at the shoulders. The broken design, recreated elsewhere. The silk slips leaving the shoulder naked, revealing the arms. Fingers so brown on the red skirt. The skirt swiftly drawn together in handfuls, now, as she mounts the stairs. The limbs perfect, the ankles fine. A knee shows. Then everything disappears. The skirt sweeps the floor, the hands are free, and the bodice unconfined.

(pp. 38–39)

Skirts, shawls, hands, walk, folds, breasts, shoulders, the naked shoulder, arm, fingers, ankles, legs, knees, the "unconfined" bodice, veiling and unveiling (a cascade, folds, waves, games, knot, glistening, breaking, recreating, revealing, showing, disappearance) – the body of a woman is "broken down" and, by the same gesture, eroticized. The new gaze that segments and divides represents the scopic drive at work. The body is read and falls apart; the object of desire constituted by this fragmentation remains out of reach. For just a moment, the subject is freed from the grip of the totalitarian and totalizing superego and changes his style and position. In Scene 13, some of the sentences have no verbs and are clearly at odds with both the story of the adventure and the questioning delusion of the second part. Like a passing angel, the passage metaphorically represents the breaking down of the maternal body, which is the precondition of reading, in other words, of the sublimation of the drive for mastery and the scopic drive. The dissection of her image by the subject's gaze – before she is again made whole by another bout of François' paranoia – preconditions the fragmentation of the maternal language through words and syllables, which can then be played with in reading, writing and poetry. During this short moment of grace, we witness the birth of the metaphor and of the subject of writing – and also of the reader's own *jouis-sens*, faced with the living signs of the Other which stands in such stark contrast to the dead signs of his psychotic world. By engendering the woman as an object, he simultaneously becomes a poet and a creator.[99]

This *père-version* (the erotizing and thus fragmenting gaze of the father on the mother's body) allows François to assume a new psychic position; it stops his hands from trying to grip and strangle. Anxiety fades away. The subject's adventure crystalizes into a precarious moment of desire. For an instant, François inhabits the place of the author, the place of grace, the place of the Angel. The latter is a figure of the birth of the metaphor; his passage leads from Perceval's deadly punch mark to François' erotic poem, in which the murder is sublimated – the mark of 0 inscribing the Symbolic in the Real of the body, the sliding of signifiers along the chain of desire, tying together the Imaginary and the Symbolic. The Angel personifies the moment of *jouis-sens* that François had already experienced as a student in his encounter with literature. It designates the enigma of some unknown force, one that momentarily expiates the Oedipal hate and guilt. It gives a name to the calm that lies beyond. We could call it *sublimation* or *oeuvre*, the Thing of the book.

*

The work deconstructed in the breaking down of the mother's body takes on the monstrous visage of the act necessary to sublimation. But for François, what is killed is first of all the *Child* as an object of the mother's sadistic jouissance; the adult will not survive this murder of the Wonder Child, of the monstrous offspring of sin. His self-destruction is thus a necessity: it drowns the incestual monster that forever enjoys being the "son of evil". Likewise, through the many recurrent child murders of her works, Anne Hébert never stops trying to kill the Wonder Child – who never stops not dying. And as we have seen, by virtue of being a figure of the ego, the hero of the Novel never stops trying to bring this ancestor and its family romance back to life.

> How long is it since I took possession of my mother's big bed? . . . Was I afraid the horror of my nights would diminish? I irritated the wound. I am it and it is me. . . . [W]hat old insomnias lie about, what fevers and unnameable terrors.
>
> (p. 35)

> I am not yet prepared for the definitive integration with the fury of the falls, nor for the even more profound abyss within me. . . . The outcome, the final flight into my despair, remains in suspense. . . . I am weary of watching the water and the fantastic images within it. . . . I am leaning out as far as possible. I want to see down into the gulf, as far down as I can. I want to lose myself in my own adventure. My sole and fearful wealth.
>
> (pp. 41, 47)

Does the lasting fascination with this madman's story and its countless interpretations derive from this potent final scream, this cry of powerlessness, the hero's leap into the void?

Is it because during the (postwar) writing of this story the inefficacy of the spoken word instituted this absolute need for literature, in order to write the paradoxical power of the "Would that I might?", "The Torrent" tells the story of a failure which paradoxically turns into a success? The novella comments on the very possibility of sublimation through reading and writing, the human being's "sole and fearful wealth", while also offering a criticism of the morbid identification with landscape, of the dream and the Imaginary as the sole means of representation, of identification based on the powerful illusion of consubstantiality between a place and its inhabitants. Escaping this magic belief – not by drowning oneself in the torrent but by separating from it and from the landscape – calls for the unconscious murder of the Great Mother, in order to transform the pain of this necessary act, an act of separation, into a production, a reparation. François' fictional account is also a healing speech because it replaces what is unthinkable by creating a bond. How, indeed, do we think of something *beyond* the Mother and her territory once "God" has become an empty signifier?

Earlier in this chapter, the two short novels by Marie Redonnet (*Hotel Splendid, Forever Valley*) showed us that only the Law of the Symbolic and our necessary alienation in it can produce a locus for transcendence, a place where the human being's name can be inscribed as a project. By envisioning an ethics of and for the subject, such a project can open up the possibility of desire.

- This Symbolic must be different from the dead *formulae* of chemistry or the mother's obsessional accounts; it is a writing of a man or a woman traversing an imaginary territory in search for a personal formulation of a question;
- This writing must bind together the Real of the suffering body, the geographical Imaginary and the universality of language.

In "The Torrent", Anne Hébert has showed us a way – impossible for François, but conceivable for herself. Only on one condition can writing be thought of as a work producing humanity, in other words, desire: namely that the unconscious subject is able to transform the stigmata on the mother's corpse/parchment into the illumination of a future book; that the breaking down of the female body (in the mother), eroticized by the Other (the father), can become materialized and metaphorized in words written on a page.

Notes

1 Millet, C. (2002). "Pourquoi et Comment". In *La Vie sexuelle de Catherine M.* Paris: Seuil, pp. i–xiv. [Translated for this edition and used with the kind permission of the publisher].

2 Let us recall this image: "Rather than withdraw from a text whose defences were so strong, he pitted all his strength in the will to seize it, obstinately refusing to withdraw his glance and still thinking himself a profound reader, even when the words were already taking hold of him and beginning to read him. He was seized, kneaded by intelligible hands, bitten by a vital tooth; he entered with his living body into the anonymous shapes of words, giving his substance to them, establishing their relationships, offering his being to the word '*be*'" (Blanchot, M. [1973]. *Thomas the Obscure.* Translated by Robert Lamberton. Barrytown, NY: Station Hill Press, pp. 25–26).

3 Let us note here the etymology of the French word *travail*, or work: "to torture with a tripalium", an instrument with three stakes. See Dubois, J., Mitterand, H., & Dauzat, A. (1993). *Dictionnaire étymologique*. Paris: Larousse, p. 778.

4 Proust, M. (2003). *In Search of Lost Time. Volume 1: The Way by Swann's*. Translated by Lydia Davis. London: Penguin, pp. 7–8.

5 Freud, S. (1908). "Creative Writers and Day-Dreaming". In *SE*, IX, p. 143.

6 This relationship between *Innerwelt* and *Umwelt*, which Lacan discusses in his 1949 paper "The Mirror Stage as Formative of the *I* Function" and in "Agressiveness in Psychoanalysis." *Écrits*. Translated by Bruce Fink (2006). New York: Norton, pp. 75–81 and 82–101.

7 Beauvoir, S. de. (1990). *All Said and Done*. London: Penguin Modern Classics, p. 499.

8 Lacan, J. (2006). *Écrits*. Translated by Bruce Fink. New York: Norton, p. 379.

9 Lacan, J. (2007). *The Seminar Book XVII, the Other Side of Psychoanalysis*. Translated by Russell Grigg. New York: Norton, p. 30.

10 Rousseau, J.-J. (1973). *Confessions*. London: Penguin Classics, p. xxv.

11 Freud, "Creative Writers and Day-Dreaming", p. 149.

12 Dayan, J. & Ribowska, M. (1979). *Simone de Beauvoir: un film de Josée Dayan et Malka Ribowska*. Text of a film portrait of Simone de Beauvoir directed by Josée Dayan. Paris: © Éditions Gallimard, p. 92 [Translated for this edition].

13 Beckett, S. (1959). *Three Novels (Molloy, Malone Dies, the Unnameable)*. New York: Grove Press, p. 267.

14 Angot, C. (2001). *Normalement*. Followed by *La peur du lendemain*. Paris: ©Editions Stock, p. 112 [Translated for this edition].

15 Lacan, *Écrits*, p. 16.

16 Rousseau, *Confessions*, p. 5.

17 Barthes, Roland (1975). "The Reality Effect". In *The Rustle of Language*, Translated by Richard Howard, New York: Hill and Wang, pp. 141–145, 175.

18 Sartre, J. P. (2000). *Nausea*. Translated by Robert Baldick. London: Penguin Modern Classics, pp. 138 and 143. Originally published 1938.

19 In his novel *Fils*, Serge Doubrovsky defines *autofiction* as "fiction dealing with strictly real events and facts; autofiction, if you wish, confiding in the adventure of language the language of an adventure, outside the wisdom and syntactic structure of the traditional or 'new' novel" (Doubrovsky, S. [1977]. *Fils*. Paris: Galatée: back cover [Translated for this edition]).

20 Angot, *Normalement*, p. 32.

21 I am borrowing this expression from Eugénie Lemoine-Luccioni. See Lemoine-Luccioni, E. (1987). *The Dividing of Women, or Women's Lot*. Translated by Marie-Laure Davenport and Marie-Christine Reguis. London: Free Association.

22 Angot, C. (1999). *L'Inceste*. Paris: Stock, 26–27. Discussing his "perverse" discovery of autofiction, Serge Doubrovsky also speaks about "pieces of my real self" that he offers to the reader: "slices of my true life [that] will be absorbed. . . . In the game of truth, you can no longer pay with words. You must pay with yourself. Directly. Unshielded. Without masks or embellishments. . . . Rousseau said, 'a man in all truth of his nature.' No more fireworks" (Doubrovsky, S. [2012]. *Le livre brisé*. Paris: Grasset, p. 330 [Translated for this edition]).

23 Lemoine-Luccioni, E. (1980). *Le rêve du cosmonaute*. Paris: ©Le Seuil, p. 139 [Translated for this edition and used with the kind permission of the publisher].

24 Redonnet, M. (1994). *Hôtel Splendid*. Translated by Jordan Stump. Lincoln: University of Nebraska Press, pp. 3–4.

25 Redonnet, M. (1994). *Forever Valley*. Translated by Jordan Stump. Lincoln: University of Nebraska Press, pp. 3–4.

26 The original trilogy was published by Editions de Minuit (Paris) between 1986 and 1987. Previously, Redonnet had published *Le mort et Cie* (1985) and *Doublures* (1986) with POL, to whom she returned with *Candy Story* (1992). She is also the author of *Tir*

et Lir (1988, Minuit) and *Silsie* (1990, Gallimard), *Le cirque Pandor* and *Nevermore* (1994, POL), *L'accord de paix* (2000, Grasset) and *Diego* (2005, Minuit). I have discussed the author's work, which was a wonderful personal discovery, in Picard, A.-M. (1994). "Dans le paysage, une figure féminine . . . à peine: le triptyque de Marie Redonnet" *The Australian Journal of French Studies*, 2, 12 (Fall), pp. 228–240; and also in "Arrêt sur image: identité et altérité chez Brossard et Redonnet", *Dalhousie French Studies, 31*, Mises en scènes du regard (Summer 1995), pp. 101–112; and "Écrire au bord du gouffre. Le *Splendid Hôtel* de Marie Redonnet". In Meurée, C. (Ed.). *Interférences littéraires, New Series série, n° 5*, "Le sujet apocalyptique", 2010, pp. 31–42.

27 "Naïve" and "native" share the same Latin origin: *nativus*, or natural.

28 Lacan, J. (1984). "Comptes rendus d'enseignements 1964–1968". *Ornicar?* 29, pp. 8–25 [Translated for this edition].

29 See "Redonne après maldonne". *Infini*, 19, Special issue "Où en est la littérature?" (Summer 1987), pp. 160–163.

30 De Certeau, M. (1992). *The Writing of History*. New York City: Columbia University Press, p. 100.

31 Lacan, J. (1997). *Seminar Book VII: The Ethics of Psychoanalysis (1959–1960)*. New York: Norton, p. 121.

32 Juranville, A. (1988). *Lacan et la philosophie*. Paris: PUF, p. 292 [Translated for this edition].

33 As the writer also says, *redonne après maldonne*, putting on her own pen name (Redonnet), could perhaps be translated as "redeal what has been misdealt". See "Redonne après maldonne."

34 Compare with *HS*: "*You might think* you were on a boat", p. 112.

35 Lacan, *The Ethics of Psychoanalysis*, p. 119.

36 Cixous, H. (1987). *L'Indiade ou l'Inde de leurs rêves, et quelques écrits sur le théâtre*. Paris: Editions du Théâtre du Soleil, p. 251 [Translated for this edition and used with the kind permission of Agence Althéa, éditions Théâtrales].

37 Cixous, H. (1999). *Osnabrück*. Paris: Editions Des Femmes-Antoinette Fouque, p. 157 [All following citations translated for this edition with the kind permission of the author and publisher]. See also Picard, A.-M. (1998). "Le Père de l'écriture, Writing within the Secret Father". In Jacobus, L. A. & Barreca R. (Eds.). *Hélène Cixous: The Lit Essays*. New York: Gordon and Breach.

38 Cixous, H. (1969). *Dedans*. Paris: Grasset © Hélène Cixous [All following citations translated for this edition with kind permission of the author].

39 Cixous, H. (1997). *Or, Les Lettres de mon père*. Paris: Editions Des Femmes-Antoinette Fouque, pp. 26–27 [All following citations translated for this edition]. We thank Editions des Femmes-Antoinette Fouque and the author for their kind permission to translate the following excerpts.

40 I borrow this expression from Lemoine-Luccioni, *Le rêve du cosmonaute*, p. 134.

41 Her very first book was in fact *Prénom de Dieu*, a collection of short stories published by Grasset in 1967, which should be read, with respect to *Dedans*, as a catalyst from which arise different figures of the father, among others.

42 Cixous, H. (1989). "From the Scene of the Unconscious to the Scene of History." In Cohen, R. (Ed.) *The Future of Literary Theory*. London: Routledge, p. 4.

43 A version of the Lacanian *parlêtre*, which, as M.-L. Lévy has pointed out to me, has long belonged to the Judaic tradition. In the latter, human nature is defined most exactly as: "*hay ha-médabèr*", the "speaking living being". It was first formulated by the Talmudic scholar, moral philosopher and mathematician Rabbi Judah Loew ben Bezalel, known also as the Maharal of Prague (1512–1609).

44 We should see this in parallel with Valentin's nightmare, which I discussed at the beginning of Chapter I. Writing plays with this loss of the favourite parent, while trying to repress or mend it with the help of fiction.

45 "First I would listen to the noise of the new word my father pronounced: for several days, I would let it mature in the air without touching it. We would get used to each other. I would never push a word too quickly. I was waiting for it to find itself a place among the familiar ones" (*Dedans*, p. 52).

46 An expression we find in the description of Beethoven's gaze in Cixous, H. (1997) *Beethoven à jamais*, Paris: Editions Des femmes-Antoinette Fouque, 1993, p. 131.

47 Lacan's rendering of Freud's *einziger Zug*.

48 "From the Scene of the Unconscious to the Scene of History". p. 2.

49 ORAN-JE (in French); Lacan, already cited, put it in the following way: "At the outset, subjectivity has no relation to the real, but rather to a syntax which is engendered by the signifying mark there" (*Écrits*, p. 51).

50 "The signifier originates from the effacing of the trace," Lacan said.

51 Cixous calls the box a *cartombe*, a hybrid of *carton* (box) and *tombe* (grave).

52 Lévy, M.-L. (1995). "La clinique et les divans de Procuste". *Les Carnets de psychanalyse 7*, Détours cliniques, pp. 51–64; especially, pp. 58–61.

53 Cixous, *Osnabrück*, p. 162.

54 Cixous, *Osnabrück*, p. 216 (both epigraphs used with the kind permission of the author and publisher Editions de Femmes-Antoinette Fouque and H. Cixous).

55 Pommier, G. (1993). *Naissance et renaissance de l'écriture*. Collection "Ecriture". Paris: P.U.F., especially "Sacralité de l'écriture." pp. 100–140.

56 According to Freud's (1926) expression in "Inhibition, Symptoms and Anxiety", in *SE*, XX, p. 36.

57 Cixous, *Osnabrück*, pp. 152–153.

58 The smallest element of meaning: *meures* is composed of three morphemes (or semes) – *meur* (to die) + *e* (present subjunctive) + *s* (second person of the singular).

59 Similar to the story by Anne Hébert I discuss later.

60 The father of writing, the Symbolic figured by and as the dead father.

61 "I say that we are active when something takes place, in us or externally to us, of which we are the adequate cause; that is, (by preceding Def.), when from our nature there follows in us or externally to us something which can be clearly and distinctly understood through our nature alone. On the other hand, I say that we are passive when something takes place in us, or follows from our nature, of which we are only the partial cause." Spinoza, B. & Morgan, M. L. (Eds.). (2006). "Part III: Concerning the Origin and Nature of Emotions". In *The Essential Spinoza: Ethics and Related Writings*. Translated by Samuel Shirley. Indianapolis, IN: Hackett Publishing, p. 62.

62 An earlier version of this chapter was published as "L'enfant du Torrent ou le sujet de l'œuvre en puissance". In Patterson, J. M. & Saint-Martin, L. (Eds.). (2006). *Anne Hébert en revue. Voix et images*. Québec: Presses universitaires du Québec, pp. 93–114.

63 *The Torrent: Novellas and Short Stories by Anne Hébert*. Translated by Gwendolyn Moore. Montréal: Harvest House, 1973. Written in 1945, Hébert's book was first published by the Editions Hurtubise in 1963, with an introduction by Harvey, Robert, *Pour un nouveau Torrent*. Montreal, Hurtubise: HMH, (pp. 7–18). For a discussion of the history of the book and its different editions, see Boucher, J.-P. (1985). "Le titre du recueil: le premier récit "Le torrent" d'Anne Hébert". *Écrits du Canada français*, 65, pp. 27–45.

64 Anne Hébert (1916–2000) who, in the words of one of her most enthusiastic readers, Robert Harvey (http:www.anne-hébert.com), "undoubtedly occupies a place of honour in the literature of Quebec", was awarded the French Prix des libraires for *Kamouraska* in 1970 and received the Prix Femina for her fifth novel, *Les Fous de Bassan*, in 1974, both published by Editions du Seuil. Living in Paris from the 1970s until her death, Hébert was published by Le Seuil (*Les chambres de bois*, 1958; and *Les enfants du sabbat*, 1975).

65 Derrida, J. (2000). "H.C. Pour la vie, c'est à dire. . ." In Calle-Gruber, M. (Ed.) *Hélène Cixous, Croisées d'une œuvre.* Paris: Galilée, pp. 130–140. Derrida's essay was published in English as *H. C. for Life, That Is to Say. . .* Translated by Laurent Milesi and Stefan Herbrechter. Stanford, CA: Stanford University Press, 2006.

66 Formal distancing. See Declerk, Renaat. (2011). "The Definition of Modality". In Patard, A. & Brisard, F. (Eds.). *Cognitive Approaches to Tense, Aspect, and Epistemic Modality.* Amsterdam: John Benjamins Publishing, pp. 21–44, p. 28.

67 Hervé Bazin's 1948 novel *Viper in the Fist* is a story of a young Jean Rezeau and his brothers, who are tormented by their mad and cruel mother, Paule, nicknamed by the children *Folcoche* (a contraction of *folle* and *coche,* a female pig). The novel is often assigned as compulsory reading for high-school students and *folcoche* has become synonymous with the figure of a tyrannical and abusive mother.

68 The same doubt exists at the end of Guy de Maupassant's short story *The Horla,* a paradigmatic tale of the "madman's search for meaning in insanity" genre, where, too, the narrator creates a discourse about the *unbewusste* that inhabits him. This doubt should be taken into account rather than replaced by Harvey's certainty: "Hence the hasty and contradictory conclusions about François' so-called 'suicide' at the end of the story. This interpretation must be rejected outright. A close reading will show that, to the contrary, François Perreault [sic] has never been so 'passionately' alive. . ." (Harvey, Robert [1982]. *Pour un nouveau Torrent.* Montreal, Hurtubise: HMH, p. 133).

69 Likewise, *The Ravishing of Lol Stein* begins with: "*Lol V. Stein est née, ici, à S. Thala*" (Lol Stein was born here, in South Thala). The deictic *ici,* in the original enclosed in commas, functions as a quilting point, tying together the fictional birth of the character's being in the world, the knowledge and perception of the subject of narration, the place of writing – with punctuation as its sign, its materialization – and the text as a chain of signifiers. We see the same symbolic efficacy in François' "I deliver myself to my own end" and in the sentence pronounced by the narrator who is in love with Lol, the insane heroine whom his story struggles to pin down: "I refuse to admit the end which is probably going to come and separate us, how easy it will be, how distressingly simple, for the moment I refuse to accept it, to accept this end, I accept the other, the end which has still to be invented, the end I do not yet know, that no one has invented: the endless end, the endless beginning of Lol Stein" (Translated by Richard Seaver, published in English as Duras, M. [1966]. *The Ravishing of Lol Stein.* New York City: Grove Press).

70 The *routard* (hobo, vagrant or simply itinerant) is an emblematic figure of Quebec literature (cf. Germaine Guévremont's 1945 novel *Le survenant* or later Jacques Poulin's *Volkswagen Blues,* 1984), which situates knowledge on the side of deterritorialization. Daniel Vaillancourt developed this idea in a conference paper *Enfances d'une notion, figure d'enfants* presented at the University of Toronto (February 1994).

71 Robert Harvey has also realized this but his "time" concerns the reinvention of the past. As P.-H. Lemieux reminds us (p. 115), Anne Hébert uses *aventure* as a keyword to describe "all poetic experience" (see Lemieux, P.-H. "Poésie, solitude rompue", *Poèmes,* Paris: Le Seuil, 1960). On the other hand, the relationships established by Lemieux between "The Torrent" and Hébert's later text follow the same direction as my approach, that is of looking for the inscription of the work of symbolization (of writing) in the hero's psychology.

72 The French *avenante* resounds with *avenir* and "adventure": to come, to become. The English "comely" might be a better translation.

73 Literally, the flow of life.

74 Reminding us of the lamp in Elisabeth Barillé's scene and of Marcel, the narrator of *In Search of Lost Time:* it too signals what is played out in the fantasmatic theatre and remains a metonymy of the scopic drive at work in reading; see Chapter II, scene 4, and Chapter III, scene 6.

75 As for Claudine, she never stops trying to account for herself, through her tyrannical discipline, to her fanatic Catholic superego; can we assume that she eventually gets her share when the "wages of sin" have been repaid, just before her death (p. 46)?

76 The moment of effacement is a beautiful representation of Lacan's conceptualization of the subject as what emerges in the gap between two signifiers, a flickering of being that is shown by the void and immediately effaced by the subsequent signifier.

77 The subject of the statement intuits this "unknown wealth" as a time to come, which will be different from his bleak present. A time and space beyond the mother, which comes to existence by virtue of this very statement, because the subject of anamnesis is right here, constructing it with his words. The "wealth" that was seen in the moment of the statement as a name of a thing (a formidable desire) in fact precisely designates the power of the narrating subject's enunciation; the child who feels cannot yet tell. But he is already in possession of the potential *oeuvre* of his adventure, like a hidden treasure of signifiers awaiting actualization and an audience. We are reminded of the construction of the autobiographical subject, who in essence says: "Already as a young child, I know I would one day write my autobiography. . . ." Sartre's *Words* perfectly illustrate this tension, between the subject as a famous writer and his child self, the future autobiographer. Based on his position, more or less established, in the Symbolic (the choice of the object of sublimation and a choice of style) and the Imaginary (an identity relying on the recognition of a certain milieu or profession), the subject seeks to retrace the steps that have led him to where he believes himself to be. And it is therefore no surprise that all the roads he chooses lead to Rome, in other words to the ego.

78 See Chapter II, "The reading eros".

79 Or, to put it otherwise, the signifiers of poets have bordered a lack within him, momentarily succeeding in representing the subject as lacking. Despair is the symptom of the ego's refusal of this representation.

80 See Mitchell, C. (1989). "La symbolique de la surdité dans *Le torrent* d'Anne Hébert". *Québec Studies*, 8, pp. 65–72.

81 And of suicide (p. 23) which foreshadows the ending's (literal) cliffhanger.

82 Tentatively, we could suggest the following formulation of the subject of "The Torrent": $(S^a/s^é)$, where S^a would be the signifiers of the mother which named the world and François' destiny forever and $s^é$ the signifieds of the deaf child who recreates his own world; the bar between them would of course be the torrent. Still, we cannot avoid the primacy of the signifier over the signified: "A phrase haunts my nights. 'You are my son, a continuation of myself.' I am linked to the damned. I am a part of her damnation, as she of mine. . . . No! No! I am responsible for nothing! I am not a free being! I repeat to you that I am not free! That I have never been free! Oh, what strikes me with such fury? The torrent surges through my head. . . . I am drawn close to the falls. I must behold my inward image. I lean over the boiling gulf. I lean over myself" (p. 41).

83 See Lemieux, "Poésie, solitude rompue", p. 122 who reduces the torrent to the ego, perhaps too hastily.

84 Earlier ("*Dé-lire* 2: deleting the name of the father"), we have seen the necessity of topography as a form of primordial writing, as shown by the narrators of Marie Redonnet's triptych.

85 Harvey puts it as follows: "This overfilling of the dream having to be lived through in the 'oeuvre'" (p. 151).

86 Having created a topography of the landscape as an ego without a subject, the work of the child's regressive Imaginary has "managed" to give form to this hate that, since his school days, had protected him from falling into complete despair and has ultimately kept him alive. The torrent and Perceval have become two imagoes of the force of the drive that had already been "felt" and predicted by the narrator and had been present since the child's grasping of the existence of a space beyond the mother. In this beyond,

she is lacking, a lack that reveals to the child that he cannot be an object of her jouis-sance and is therefore himself lacking. François' refusal to return to school is a sign of this existence of the subject beyond the mother. By refusing to be her phallic extension, the "continuation" of her desire to take revenge on everyone, the adolescent says *yes* to his emerging desire, one that is intertwined with and constructed upon hatred.

87 "For what even end did I wish to free him? Was it to unleash the evil in me?" (p. 25). "What atrocious battle had consumed me? Had I fought the Angel face to face? I did not want to know" (p. 26). Or: "I turned to Perceval. [. . .] He had been cruelly hobbled; *yet* that did not prevent him from struggling" (pp. 24–25, my emphasis). This *yet* marks an entrance into imaginary identification. His hatred is "ripened and concentrated", while François' own is "inferior and cowardly". Therefore the horse must be allowed to "be himself in the world": we may smile at this expression, which sums up the therapeutic aims of psychoanalysis, with the anamnesis as its beginning. This reminds me of my first impression upon reading Hébert's text, namely that François is speaking as a psychologist. Further: "The use of physical force. . . . Brutality – the last recourse of those who have lost their inner power" (p. 34). It seems that what is transmitted through the narrator's discourse is the author's knowledge about writing as a mode of sublimation.

88 De Troyes, C. (1999). *Perceval, the Story of the Grail.* Translated by Burton Raffel. New Haven: Yale University Press; see, for example, line 1980.

89 A name we are therefore going to keep as a signifier of literature, a kind of indivisible hieroglyph. This ideogrammatic quality opens it up to all kinds of interpretations, each reader being able to project his own theory and ideas into it: for example, Mitchell (p. 67) understands it as "Père-céphal", and so on.

90 Lines 3188–3189, 3230–3241, 4591–4613.

91 Lines 408 and 3451.

92 "The Torrent," p. 40.

93 See pages 26–28, 34, 36, 41–42, 46–47.

94 Thus facing the danger of regressing into animism, where the Great Whole of Nature becomes saturated with meaning and intention and inhabited by the evil eye, the bad Mother: "The rain, the wind, the clover, the leaves have become the elements of my life . . . I am not yet ripe for the ultimate flight, for the final commitment to the cosmic forces. I do not yet have the permanent right to say to the tree, 'My brother,' and to the falls, 'Here I am.'" (p. 27).

95 It would be useful to look at the way in which these dimensions are transformed and reorganized in the figure of Perceval Brown, the mad child of Griffin Creek. We could even argue that in Perceval's story, the horse of "The Torrent" reappears – in the sofa: "A quilted, shiny black sofa. Like a shiny black horse. With blue reflections" (Hébert, A. [1982]. *Les fous de Bassan*, Paris: Le Seuil, Points, p. 140).

96 To return to Lacan's reformulation of the Cartesian cogito: *I think where I am not; I am where I do not think.*

97 "The elements of a dream. Or of something to be undertaken? I sensed that there would soon emerge from my torment the monstrous visage of either the one or the other" (p. 24, my emphasis).

98 In the Lacanian sense, the Other would have been the witness of the subject's jubila-tion before his own (future) image in the mirror and he is thus *presupposed* to have been present to this *jouissance*, thus becoming the place of Being – of the (complete) Being the subject has lost through the intervention of the Symbolic. The Other is now going to haunt the subject as a depositary of a knowledge about this completeness of Being. François gives us a perfect definition of this while speaking about the cat: "When I saw the cat for the last time, I was eyeing the broken body of my mother. The beast, conscious, out of reach, *kept* staring at me, a look fixed from time immemorial.

Someone had surprised me, then? Someone had been contemplating me without inter-
ruption, untiringly? Someone had known me, at that moment when I no longer had any
knowledge of myself?" (p. 137). The author's emphasis suggests the mother's indel-
ible mark on the child, with the feline gaze as its phantom, but also the excluded third
in possession of knowledge about my (lost) Being.

99 Paul-Laurent Assoun describes the relationship between perversion, a version of
Woman and writing: "While the neurotic, who is caught up in a relationship to a
forbidden woman, uses his fantasy of Woman as a support for his writing, the pervert, stunned by the denial [of her castration] he maintains in his relationship with a
woman (originally the Mother), converts [his fantasmatic] Woman into a challenge
that provokes him to write, a defiance which becomes an offense. This is the bond, the
imaginary ligation, between the pervert and Woman" – and literature, we could add,
following Assoun's logic (cf. Assoun, P.-L. [1996]. *Le pervers et la femme*. Paris: Ed.
Economica, p. 11 [Translated for this edition]).

Conclusion

Reading as a critique of maternal jouissance

In 1975, Serge Leclaire wrote:

> Always already caught up in a dreamlike third person (he will be a great man, she will marry a prince . . .) and in the seduction and bidding of a second person (will you answer my wishes? are you coming?), the story starts only in the first person: no, "I" is not that. The subject is born and reborn solely from a constant disentanglement of body and words, from a perpetually repeatable crossing of the grid of signifiers, from the ghostly, hallucinated reunion with the lost but immediately present object, right there, so very close to us.[1]

This lost primordial object is, first of all, myself: a total being still unspoilt by language.[2] "It's an old story," the psychoanalyst Serge Leclaire concludes, "and with it, everything begins again and again: a child to kill, a delivery to go through".

This is the story this book has been trying to tell, showing that both nonreaders and poets alike participate, whether unwittingly or working with the semblance of the written trace, in a certain refusal of this unravelling of the body and words. Such disentanglement would equal murdering the Little Believer, the subject before the letter, as well as killing God in his paradise – the mother tongue, Being's native land.

Writers describe this deadly struggle with words, their effect of thingness, their arbitrariness and the desire of the Other concealed in them. We have learned everything from writers, as I hope it will have been made clear in the fourteen scenes I have extracted from their books, and thus separated from the creative gesture that had pressed onto the blank page to consort with its void.

Scene 14

The mistress collects our papers. She is going to examine them, indicate the mistakes in red ink in the margin, then count them up and give the work a mark. Nothing can equal the fairness of the mark she will write under my name. It is justice itself, it is equity. It alone gives rise to that trace of approbation on the mistress's face when she looks at me. I am nothing other than what I have written. Nothing that I don't know, that people project on to me, that they foist on to me without my knowledge, as they are always doing there, outside, in my other life. . . . I am completely protected from whims and caprices, from obscure, disturbing movements. . . . And also, nothing reaches here of that love, "our love", as Mama calls it . . . which gives rise to something in me that hurts, which, in spite of the pain, I am supposed to cultivate, to nurture, and which, ignobly, I try to stifle. No trace of all that here. Here, I am in security. . . . Law, which everyone has to respect, protects me. Everything that happens to me here can only depend on me.[3]

We see that little Nathalie chooses the symbolic order instituted by the school to protect herself from the mother's confused and troubling demand for love. The thing is that in the presence of her mother, she can no longer tell which one of them really provokes these movements. There is no space between them, no third term that would allow the child to think for herself. However, at school, the writer remembers, "the only aim of the solicitude, the concern which surrounds me here, is to help me to possess, to accomplish, what I myself desire, what gives me, me first and foremost, such pleasure" (Sarraute, 2013, p. 149). As it is often the case with girls, she too understands that she has everything to gain in the classroom. By submitting herself to the laws of grammar and spelling, she becomes a subject of the law, equal to all humans, beyond the reach of her mother's jouissance and control. My mother, the child tells herself, "perceives behind me" images "which I mask"; in other words, she does not see me for what I am. The power exerted by the young Russian woman over her daughter is in a sense denounced by the scene at the school where "I am nothing other than what I have written. Nothing that I don't know, that people project on to me" (p. 148).

One day at the hairdresser, Nathalie Sarraute remembers, the child made a terrifying comparison: her mother, admired and revered for her beauty and goddesslike completeness, "isn't as beautiful" as the hairdresser's doll in the window! Writing from the little girl's perspective, the author continues:

Now that this idea has entrenched itself in me, it is not just a matter of willpower for me to dislodge it. I can force myself to uproot it, to put another idea in its place, but only for a time . . . it is still there. . . . It seems that trying to keep it down, to suppress it, only increases its growth. It is the proof, the sign of what I am: a child who doesn't love its mother. A child who bears the stigma of something that separates it, that outlaws it from other children. . . .

(p. 86)

This *unheimlich* idea makes a dent in the mother's completeness; it finds her "lacking" and by doing so draws a line between her and her daughter, creating a gap in which "the subject will be able to posit herself as a remainder", as Marc

Léopold Lévy puts it.[4] The *subject-to* is cast into existence, into a space of solitude, guilt and misery, the space beyond the mother: "The disease was in me", Sarraute writes (p. 88). The previous mother–daughter identification gives way to the rejection of the mother into a foreign space: she but not myself. This moment of crisis is similar to Sartre's experience before his reading mother: the daughter does not yet have her own image or desire, but she can no longer find herself in the mother's gaze.

The Greek word κρισις is etymologically complex; it means the action and ability to distinguish, to separate and thus to decide and, as a consequence, to judge and pronounce a sentence; last, it implies something that decides or brings about a resolution.[5] The fact that it becomes possible to *criticize* the mother (that she becomes a possible object of judgment) offers the daughter a way out of the "obscure, disturbing movements" of the maternal jouissance in which she is caught up. Sarraute is aware – and tells us so in these two scenes – that the access to reading and writing is conditioned by a process of delegitimization of the mother, by her decompletion. This moment of de-idealization is often described as the foundational separation preceding the life choice of certain writers: "I stopped trying to copy her", Annie Ernaux says about her mother in her foundational text, *A Woman's Story*: "I found my own mother's attitude brash. I averted my eyes when she uncorked a bottle, holding it locked between her knees. I was ashamed of her brusque manners and speech, especially when I realized how alike we were."[6] Likewise, the Belgian author and psychoanalyst Jacqueline Harpman describes her mother: "Poor Rose, always missing out on everything?" And she continues: "That would be fine, if only in the middle of all that she had not also missed out on me. Here, all compassion is fatal: it could legitimize her and thus oppress me. In this story, it is either I or she."[7]

The delegitimization happens as a test or a rite of initiation; it is both enabled and solicited by writing in the same paradoxical entwining that joins the "chosen" mode of sublimation, as we have seen previously, to the impossible matricide that is either at work in the project itself (Cixous, see Chapter III, scene 11) or acts as its imaginary foundation (see Hébert, Chapter III, "*Dé-lire* 4"). As a "dream solution", writing works to prevent "the powerlessness of maternal identification in feminine jouissance", argues the writer and psychoanalyst Eugénie Lemoine-Luccioni.[8] In the best cases, the father's word-plays in the mother tongue helps the daughter escape being annihilated in the mother's image. In her enraged account, aptly named *La Fille démantelée* ("The Dismantled Daughter"), Harpman also speaks about this fierce struggle to make language (not) produce a separation.

> If there can only be battle between her and myself, then at least let us always be fighting, let us forever scream at each other, hit each other, let us always remain locked in this mortal embrace. I have never had her love – do I have to lose my hatred as well?
>
> (p. 236)

Like Marcel Proust and Samuel Beckett, she too can only disturb the omnipotence of the Mother, her position as the God of language, after the death of her real mother. The novel should therefore not be considered as a sepulchre for the Mother, as Harpman would have it. Instead, it is a mausoleum for the daughter's hatred, a sign of her lingering attachment, which in fact has prevented her from writing.[9] Writing allows her to restate the necessity of separation, of cutting the link, even if it is only to love the mother better, to rebuild their connection through the texture of the text.

> I can see that, page after page, I am bound to let her go and I can't imagine having nothing more to say to her. Oh how I wish I could start the book again from the beginning! When my mother was still alive and I hated her. See, now I'm really going crazy, soon I'll be crying over her death. . . .
>
> Throughout the pages devoted to her, I've found nothing worthy of praise in her. She was beautiful, they told me, but what is her beauty to me? The beauty of mothers is the father's affair. She was greedy, envious, ignorant and stupid. So what should I think of myself, if I find myself loving her?
>
> (pp. 236–237)

We see that the mother is criticized for having been flawed, for not having been perfect. When writing recreates her as a character, she becomes human. The hatred is made relative by the arbitrariness of the signifier. The exigencies of narrative and its syntax have opened up a gap, a space of play.

Writers try to invent their own language, one that would no longer belong to the mother. By doing so, they produce a textual body to make up for the truly separate body they are lacking. Harpman's narrator Edmée is able to turn this new space into the place of the excluded third, from which the subject can glimpse the mother's image, yet no longer seeks there her own reflection as the "perfect daughter". The Mother becomes a woman – for the father. No more need to ask for exclusive love and absolute recognition; the Oedipus complex has been resolved and this woman's indifference or even hatred towards her no longer affects the daughter (even *post mortem*). A necessary step towards the freedom of thought, this delegitimization is the price to be paid by the Other woman, so that the female subject becomes able to love with no demand for a reply and thus no anguish.

❖

> Mythological figures who are blind or lame, one-eyed or one-armed, are familiar the world over; and we find them disturbing because we believe their condition to be one of deficiency. But just as a system, made discrete through the removal of certain elements becomes logically richer, although numerically poorer, so myths often confer a positive significance on the disabled and the sick, who embody modes of mediation.[10]

Following this passage from Levi-Strauss, Gerard Haddad continues his own argument:

> After the sick, blind and lame, Levi-Strauss adds another surprising character to the series: "The secluded" implies a particular attitude toward female society, from which [he] refuses to be separated; on the contrary, he tries to take refuge in it. . . . The secluded character, the recluse, is in this case the sort of boy who, as we say, "clings to his mother's apron-strings".[11]

Have the illiterate, who are secluded from the Symbolic, become the new version of the disabled and lame? If illiteracy (reading difficulties) is a socioanthropological symptom, it also shows that the culture of reading and writing is beneficial for civilization in so far as it separates us from our mothers' skirts. Marc-Alain Ouaknin reminds us that the *Talmud* begins by a true "treatise on reading", one that is dedicated to the rules, postures and rhythms proper to the reading of key passages of the Hebrew prayer, "*Shema Yisrael*". He then puts forth the following hypothesis: "As if before entering into ethics as something that surpasses culture, or more accurately before entering into a non-barbaric human culture, we first needed to learn how to read. In the beginning there is reading."[12]

Perhaps literature and the reading body – the figure embodying reading's effects – are our prayer: a prayer to the self as our hero made of words, the subject's prayer to the Symbolic and its imaginary enticements. Or surely the novel, including its autofictional forms, tells the story of a desire for separation, for breaking out of the confinement of the mother's skirts and her magical language. This is true even when the subject, the poet in abeyance, remains an illiterate who delirates the laws of the Symbolic using the word-things of the mother's jouissance. When we finally reach it as readers, the Thing of the Book ultimately always produces an extrication, decompleting the mother's body through the letters of another language.

Notes

1 Leclaire, S. (1998). *A Child Is Being Killed: On Primary Narcissism and the Death Drive* (1975). Stanford, CA: Stanford University Press, p. 53.
2 Lévy, M. L. (2003). *Critique de la jouissance comme Une: leçons de psychanalyse*, Toulouse: Erès, pp. 73–75, among others.
3 Sarraute, N. (2013). *Childhood*. Translated by Barbara Wright, with a foreword by Alice Kaplan. Chicago, IL: University of Chicago Press, pp. 148–149.
4 Lévy, M.-L. (2005). "De la nécessité du négatif dans le transfert." *La clinique lacanienne*, 2(9), pp. 181–190, 183. DOI 10.3917/cla.009.0181
5 Bailly, A. (1901). *Abrégé du dictionnaire grec-français*. Paris: Hachette, p. 512.
6 Ernaux, A. (2011). *A Woman's Story*. New York, NY: Seven Stories Press, p. 50.
7 Harpman, J. (1994). *La Fille démantelée*. Brussels: Editions Labor, p. 45.
8 Lemoine-Luccioni, E. (1980). *Le Rêve du cosmonaute*. Paris: Le Seuil, p. 139.
9 See Harpman, for example p. 78, where the daughter grows thin because of there being "too much of the mother's body". In the body, hatred has maintained the rage alive

after she has been abandoned by her parents at only three weeks old (until she was ten years of age, they would only see her for a few months every year). Writing emerges "against the mother" after twenty years of analysis. Breaking the hold of hatred must have been too dangerous for the unconscious subject who relied on it to defy her parents' own hatred, their designation of her as a "piece of shit".

10 Levi-Strauss, C. (1975). *The Raw and the Cooked*. Translated by J. and D. Weightman. New York City: Harper & Row, p. 53.
11 Haddad, G. (1984). *Manger le livre*. Paris: Grasset et Fasquelle, p. 128.
12 Ouaknin, M.-A. (1994). *Bibliothérapie. Lire c'est guérir*. Paris: Points, p. 292 [Translated for this edition].

Works cited

Adler, L. & Bollman, S. (2008). *Women Who Read Are Dangerous*. London: Merrell Publishers.

Angot, C. (1999). *L'Inceste*. Paris: Stock.

Angot, C. (2001). *Normalement, suivi de La peur du lendemain*. Paris: Stock.

Assoun, P.-L. (1993). "La Lettre. Pour une métapsychologie du lire." In: *Introduction à la métapsychologie Freudienne*. Paris: PUF.

Assoun, P.-L. (1996). *Le pervers et la femme*. Paris: Ed. Economica.

Bailly, A. (1901). *Abrégé du dictionnaire grec-français*. Paris: Hachette.

Barillé, E. (1989). *Body of a Girl*. Translated by Hubert Gibbs. London: Quartet Books.

Barthes, R. (1975). "The Reality Effect." In: *The Rustle of Language*. Translated by Richard Howard. New York: Hill and Wang.

Beckett, S. (1959). *Three Novels (Molloy, Malone Dies, The Unnameable)*. New York: Grove Press.

Beizer, J. (1993). "Reading Women: The Novel in the Text of Hysteria." *Compar(a)ison*, 1: 57–74.

Benveniste, E. (1971). "The Nature of Pronouns" (1956). In: *Problems of General Linguistics*. Coral Gables, FL: University of Miami Press, pp. 217–222.

Blanchot, M. (1973). *Thomas the Obscure*. Translated by Rober Lamberton. Barrytown, NY: Station Hill Press.

Blanchot, M. (1989). *The Space of Literature* (1955). Translated by Ann Smock. Lincoln, NE: University of Nebraska Press.

Bobin, C. (1991). *Une petite robe de fête*. Paris: Gallimard.

Bonnet, C. & Tamine-Gardes, J. (1984). *Quand l'enfant parle du langage: Connaissance et conscience du langage chez l'enfant*. Paris: Pierre Mardaga.

Boucher, J.-P. (1985). "Le titre du recueil: le premier récit 'Le torrent' d'Anne Hébert." *Ecrits du Canada français*, 65: 27–45.

Breuer, J. & Freud, S. (1893). "On The Psychical Mechanism of Hysterical Phenomena." In: Strachey, J. (Ed). *The Standard Edition of the Complete Psychological Works of Sigmund Freud*, Volume II (1893–1895): Studies on Hysteria. London: The Hogarth Press and the Institute of Psycho-Analysis, pp. 1–17.

Calvino, I. (1998). *If on a Winter's Night a Traveller*. Translated by William Weaver. London: Vintage.

Chiantaretto, J.-F. (1995). *De l'Acte autobiographique: le psychanalyste et l'écriture autobiographique*. Paris: Editions Champ Vallon.

Cixous, H. (1967). *Prénom de Dieu*. Paris: Grasset.

Cixous, H. (1969). *Dedans*. Paris: Grasset.

Cixous, H. (1987). *L'Indiade ou l'Inde de leurs rêves, et quelques écrits sur le théâtre*. Paris: Editions du Théâtre du Soleil.

Cixous, H. (1989). "From the Scene of the Unconscious to the Scene of History." In: Cohen, R. (Ed). *The Future of Literary Theory*. London: Routledge, pp. 1–18.

Cixous, H. (1993). *Beethoven à jamais, ou L'existence de Dieu*. Paris: Editions Des femmes.

Cixous, H. (1997). *Or, Les Lettres de mon père*. Paris: Editions Des Femmes-Antoinette Fouque.

Cixous, H. (1999). *Osnabrück*. Paris: Editions Des Femmes-Antoinette Fouque.

Dayan, J. & Ribowska, M. (1979). *Simone de Beauvoir: un film de Josée Dayan et Malka Ribowska*. Paris: © Éditions Gallimard.

De Beauvoir, S. (1990). *All Said and Done*. London: Penguin Modern Classics.

Decaunes, L. (1976). *Clefs pour la lecture*. Paris: Seghers.

De Certeau, M. (1992). *The Writing of History*. New York City: Columbia University Press.

Derrida, J. (2006). *H. C. for Life, That Is to Say. . .* Translated by Laurent Milesi and Stefan Herbrechter. Stanford, CA: Stanford University Press, 2006.

De Troyes, C. (1999). *Perceval, the Story of the Grail*. Translated by Burton Raffel. New Haven: Yale University Press.

Doubrovsky, S. (1977). *Fils*. Paris: Galatée.

Doubrovsky, S. (1982). "Phallotexte et gynotexte dans *La Nausée*: 'Feuillet sans date'." In: Issacharoff, M. & Vilquin, J.-Cl. (Eds). *Sartre et la mise ne signe*. Paris: Klincsieck, French Forum, pp. 31–55.

Doubrovsky, S. (1989). *Le livre brisé*. Paris: Grasset.

Dubois, J., Mitterand, H., & Dauzat, A. (1993). *Dictionnaire étymologique*. Paris: Larousse.

Duras, M. (1966). *The Ravishing of Lol Stein*. New York City: Grove Press.

Ernaux, A. (2011). *A Woman's Story*. New York: Seven Stories Press.

Faguet, É. (1912). *L'Art de lire*. Paris: Hachette.

Ferron, C. (1987). "Qu'est-ce que c'est que ça?" *La Psychanalyse de l'enfant*, 3(4): 105–124.

Ferron, C. (1990). "Enfants non-lecteurs en thérapie." *Perspectives psychiatriques*, 24(IV): 262–265.

Flaubert, G. (1994). *Madame Bovary*. London: Wordsworth Editions.

Freud, S. (1901). "The Psychopathology of Everyday Life: 'Forgetting, Slips of the Tongue, Bungled Actions, Superstitions and Errors'." In *SE* 6: vii–296.

Freud, S. (1905). "Three Essays on the Theory of Sexuality." In *SE*, 7: 123–246.

Freud, S. (1908). "Creative Writers and Day-Dreaming." In *SE*, 9: 141–154.

Freud, S. (1908). "On the Sexual Theories of Children." In *SE*, 9: 205–226.

Freud, S. (1909). "Analysis of a *Phobia* in a *Five-Year-Old Boy*." In *SE*, 10: 3–141.

Freud, S. (1909). "Family Romances." In *SE*, 9: 235–242.

Freud, S. (1909). "Notes Upon a Case of Obsessional Neurosis." In *SE*, 10: 151–318.

Freud, S. (1913). "The Disposition to Obsessional Neurosis, a Contribution to the Problem of the Choice of Neurosis." In *SE*, 12: 311–326.

Freud, S. (1913). "Totem and Taboo." In *SE*, 13: vii–162.

Freud, S. (1919). "The 'Uncanny'." In *SE*, 17: 217–256.

Freud, S. (1923). "The Ego and the Id." In *SE*, 19: 1–66.

Freud, S. (1925). "A Note Upon the 'Mystic Writing-Pad'." In *SE*, 19: 225–232.

Freud, S. (1926). "Inhibitions, Symptoms and Anxiety." In *SE*, 20: 75–176.

Freud, S. (1953). *On Aphasia: A Critical Study* (1891). Translated by E. Stengel. New York: International Universities Press, Inc.

Haddad, G. (1984). *Manger le livre*. Paris: Grasset et Fasquelle.

Harpman, J. (1994). *La fille démantelée*. Brussels: Editions Labor.

Harvey, R. (1982). *Pour un nouveau Torrent*. Hurtubise: HMH.

Hassoun, P., Maillet, C., & Rabant, C. (1988). "Entretien avec Hélène Cixous." *Patio*, 10. 61–67.

Hébert, A. (1973). *The Torrent: Novellas and Short Stories by Anne Hébert*. Translated by Gwendolyn Moore. Montréal: Harvest House.

Hébert, A. (1982). *Les Fous de Bassan*. Paris: Le Seuil.

Jean, R. (1998). *La Lectrice*. Paris: Éditions J'ai Lu.

Juranville, A. (1988). *Lacan et la philosophie*. Paris: PUF.

Kaufmann, P. (Ed.) (1993). *L'Apport Freudien*. Paris: Bordas.

Kugler, M., Meljac, C., Auzanneau, M., Bounes, M., Bailly, L., Preneron, C., Ferron C., Giannopulu, I., Lemmel, G., Lenoble, E., Picard, A.-M. (2000). "Les échecs en lecture respectent-ils la parité? (1st part) Filles, garçons et lecture: vue d'ensemble sur les travaux récents." *Neuropsychiatrie de l'enfance et de l'adolescence*, 48: 487–498.

Kugler, M., Meljac, C., Auzanneau, M., Bounes, M., Bailly, L., Preneron, C., Ferron C., Giannopulu, I., Lemmel, G., Lenoble, E., Picard, A.-M. (2001). "Les échecs en lecture respectent-ils la parité? (2e partie) Filles et échecs et lecture: bilan de quinze ans d'expérience clinique." *Neuropsychiatrie de l'enfance et de l'adolescence*, 49: 53–71.

Lacan, J. (1970). "Radiophonie." *Scilicet*, 2–3: 55–99.

Lacan, J. (1973). "L'étourdit." *Scilicet*, 4: 5–51.

Lacan, J. (1984). "Comptes rendus d'enseignements 1964–1968." *Ornicar?* 29: 8–25.

Lacan, J. (1990). *Television*. Translated by Denis Hollier, Rosalind Krauss, and Annette Michelson. New York City: W.W. Norton.

Lacan, J. (1997). *The Seminar, Book VII, The Ethics of Psychoanalysis*. Translated by Dennis Porter. New York: Norton.

Lacan, J. (1999). *The Seminar, Book XX, Encore. The Limits of Love and Knowledge*. Translated by Bruce Fink. New York: Norton.

Lacan, J. (2006). *Écrits*. Translated by Bruce Fink. New York City: W.W. Norton.

Lacan, J. (2007). *The Seminar, Book XVII, the Other Side of Psychoanalysis*. Translated by Russel Grigg. New York: Norton.

Lacan, J., Miller, J-A. & Fink, B. (1999). *On Feminine Sexuality, the Limits of Love and Knowledge: The Seminar of Jacques Lacan*, "Book XX, Encore." New York: W.W. Norton, p. 9.

Lafont, R. (Ed.) (1984). *Anthropologie de l'écriture*. Paris: Centre de création industrielle, Centre George Pompidou.

Leclaire, S. (1998). *A Child Is Being Killed: On Primary Narcissism and the Death Drive* (1975). Stanford, CA: Stanford University Press.

Lemieux, P.-H. (1960). "Poésie, solitude rompue." *Poèmes*. Paris: Le Seuil.

Lemoine-Luccioni, E. (1980). *Le rêve du cosmonaute*. Paris: Le Seuil.

Lemoine-Luccioni, E. (1987). *The Dividing of Women, or Women's Lot*. Translated by Marie-Laure Davenport and Marie-Christine Reguis. London: Free Association.

Levi-Strauss, C. (1975). *The Raw and the Cooked*. Translated by J. and D. Weightman. New York City: Harper & Row.

Lévy, A. (2004). *La leçon d'alphabet*. Paris: Editions Vert et Bleu.

Lévy, M.-L. (1995). "La clinique et les divans de Procuste." *Les Carnets de psychanalyse*, 7: 51–64.

Lévy, M.-L. (1996). "La Cigogne et le kabbaliste ou du comment et du pourquoi." In Picard, A.-M. (Ed). *L'imaginaire de la théorie. Texte*, 17/18. Toronto: University of Toronto Press, pp. 233–242.

Lévy, M.-L. (2003). *Critique de la jouissance comme Une: leçons de psychanalyse*, Toulouse: Erès.

Lévy, M.-L. (2005) "De la nécessité du négatif dans le transfert." *La clinique lacanienne*, 2(9): 181–190, 183. DOI 10.3917/cla.009.0181

Malka, V. (2006). *Mots d'esprit de l'humour juif.* Paris: Le Seuil.

Massin, R. (1970). *Letter and Image.* New York City: Van Nostrand Reinhold.

McDougall, J. (1985). *Theatres of the Mind. Illusion and Truth on the Psychoanalytic Stage.* London: Basic Books.

Melman, C. (1984). *Nouvelles Etudes sur l'hystérie.* Paris: Editions Joseph Clims.

Millet, C. (2002). "Pourquoi et comment". In: *La Vie sexuelle de Catherine M.* Paris: Seuil, i–xiv.

Mitchell, C. (1989). "La symbolique de la surdité dans 'Le torrent' d'Anne Hébert." *Québec Studies*, 8: 65–72.

Ouaknin, M.-A. (1994). *Bibliothérapie. Lire, c'est guérir.* Paris: Le Seuil.

Ouaknin, M.-A. (1997). *Les Mystères de l'alphabet.* Paris: Ed. Assouline.

Patard, A. & Brisard, F. (2011). *Cognitive Approaches to Tense, Aspect, and Epistemic Modality.* Amsterdam: John Benjamins Publishing.

Patterson, J. M. & Saint-Martin, L. (Eds.) (2006). *Anne Hébert en revue. Voix et images*, (Special Issue).

Picard, A.-M. (1994). "Dans le paysage, une figure féminine . . . à peine: le triptyque de Marie Redonnet." *The Australian Journal of French Studies*, 2 (12): 228–240.

Picard, A.-M. (1995). "Arrêt sur image: identité et altérité chez Brossard et Redonnet." *Dalhousie French Studies*, 31: 101–112.

Picard, A.-M. (1998). "Le Père de l'écriture, Writing within the Secret Father." In: Jacobus, L. A. & Barreca, R. (Eds). *Hélène Cixous: The Lit Essays.* New York: Gordon and Breach, pp. 23–57.

Picard, A.-M. (2010). "Écrire au bord du gouffre: Le *Splendid Hôtel* de Marie Redonnet." In: Meurée, C. (Ed). *Interférences littéraires*, Nouvelle série, n° 5, "Le sujet apocalyptique," pp. 31–42.

Picard, M. (1986). *La lecture comme jeu.* Paris: Minuit.

Pommier, G. (1993). *Naissance et renaissance de l'écriture.* Paris: P.U.F.

Préneron, C., Meljac, C., & Netchine, S. (1994). *Des enfants hors du lire.* Paris: Bayard.

Proust, M. (1996). *In Search of Lost Time: Time Regained* (1913). London: Vintage.

Proust, M. (2003). *In Search of Lost Time. The Way by Swann's.* London: Penguin.

Proust, M. & Ruskin, J. (2011). *On Reading* (1904). London: Hesperus.

Redonnet, M. (1987). "Redonne après maldonne." *Infini*, 19: 160–163.

Redonnet, M. (1994). *Forever Valley.* Translated by Jordan Stump. Lincoln: University of Nebraska Press.

Redonnet, M. (1994). *Hôtel Splendid.* Translated by Jordan Stump. Lincoln: University of Nebraska Press.

Redonnet, M. (1994). *Rose Melie Rose.* Translated by Jordan Stump. Lincoln: University of Nebraska Press.

Rey, J.-M. (1982). "Petite préface à la lecture." *L'Écrit du temps* (Spring 1982): 65–68.

Rilke, R. M. (1990). *The Notebooks of Malte Laurids Brigge: A Novel* (1929). Translated by Stephen Mitchell. New York: Random House.

Rousseau, J.-J. (1973). *Confessions.* London: Penguin Classics.

Sarraute, N. (2013). *Childhood.* Translated by Barbara Wright. Chicago, IL: University of Chicago Press.

Sartre, J.-P. (1956). *Being and Nothingness.* Translated by Hazel E. Barnes. New York: Philosophical Library.

Sartre, J.-P. (2000). *Words.* London: Penguin Books.

Sartre, J.-P. (2000). *Nausea.* Translated by Robert Baldick. London: Penguin Modern Classics. Originally published 1938.

Spinoza, B. & Morgan, M. L. (Eds.) (2006). "Part III: Concerning the Origin and Nature of Emotions." In: *The Essential Spinoza: Ethics and Related Writings.* Translated by Samuel Shirley. Indianapolis, IN: Hackett Publishing, 61–101.

Strachey, J. (1930). "Some Unconscious Factors in Reading." *The International Journal of Psychoanalysis*, IX: 322–331.

Winnicott, W. D. (1971). *Playing and Reality.* London: Routledge.

Index

For Product Safety Concerns and Information please contact our EU
representative GPSR@taylorandfrancis.com
Taylor & Francis Verlag GmbH, Kaufingerstraße 24, 80331 München, Germany

9 781138 796034